THE GIRL

HE DRAG

OOK 1

PTED BY DENISE MINA

BY LEONARDO MANC

RS BY GIULIA BRUSC

RS BY STEVE WANDS

ON THE NOVEL THE GIRL WITH THE

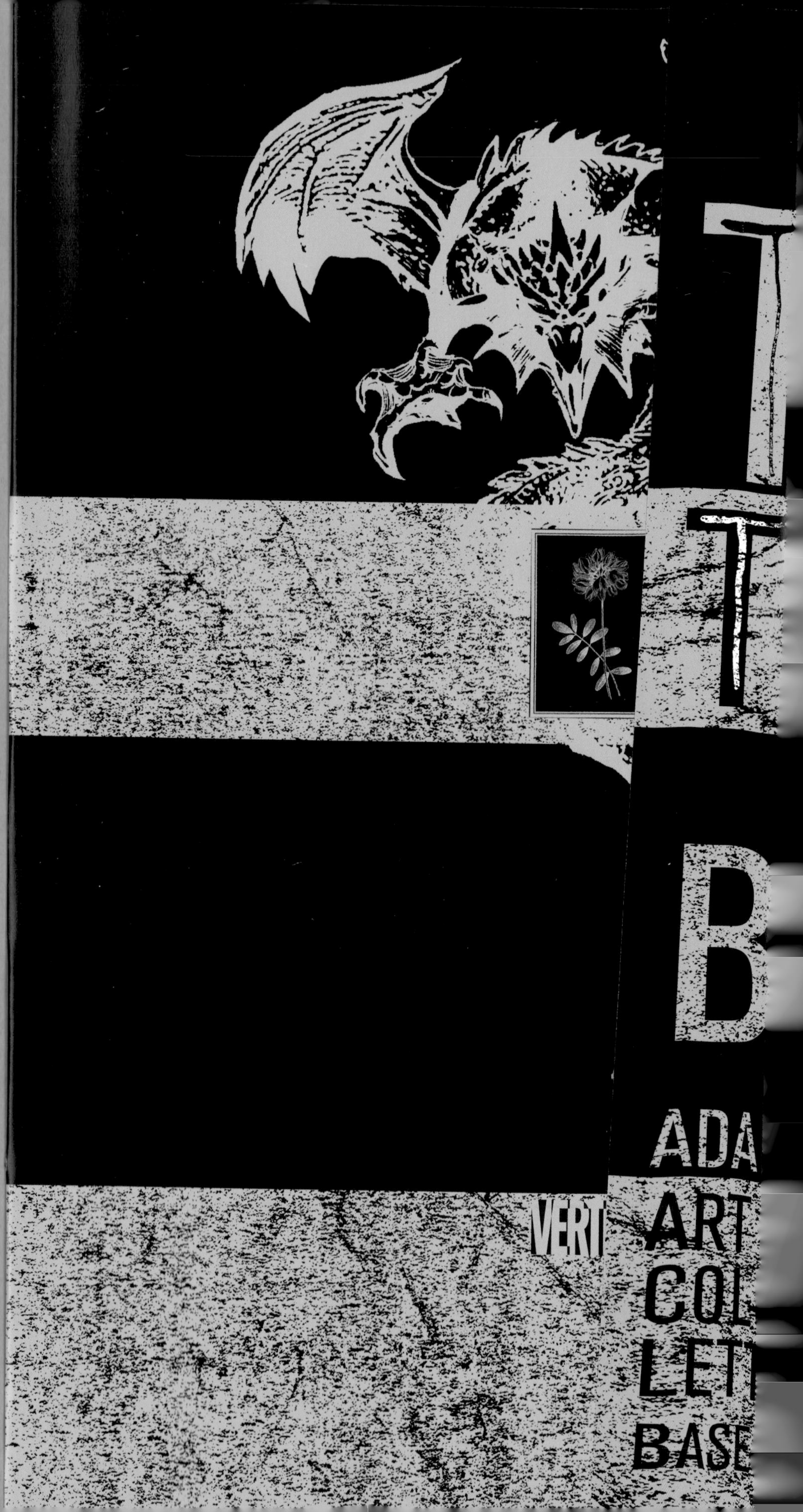
VERT
ADA
ART
COL
BASE

RL WITH

ON TATTOO

AND ANDREA MUTTI
AND PATRICIA MULVIHILL
COVER BY LEE BERMEJO
DRAGON TATTOO BY STIEG LARSSON

Will Dennis Editor Mark Doyle Associate Editor Robbin Brosterman Design Director – Books Louis Prandi Publication Design

Karen Berger Senior VP – Executive Editor, Vertigo Bob Harras VP – Editor-in-Chief

Diane Nelson President Dan DiDio and Jim Lee Co-Publishers Geoff Johns Chief Creative Officer John Rood Executive VP – Sales, Marketing and Business Development
Amy Genkins Senior VP – Business and Legal Affairs Nairi Gardiner Senior VP – Finance Jeff Boison VP – Publishing Operations Mark Chiarello VP – Art Direction and Design
John Cunningham VP – Marketing Terri Cunningham VP – Talent Relations and Services Alison Gill Senior VP – Manufacturing and Operations Hank Kanalz Senior VP – Digital
Jay Kogan VP – Business and Legal Affairs, Publishing Jack Mahan VP – Business Affairs, Talent Nick Napolitano VP – Manufacturing Administration
Sue Pohja VP – Book Sales Courtney Simmons Senior VP – Publicity Bob Wayne Senior VP – Sales

Library of Congress Cataloging-in-Publication Data

Mina, Denise.
The girl with the dragon tattoo. Book 1 / Denise Mina, Leonardo Manco, Andrea Mutti.
p. cm.
ISBN 978-1-4012-3557-4 (alk. paper)
1. Crime--Sweden--Comic books, strips, etc. 2. Graphic novels. I. Manco, Leonardo. II. Mutti, Andrea, 1973- III. Larsson, Stieg, 1954-2004. Girl with the dragon tattoo. IV. Title.
PN6737.M57657 2012
741.5'942--dc23
2012030613

SUSTAINABLE
FORESTRY
INITIATIVE

Certified Chain of Custody
At Least 25% Certified Forest Content

www.sfiprogram.org
SFI-01042
APPLIES TO TEXT STOCK ONLY

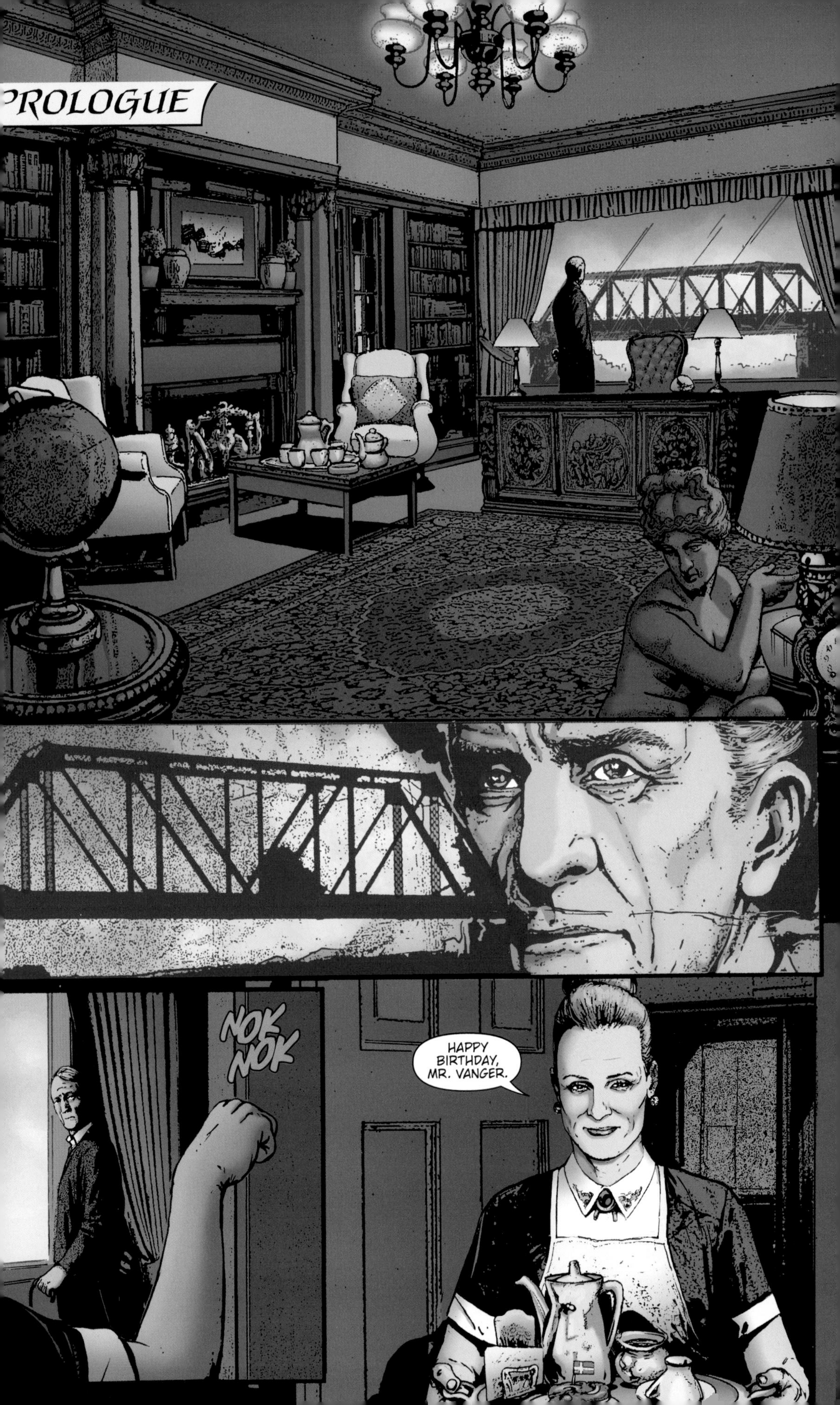
PROLOGUE
NOK NOK
HAPPY BIRTHDAY, MR. VANGER.

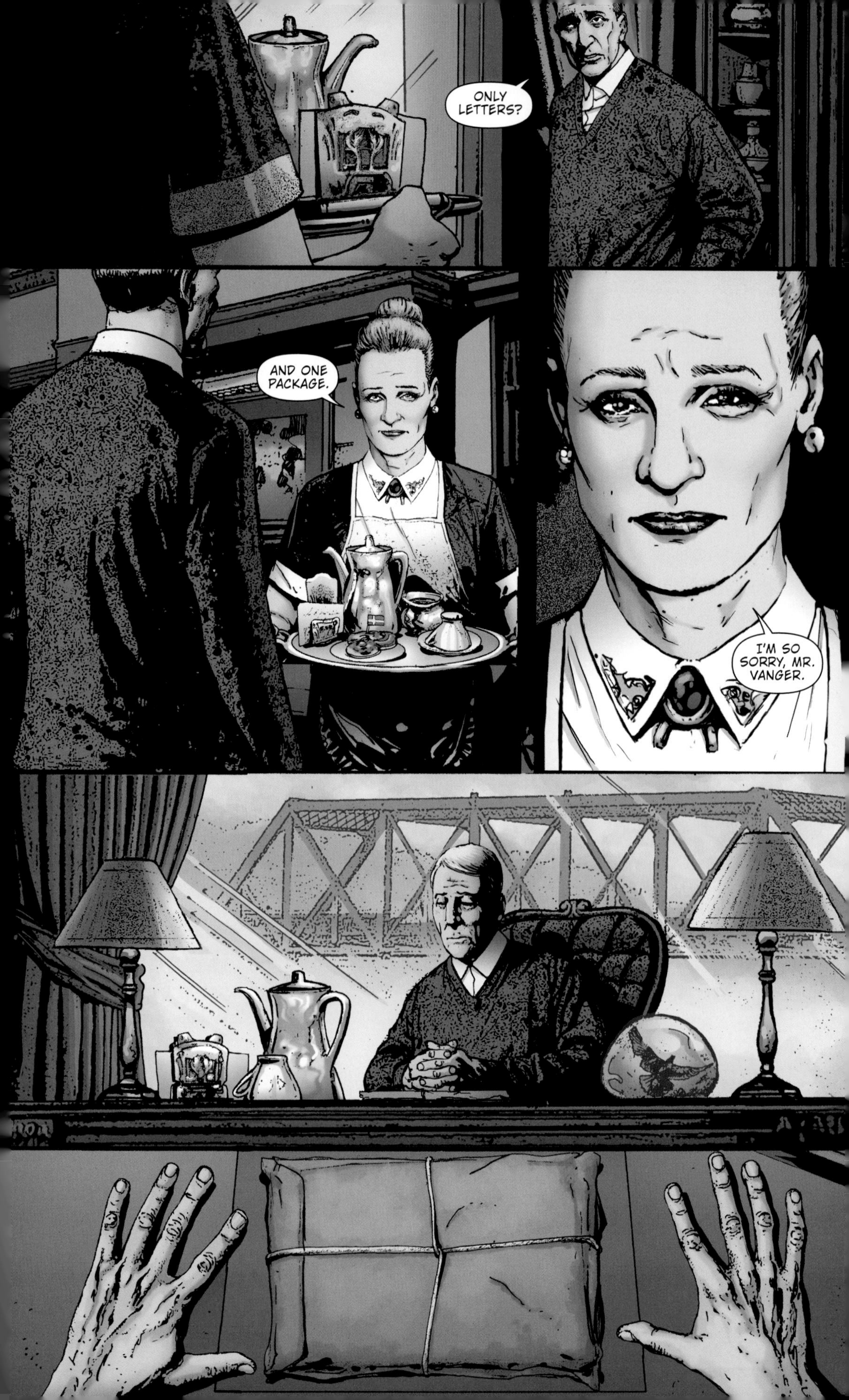
ONLY LETTERS?
AND ONE PACKAGE.
I'M SO SORRY, MR. VANGER.

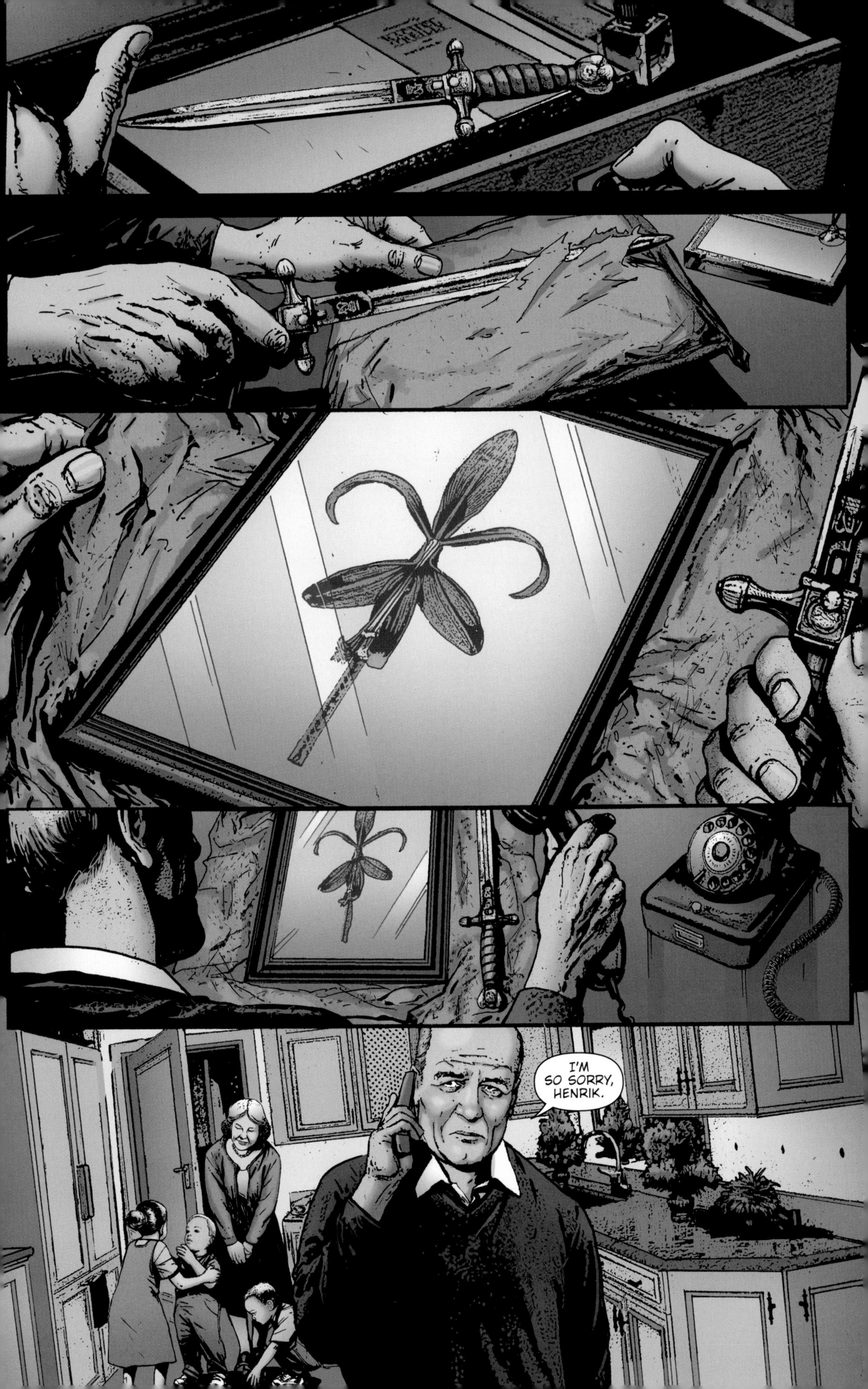
I'M SO SORRY, HENRIK.

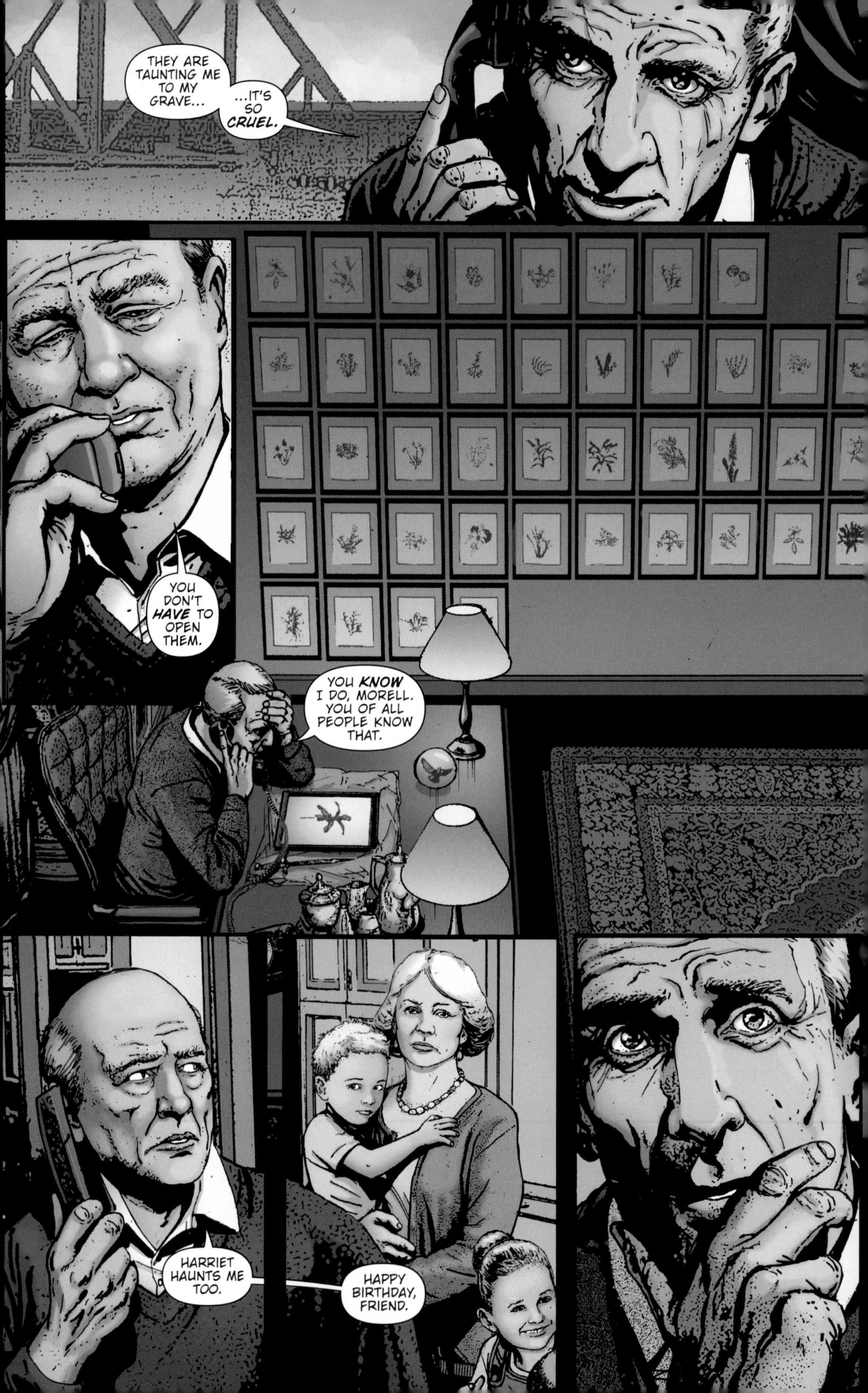
THEY ARE TAUNTING ME TO MY GRAVE...
...IT'S SO CRUEL.
YOU DON'T HAVE TO OPEN THEM.
YOU KNOW I DO, MORELL. YOU OF ALL PEOPLE KNOW THAT.
HARRIET HAUNTS ME TOO.
HAPPY BIRTHDAY, FRIEND.

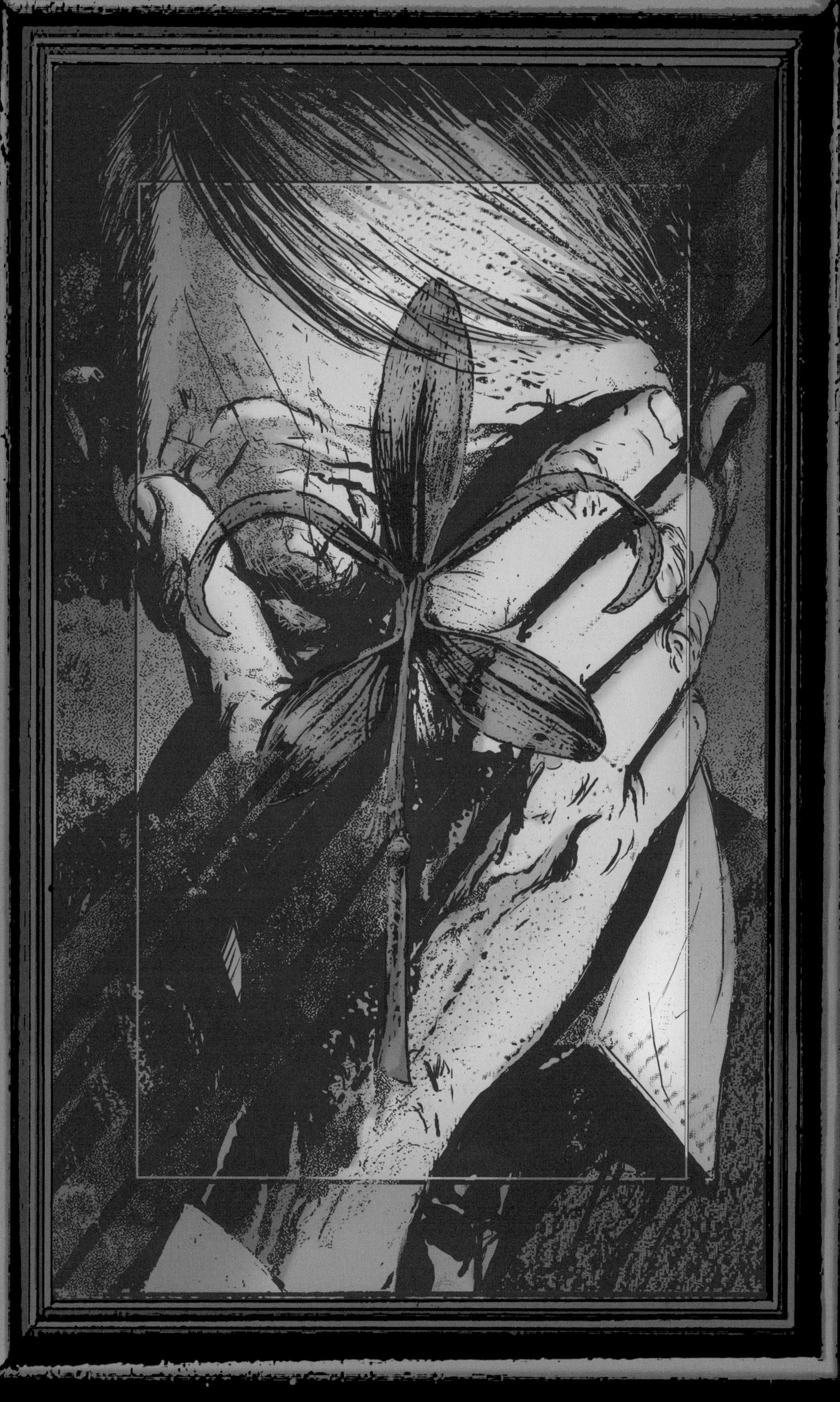

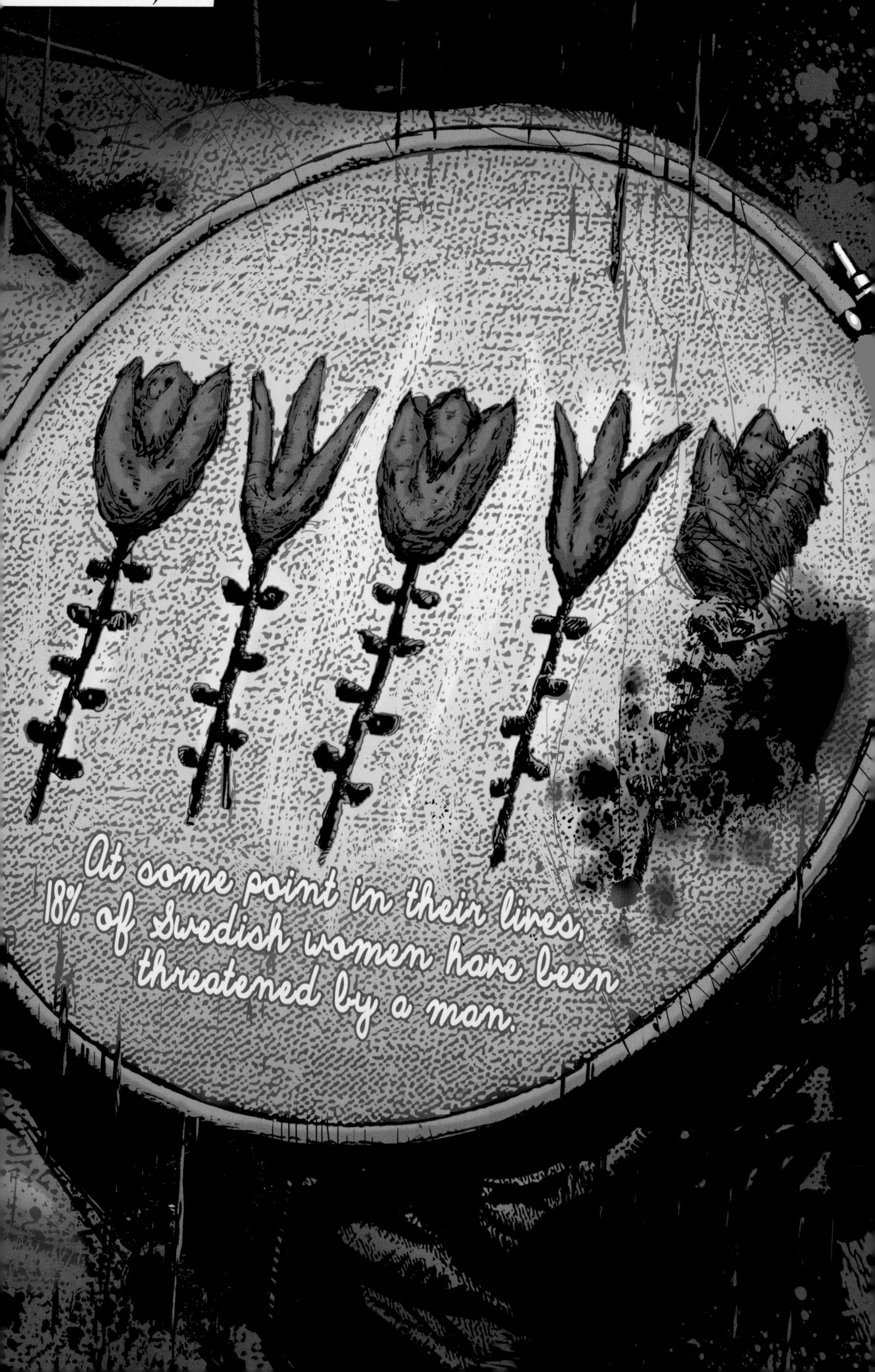
At some point in their lives,
18% of Swedish women have been
threatened by a man.

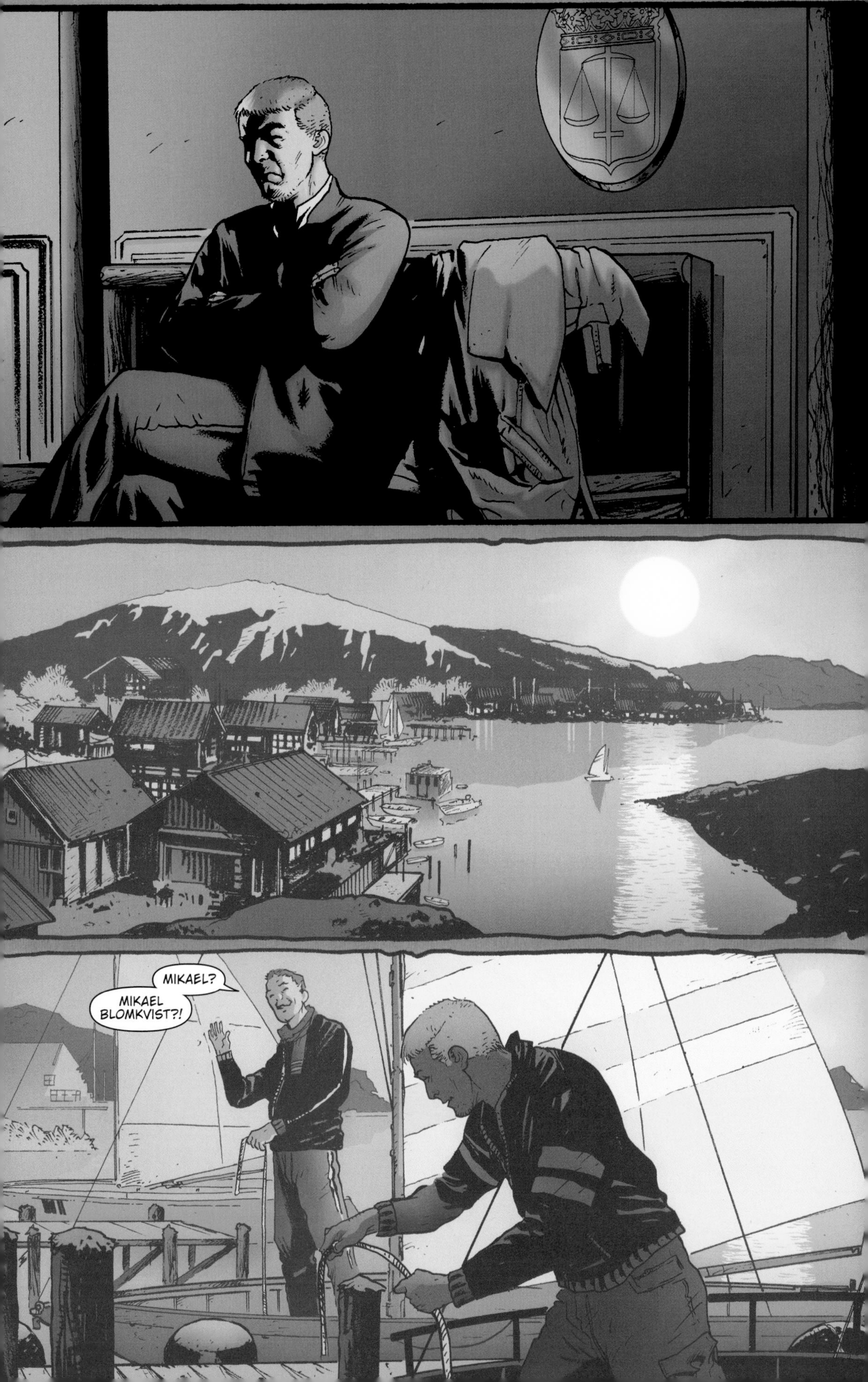
MIKAEL?
MIKAEL BLOMKVIST?!

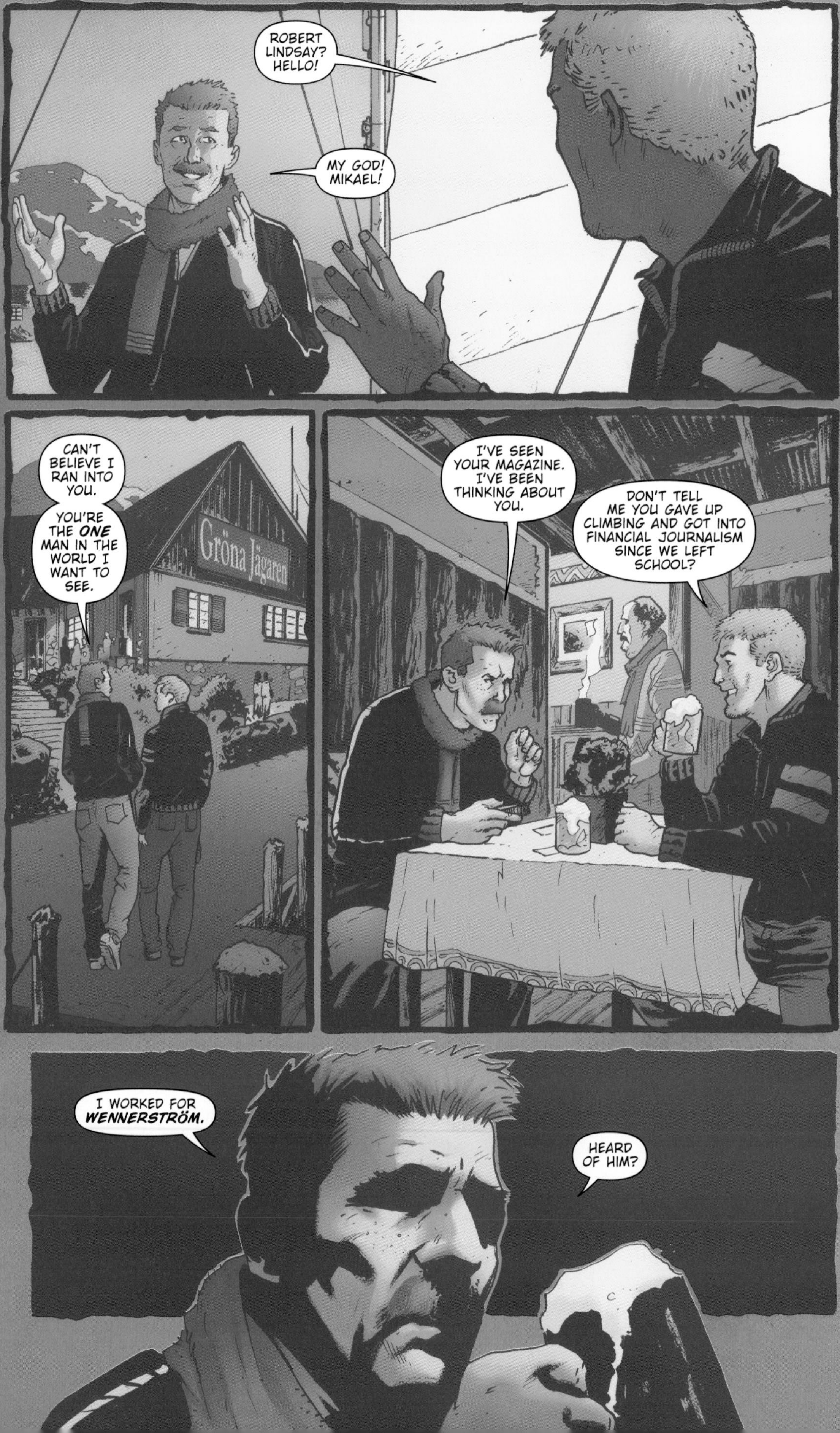
ROBERT LINDSAY? HELLO!
MY GOD! MIKAEL!
CAN'T BELIEVE I RAN INTO YOU.
YOU'RE THE ONE MAN IN THE WORLD I WANT TO SEE.
Gröna Jägaren
I'VE SEEN YOUR MAGAZINE. I'VE BEEN THINKING ABOUT YOU.
DON'T TELL ME YOU GAVE UP CLIMBING AND GOT INTO FINANCIAL JOURNALISM SINCE WE LEFT SCHOOL?
I WORKED FOR WENNERSTRÖM.
HEARD OF HIM?

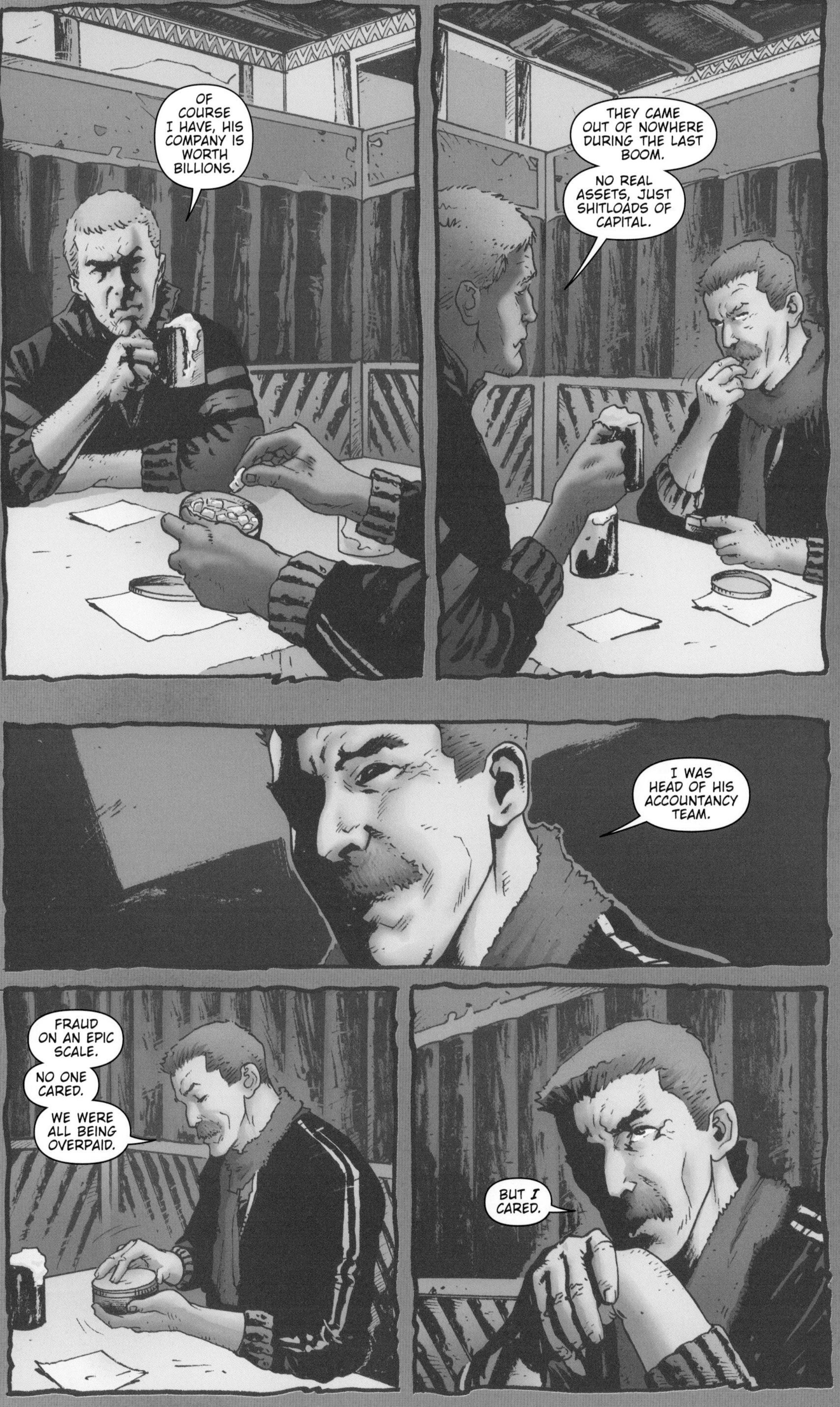
OF COURSE I HAVE, HIS COMPANY IS WORTH BILLIONS.
THEY CAME OUT OF NOWHERE DURING THE LAST BOOM.
NO REAL ASSETS, JUST SHITLOADS OF CAPITAL.
I WAS HEAD OF HIS ACCOUNTANCY TEAM.
FRAUD ON AN EPIC SCALE.
NO ONE CARED.
WE WERE ALL BEING OVERPAID.
BUT *I* CARED.

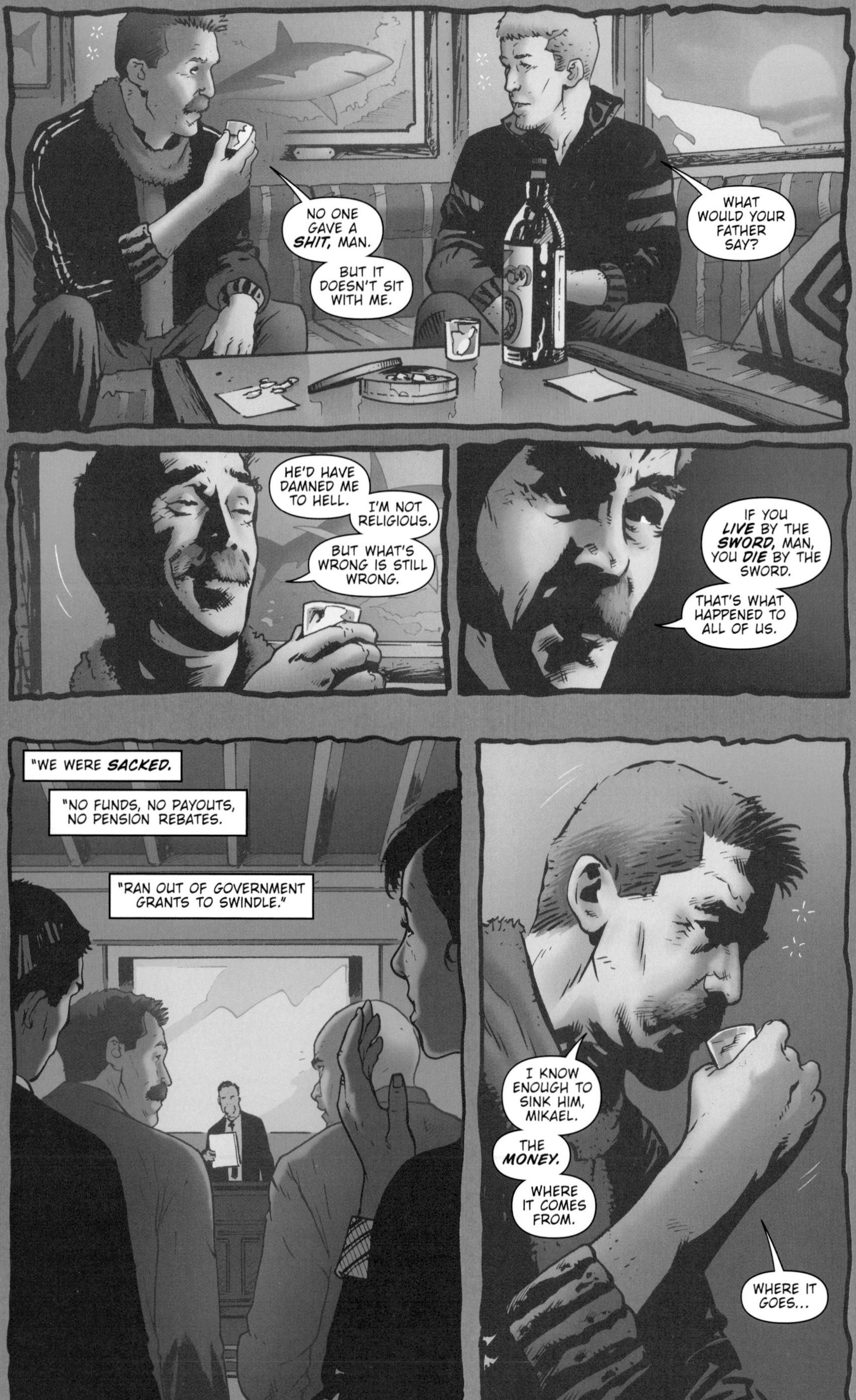
NO ONE GAVE A SHIT, MAN.
BUT IT DOESN'T SIT WITH ME.
WHAT WOULD YOUR FATHER SAY?
HE'D HAVE DAMNED ME TO HELL.
I'M NOT RELIGIOUS.
BUT WHAT'S WRONG IS STILL WRONG.
IF YOU LIVE BY THE SWORD, MAN, YOU DIE BY THE SWORD.
THAT'S WHAT HAPPENED TO ALL OF US.
"WE WERE SACKED.
"NO FUNDS, NO PAYOUTS, NO PENSION REBATES.
"RAN OUT OF GOVERNMENT GRANTS TO SWINDLE."
I KNOW ENOUGH TO SINK HIM, MIKAEL.
THE MONEY.
WHERE IT COMES FROM.
WHERE IT GOES...

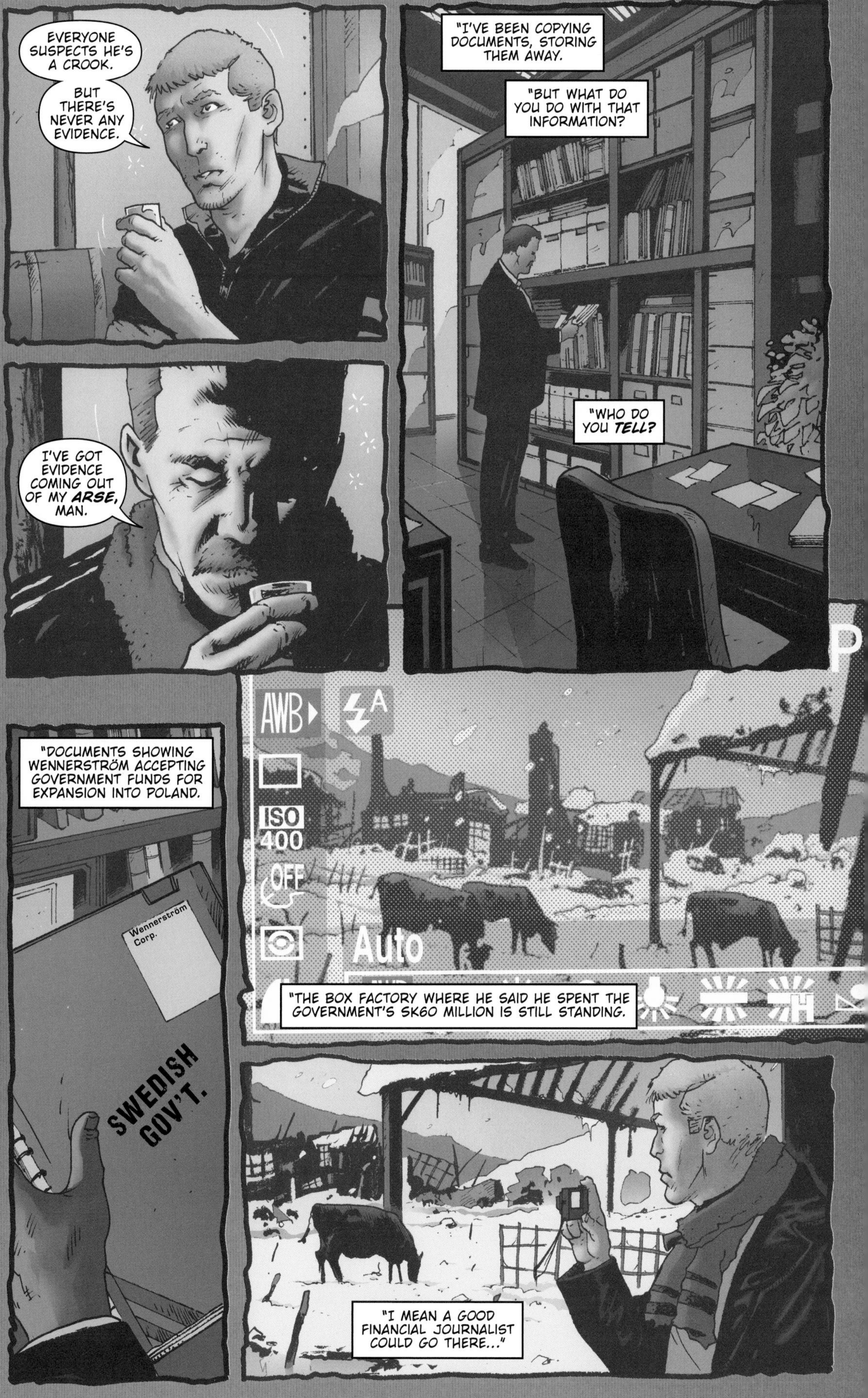
EVERYONE SUSPECTS HE'S A CROOK.
BUT THERE'S NEVER ANY EVIDENCE.
"I'VE BEEN COPYING DOCUMENTS, STORING THEM AWAY.
"BUT WHAT DO YOU DO WITH THAT INFORMATION?
I'VE GOT EVIDENCE COMING OUT OF MY **ARSE,** MAN.
"WHO DO YOU **TELL?**
"DOCUMENTS SHOWING WENNERSTRÖM ACCEPTING GOVERNMENT FUNDS FOR EXPANSION INTO POLAND.
Wennerström Corp.
SWEDISH GOV'T.
AWB
ISO 400
OFF
Auto
"THE BOX FACTORY WHERE HE SAID HE SPENT THE GOVERNMENT'S SK60 MILLION IS STILL STANDING.
"I MEAN A GOOD FINANCIAL JOURNALIST COULD GO THERE..."

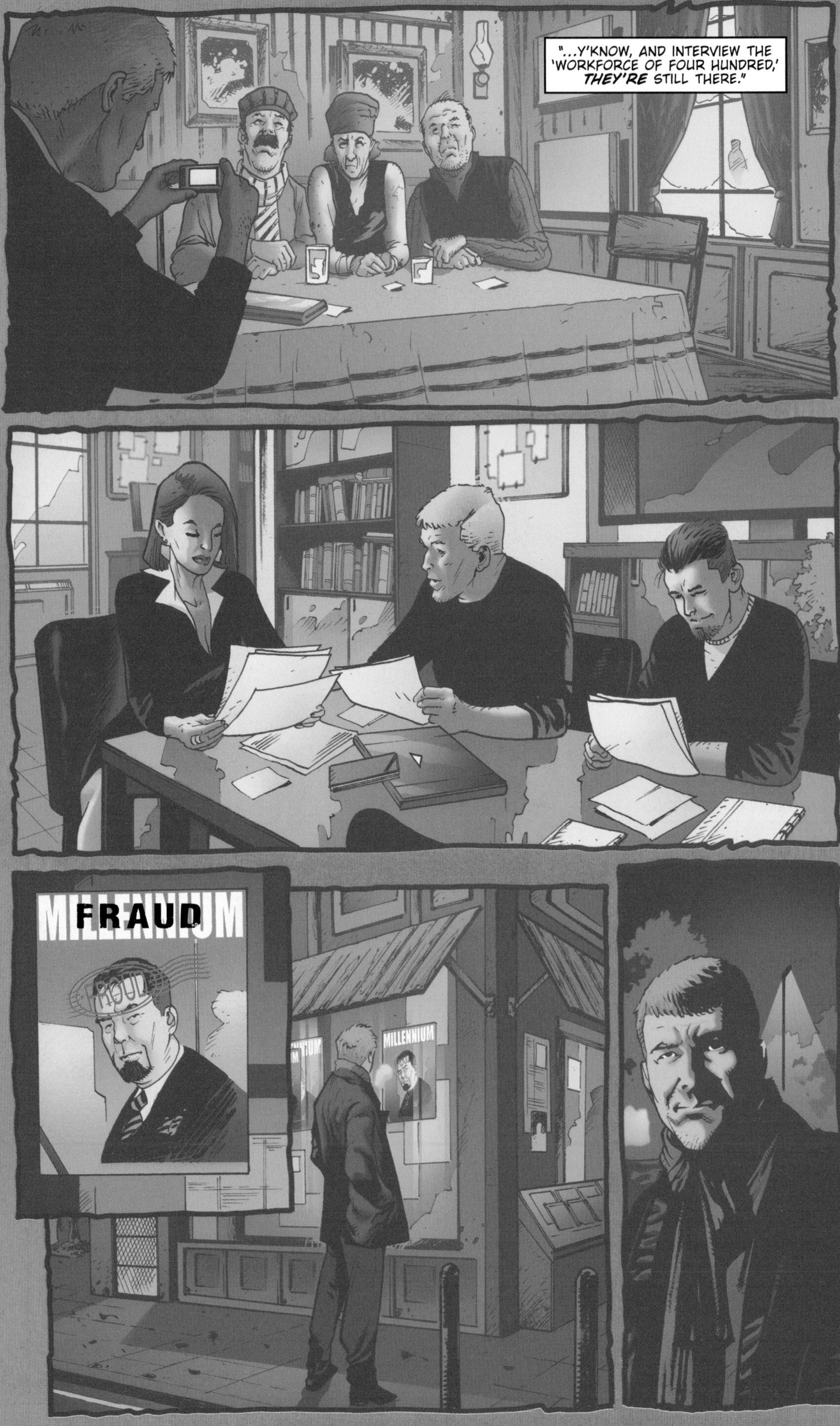
"...Y'KNOW, AND INTERVIEW THE 'WORKFORCE OF FOUR HUNDRED,' ***THEY'RE*** STILL THERE."
MILLENNIUM
FRAUD
MILLENNIUM

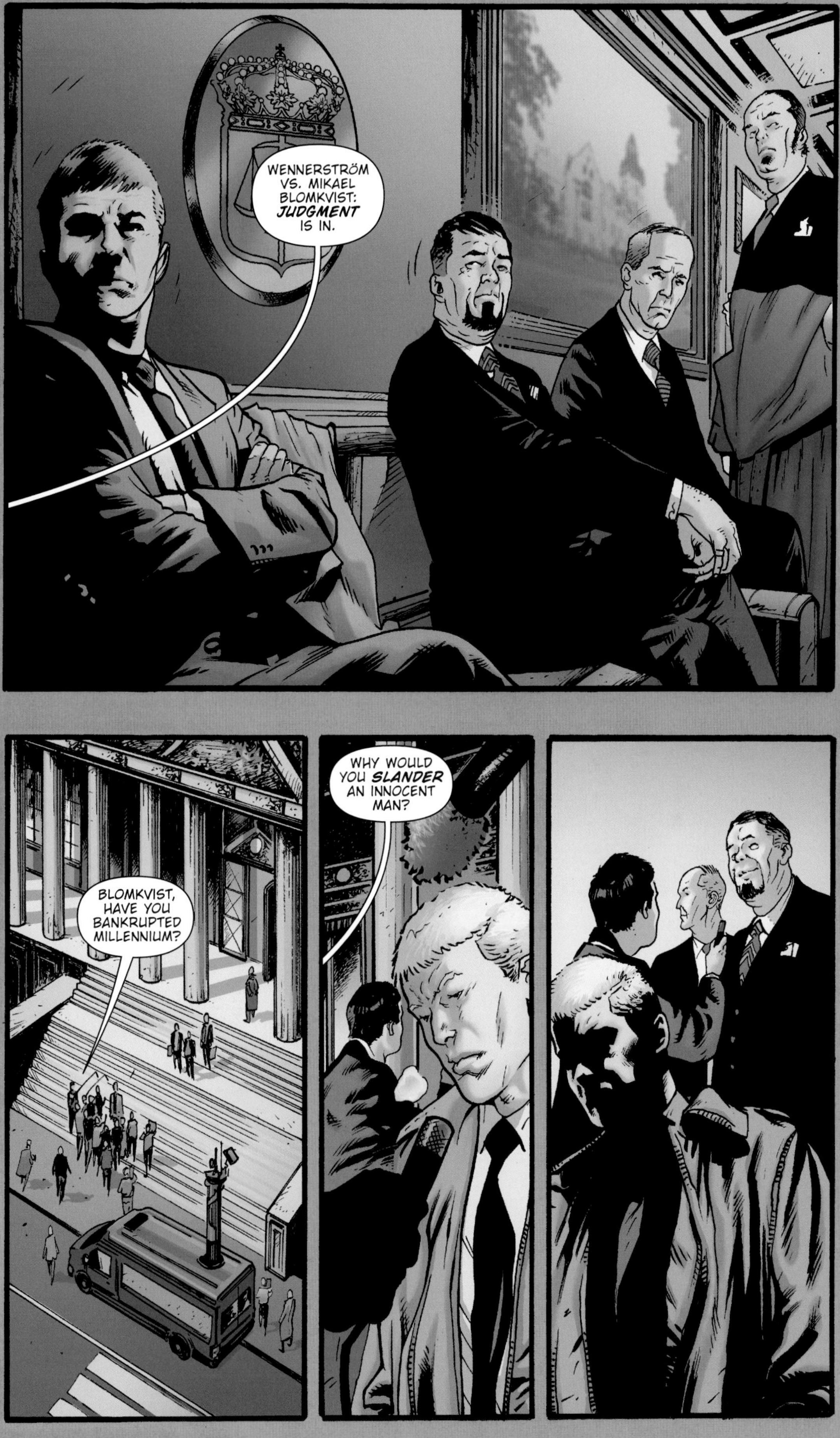
WENNERSTRÖM VS. MIKAEL BLOMKVIST: JUDGMENT IS IN.
BLOMKVIST, HAVE YOU BANKRUPTED MILLENNIUM?
WHY WOULD YOU SLANDER AN INNOCENT MAN?

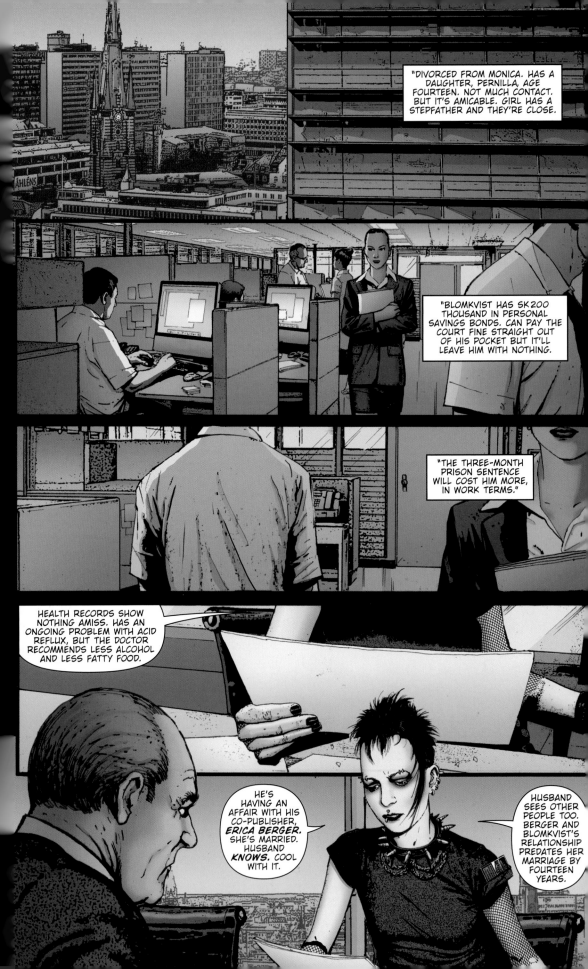

"DIVORCED FROM MONICA. HAS A DAUGHTER, PERNILLA, AGE FOURTEEN. NOT MUCH CONTACT. BUT IT'S AMICABLE. GIRL HAS A STEPFATHER AND THEY'RE CLOSE.

"BLOMKVIST HAS SK200 THOUSAND IN PERSONAL SAVINGS BONDS. CAN PAY THE COURT FINE STRAIGHT OUT OF HIS POCKET BUT IT'LL LEAVE HIM WITH NOTHING.

"THE THREE-MONTH PRISON SENTENCE WILL COST HIM MORE, IN WORK TERMS."

HEALTH RECORDS SHOW NOTHING AMISS. HAS AN ONGOING PROBLEM WITH ACID REFLUX, BUT THE DOCTOR RECOMMENDS LESS ALCOHOL AND LESS FATTY FOOD.

HE'S HAVING AN AFFAIR WITH HIS CO-PUBLISHER, *ERICA BERGER.* SHE'S MARRIED. HUSBAND *KNOWS.* COOL WITH IT.

HUSBAND SEES OTHER PEOPLE TOO. BERGER AND BLOMKVIST'S RELATIONSHIP PREDATES HER MARRIAGE BY FOURTEEN YEARS.

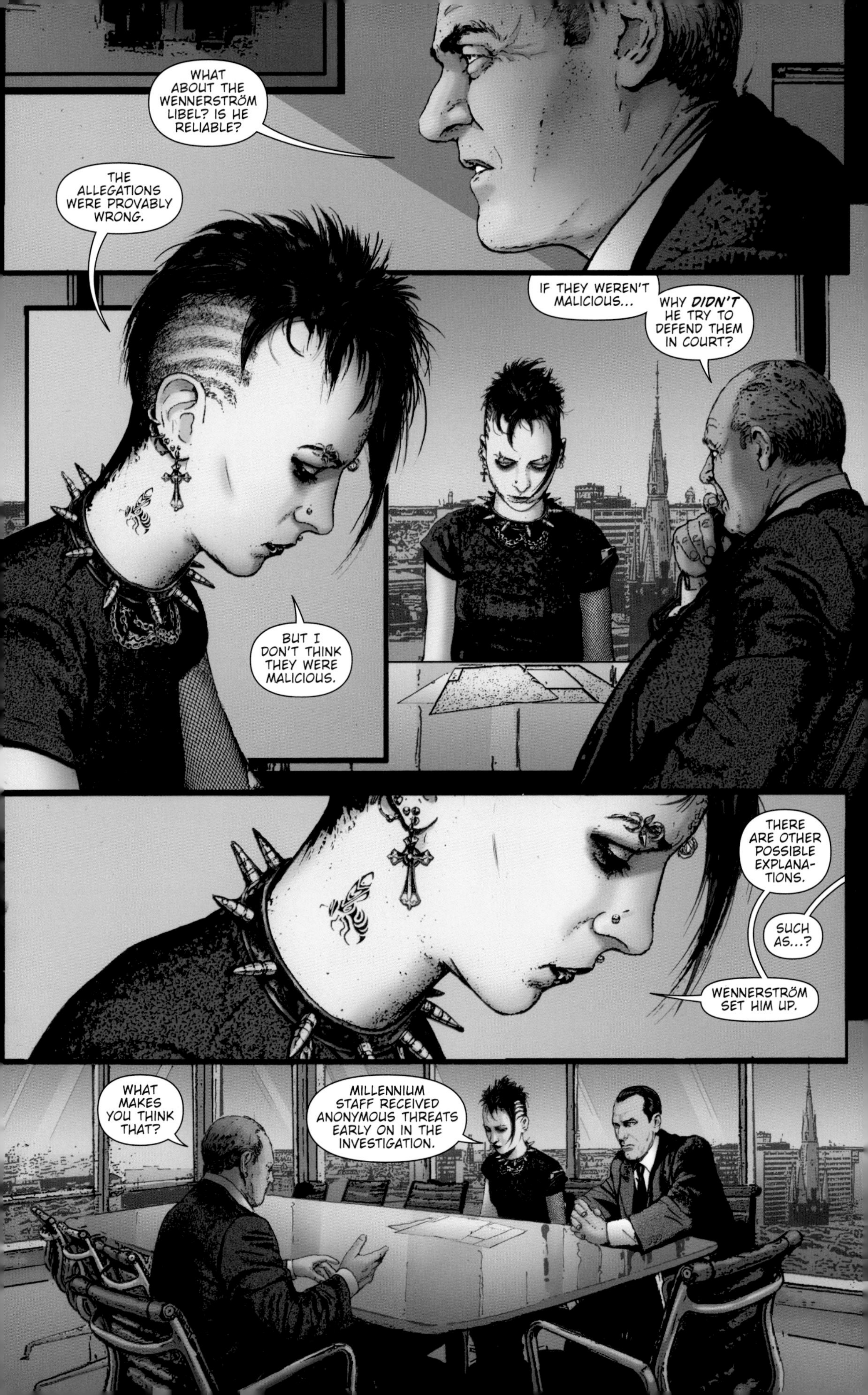
WHAT ABOUT THE WENNERSTRÖM LIBEL? IS HE RELIABLE?
THE ALLEGATIONS WERE PROVABLY WRONG.
BUT I DON'T THINK THEY WERE MALICIOUS.
IF THEY WEREN'T MALICIOUS...
WHY ***DIDN'T*** HE TRY TO DEFEND THEM IN COURT?
THERE ARE OTHER POSSIBLE EXPLANA-TIONS.
SUCH AS...?
WENNERSTRÖM SET HIM UP.
WHAT MAKES YOU THINK THAT?
MILLENNIUM STAFF RECEIVED ANONYMOUS THREATS EARLY ON IN THE INVESTIGATION.

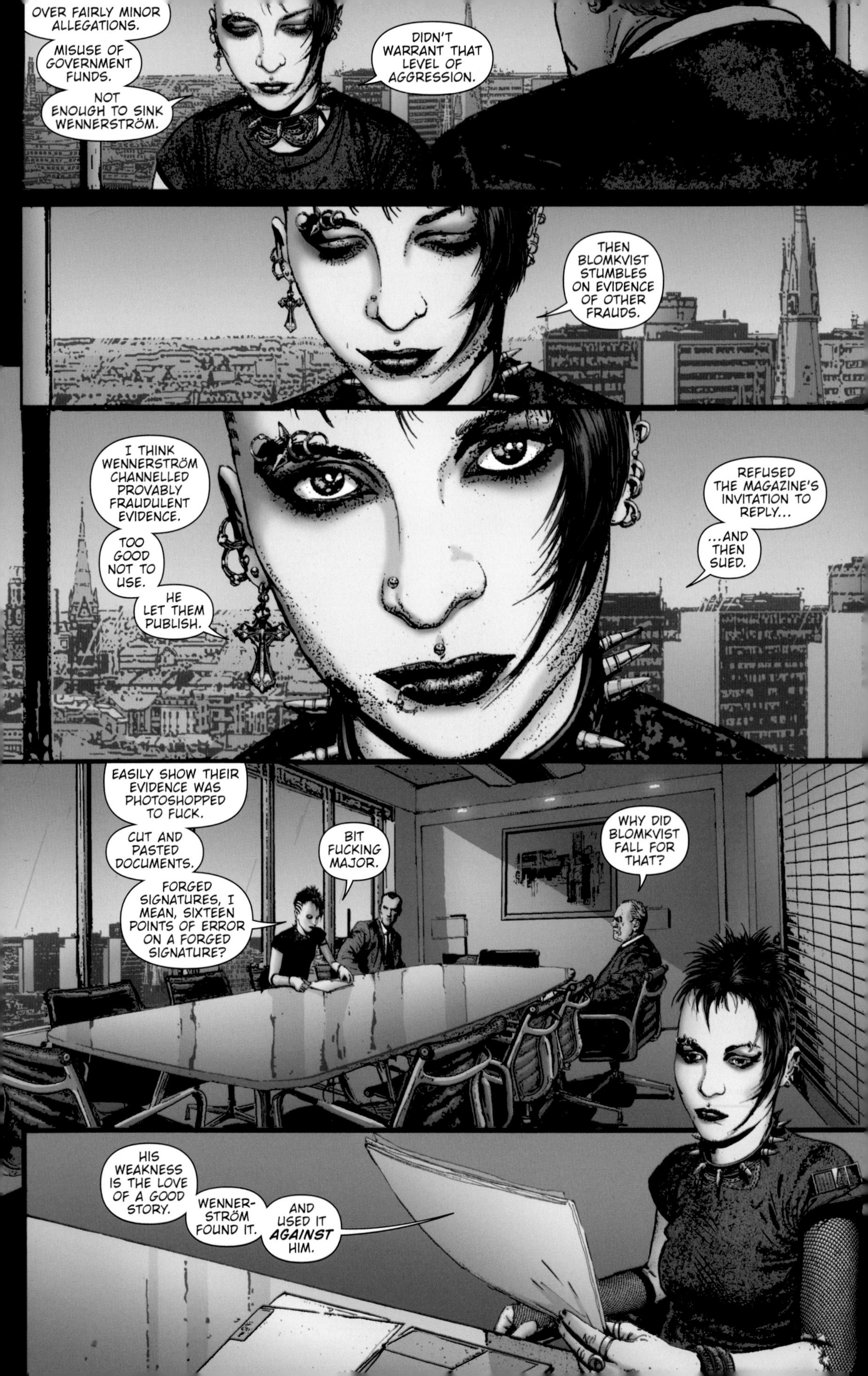
OVER FAIRLY MINOR ALLEGATIONS.
MISUSE OF GOVERNMENT FUNDS.
NOT ENOUGH TO SINK WENNERSTRÖM.
DIDN'T WARRANT THAT LEVEL OF AGGRESSION.
THEN BLOMKVIST STUMBLES ON EVIDENCE OF OTHER FRAUDS.
I THINK WENNERSTRÖM CHANNELLED PROVABLY FRAUDULENT EVIDENCE.
TOO GOOD NOT TO USE.
HE LET THEM PUBLISH.
REFUSED THE MAGAZINE'S INVITATION TO REPLY...
...AND THEN SUED.
EASILY SHOW THEIR EVIDENCE WAS PHOTOSHOPPED TO FUCK.
CUT AND PASTED DOCUMENTS.
FORGED SIGNATURES, I MEAN, SIXTEEN POINTS OF ERROR ON A FORGED SIGNATURE?
BIT FUCKING MAJOR.
WHY DID BLOMKVIST FALL FOR THAT?
HIS WEAKNESS IS THE LOVE OF A GOOD STORY.
WENNERSTRÖM FOUND IT.
AND USED IT *AGAINST* HIM.

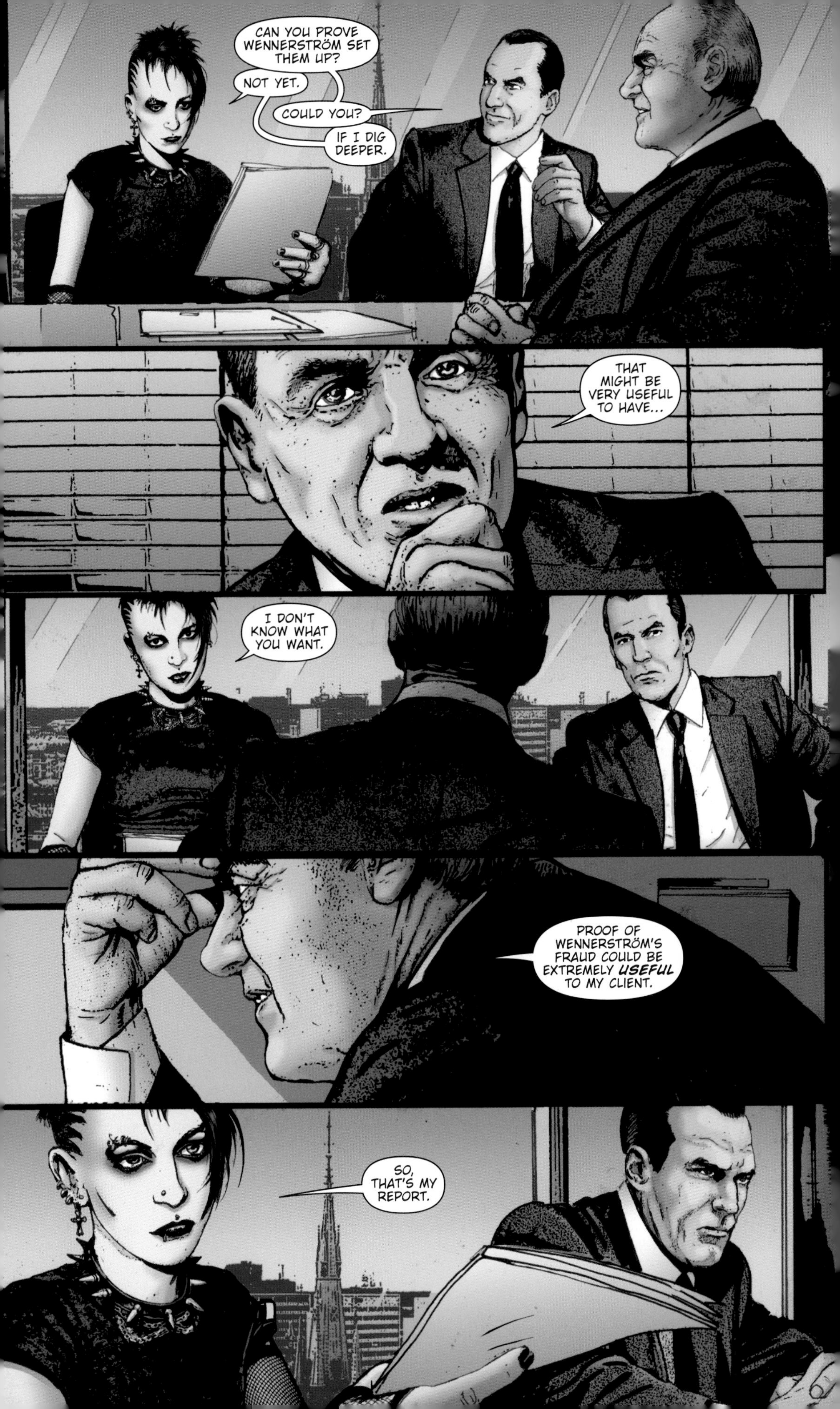

CAN YOU PROVE WENNERSTRÖM SET THEM UP?
NOT YET.
COULD YOU?
IF I DIG DEEPER.
THAT MIGHT BE VERY USEFUL TO HAVE...
I DON'T KNOW WHAT YOU WANT.
PROOF OF WENNERSTRÖM'S FRAUD COULD BE EXTREMELY *USEFUL* TO MY CLIENT.
SO, THAT'S MY REPORT.

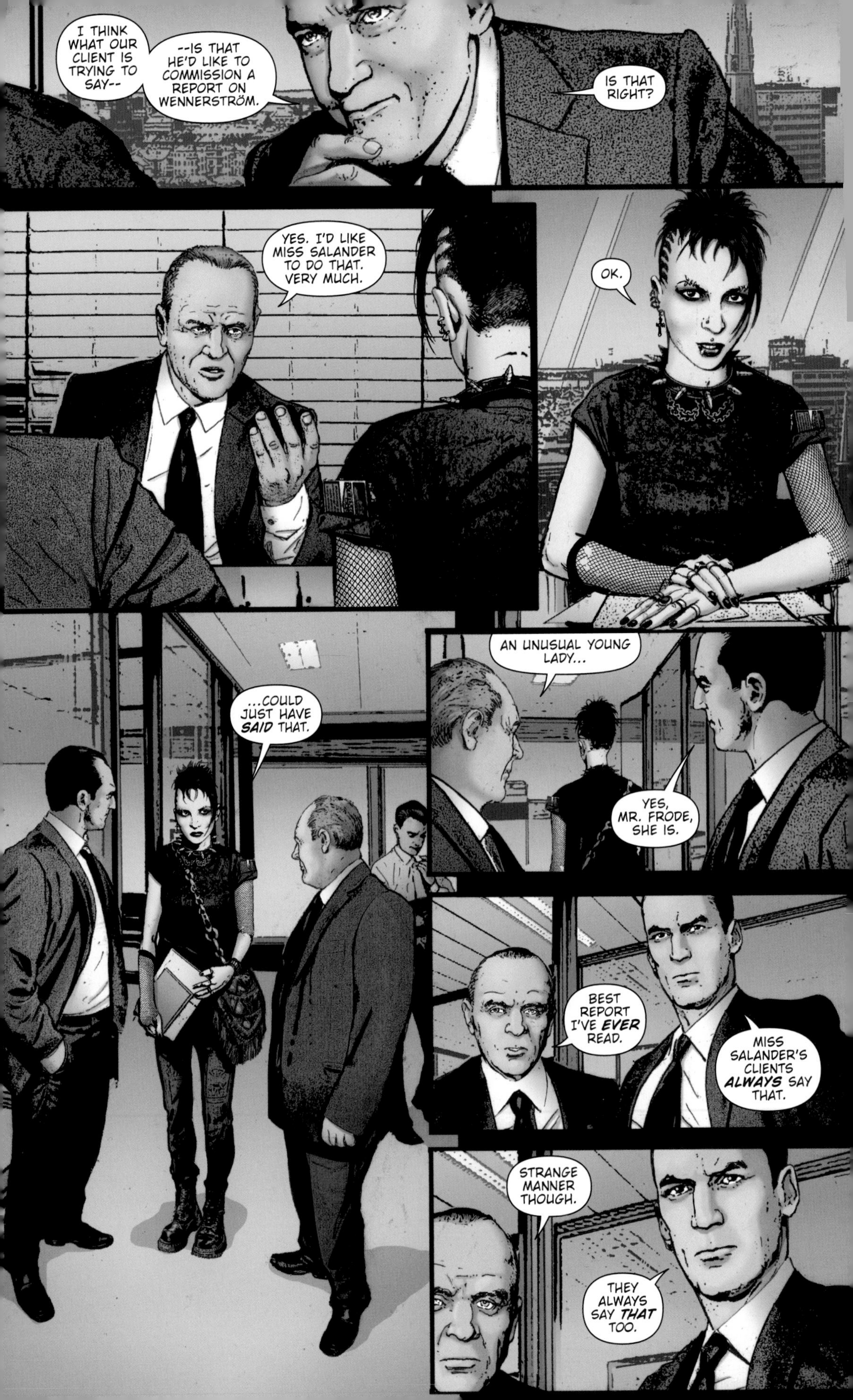
I THINK WHAT OUR CLIENT IS TRYING TO SAY--
--IS THAT HE'D LIKE TO COMMISSION A REPORT ON WENNERSTRÖM.
IS THAT RIGHT?
YES. I'D LIKE MISS SALANDER TO DO THAT. VERY MUCH.
OK.
...COULD JUST HAVE SAID THAT.
AN UNUSUAL YOUNG LADY...
YES, MR. FRODE, SHE IS.
BEST REPORT I'VE EVER READ.
MISS SALANDER'S CLIENTS ALWAYS SAY THAT.
STRANGE MANNER THOUGH.
THEY ALWAYS SAY THAT TOO.

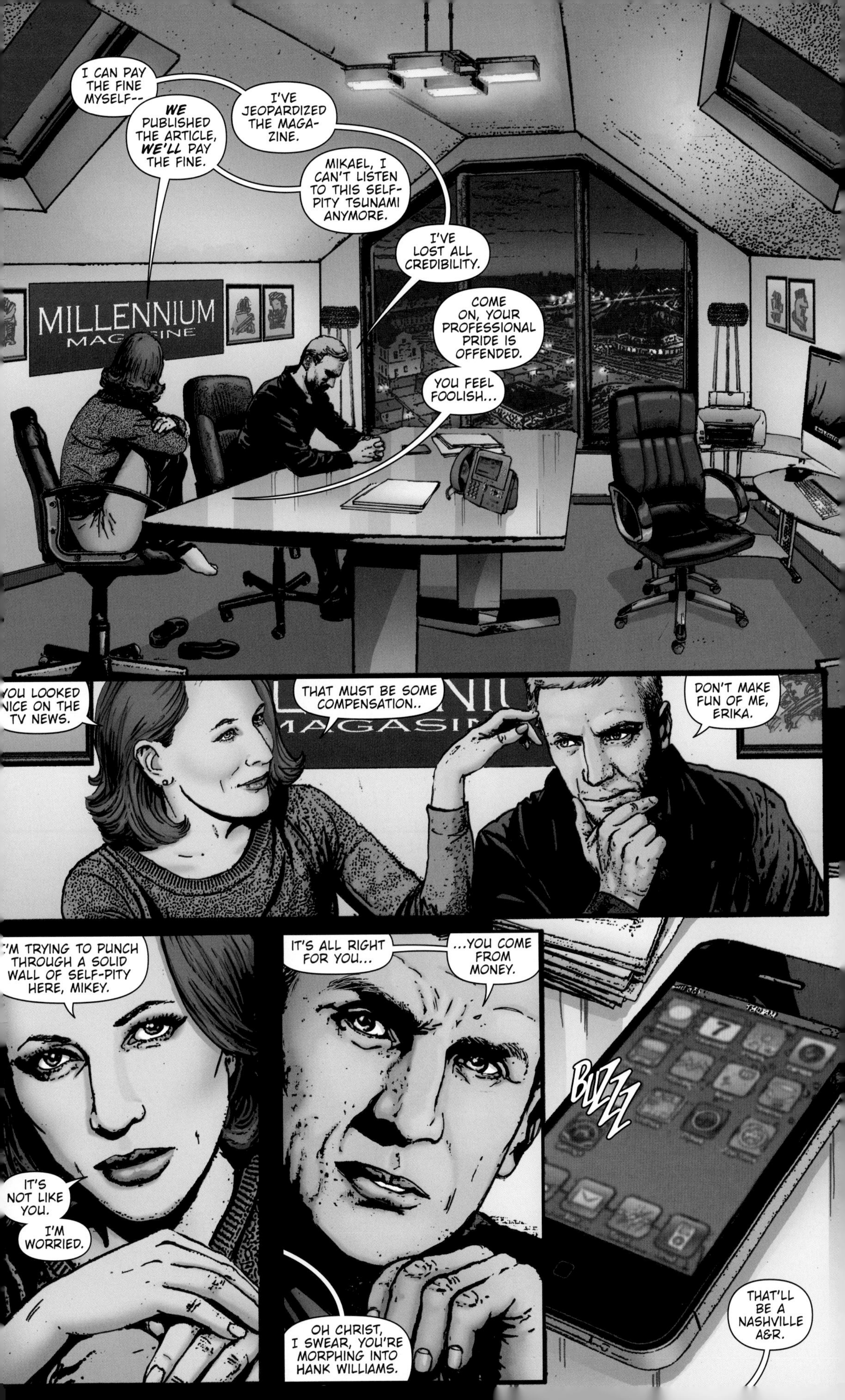
I CAN PAY THE FINE MYSELF--
WE PUBLISHED THE ARTICLE, WE'LL PAY THE FINE.
I'VE JEOPARDIZED THE MAGA- ZINE.
MIKAEL, I CAN'T LISTEN TO THIS SELF- PITY TSUNAMI ANYMORE.
I'VE LOST ALL CREDIBILITY.
COME ON, YOUR PROFESSIONAL PRIDE IS OFFENDED.
YOU FEEL FOOLISH...
MILLENNIUM MAGAZINE
YOU LOOKED NICE ON THE TV NEWS.
THAT MUST BE SOME COMPENSATION..
DON'T MAKE FUN OF ME, ERIKA.
I'M TRYING TO PUNCH THROUGH A SOLID WALL OF SELF-PITY HERE, MIKEY.
IT'S NOT LIKE YOU.
I'M WORRIED.
IT'S ALL RIGHT FOR YOU...
...YOU COME FROM MONEY.
OH CHRIST, I SWEAR, YOU'RE MORPHING INTO HANK WILLIAMS.
BUZZZ
THAT'LL BE A NASHVILLE A&R.

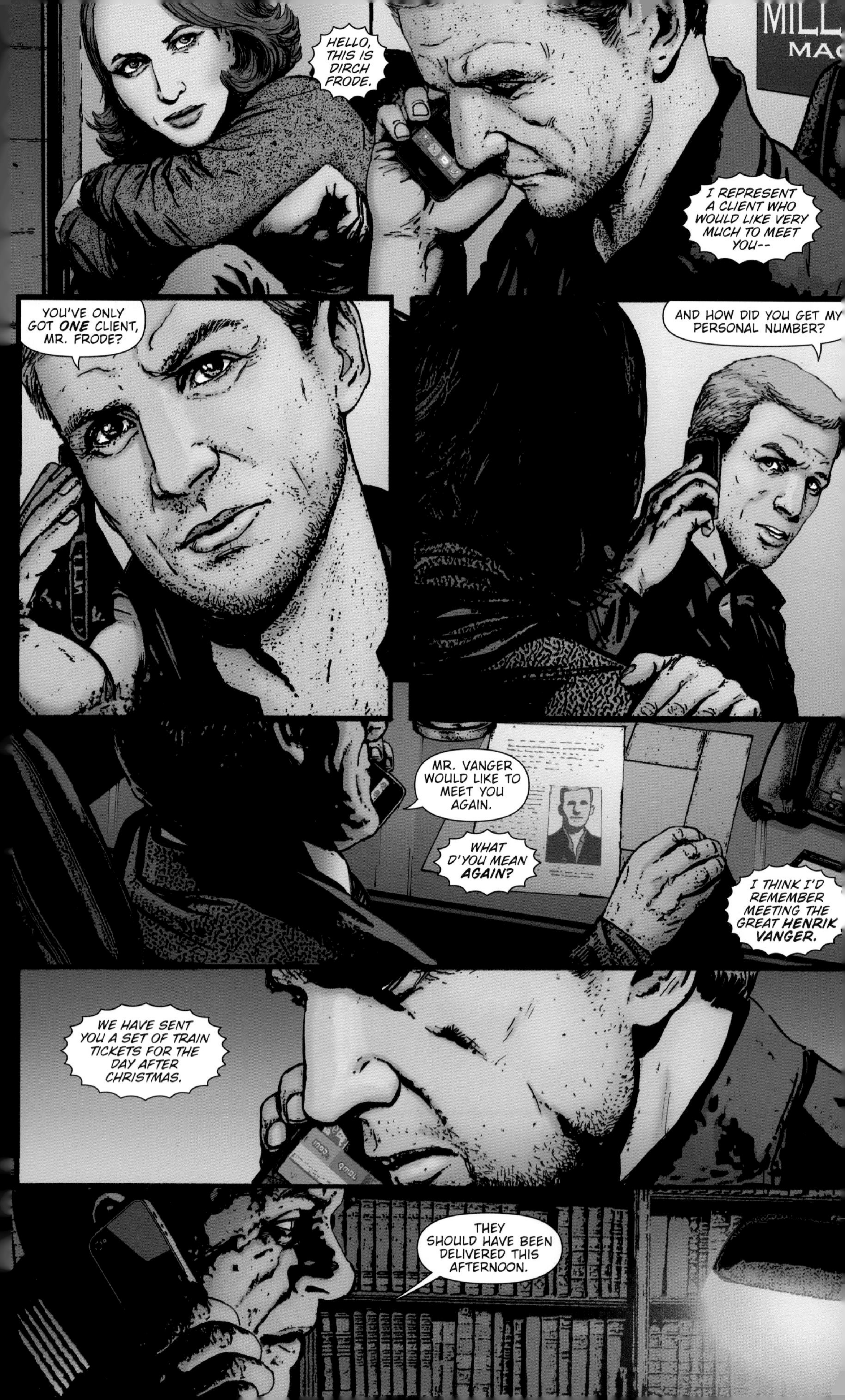
HELLO, THIS IS DIRCH FRODE.
I REPRESENT A CLIENT WHO WOULD LIKE VERY MUCH TO MEET YOU--
YOU'VE ONLY GOT **ONE** CLIENT, MR. FRODE?
AND HOW DID YOU GET MY PERSONAL NUMBER?
MR. VANGER WOULD LIKE TO MEET YOU AGAIN.
WHAT D'YOU MEAN **AGAIN?**
I THINK I'D REMEMBER MEETING THE GREAT **HENRIK VANGER.**
WE HAVE SENT YOU A SET OF TRAIN TICKETS FOR THE DAY AFTER CHRISTMAS.
THEY SHOULD HAVE BEEN DELIVERED THIS AFTERNOON.

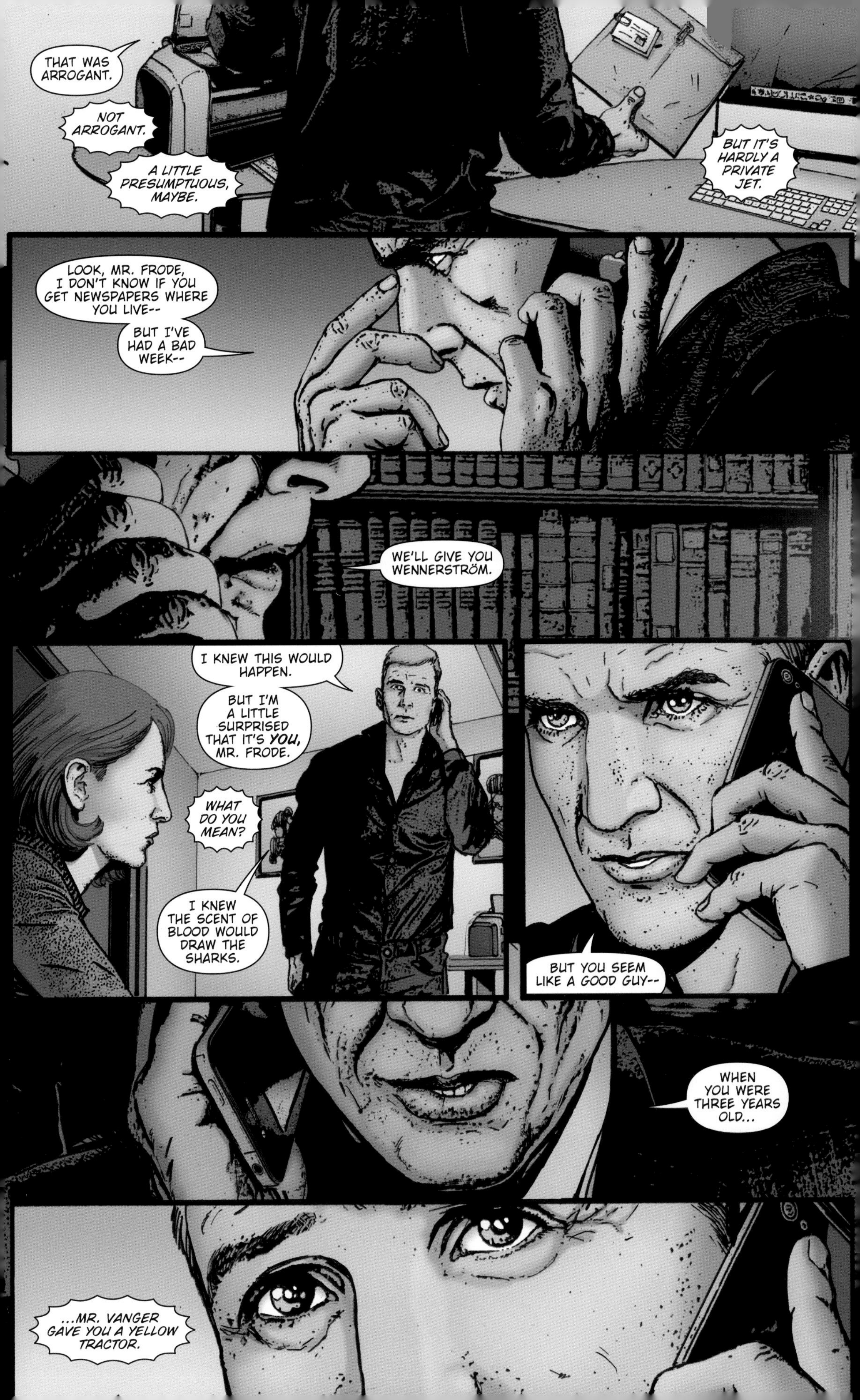
THAT WAS ARROGANT.
NOT ARROGANT.
A LITTLE PRESUMPTUOUS, MAYBE.
BUT IT'S HARDLY A PRIVATE JET.
LOOK, MR. FRODE, I DON'T KNOW IF YOU GET NEWSPAPERS WHERE YOU LIVE--
BUT I'VE HAD A BAD WEEK--
WE'LL GIVE YOU WENNERSTRÖM.
I KNEW THIS WOULD HAPPEN.
BUT I'M A LITTLE SURPRISED THAT IT'S YOU, MR. FRODE.
WHAT DO YOU MEAN?
I KNEW THE SCENT OF BLOOD WOULD DRAW THE SHARKS.
BUT YOU SEEM LIKE A GOOD GUY--
WHEN YOU WERE THREE YEARS OLD...
...MR. VANGER GAVE YOU A YELLOW TRACTOR.

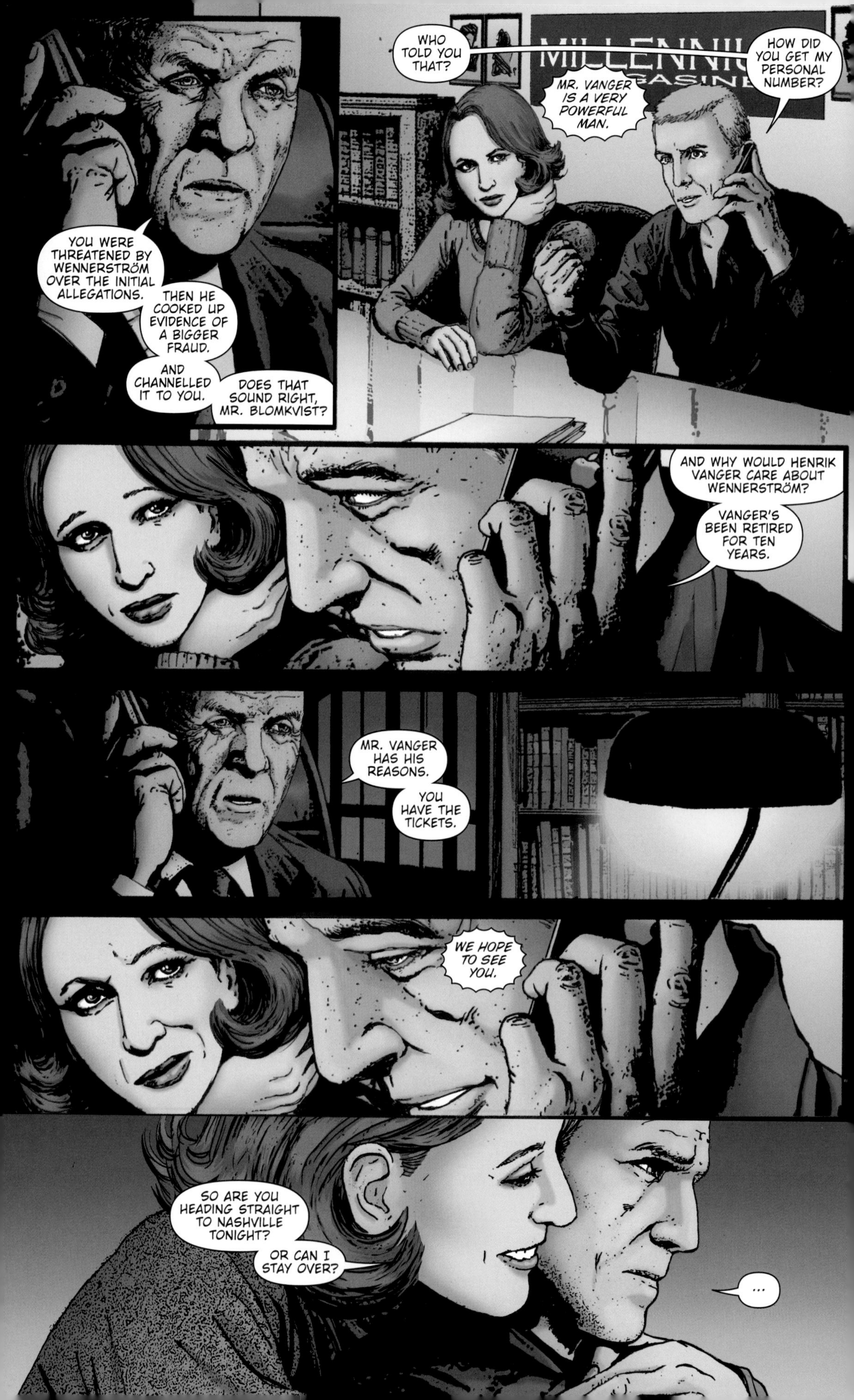
YOU WERE THREATENED BY WENNERSTRÖM OVER THE INITIAL ALLEGATIONS.
THEN HE COOKED UP EVIDENCE OF A BIGGER FRAUD.
AND CHANNELLED IT TO YOU.
DOES THAT SOUND RIGHT, MR. BLOMKVIST?
WHO TOLD YOU THAT?
HOW DID YOU GET MY PERSONAL NUMBER?
MR. VANGER IS A VERY POWERFUL MAN.
AND WHY WOULD HENRIK VANGER CARE ABOUT WENNERSTRÖM?
VANGER'S BEEN RETIRED FOR TEN YEARS.
MR. VANGER HAS HIS REASONS.
YOU HAVE THE TICKETS.
WE HOPE TO SEE YOU.
SO ARE YOU HEADING STRAIGHT TO NASHVILLE TONIGHT?
OR CAN I STAY OVER?
...

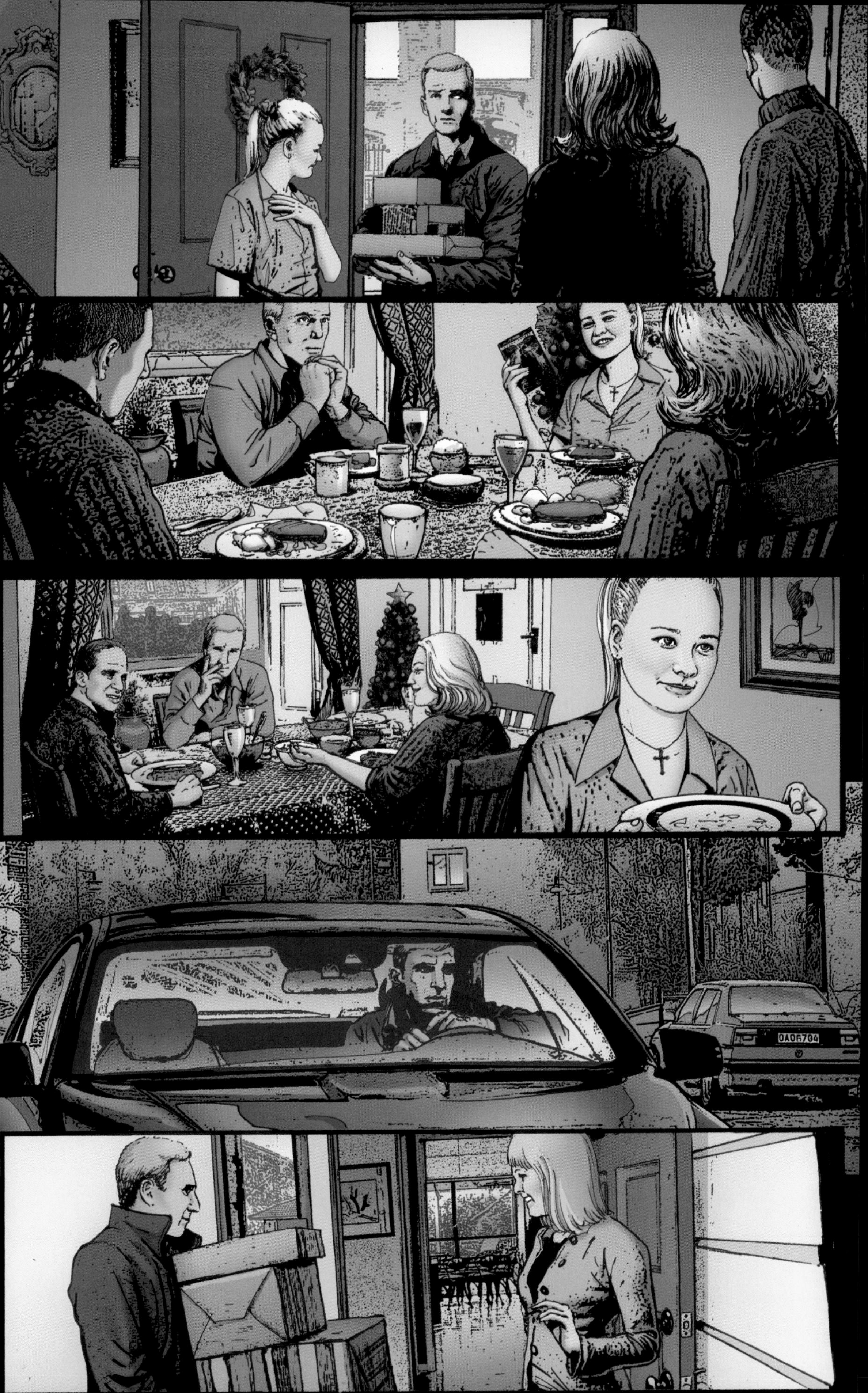

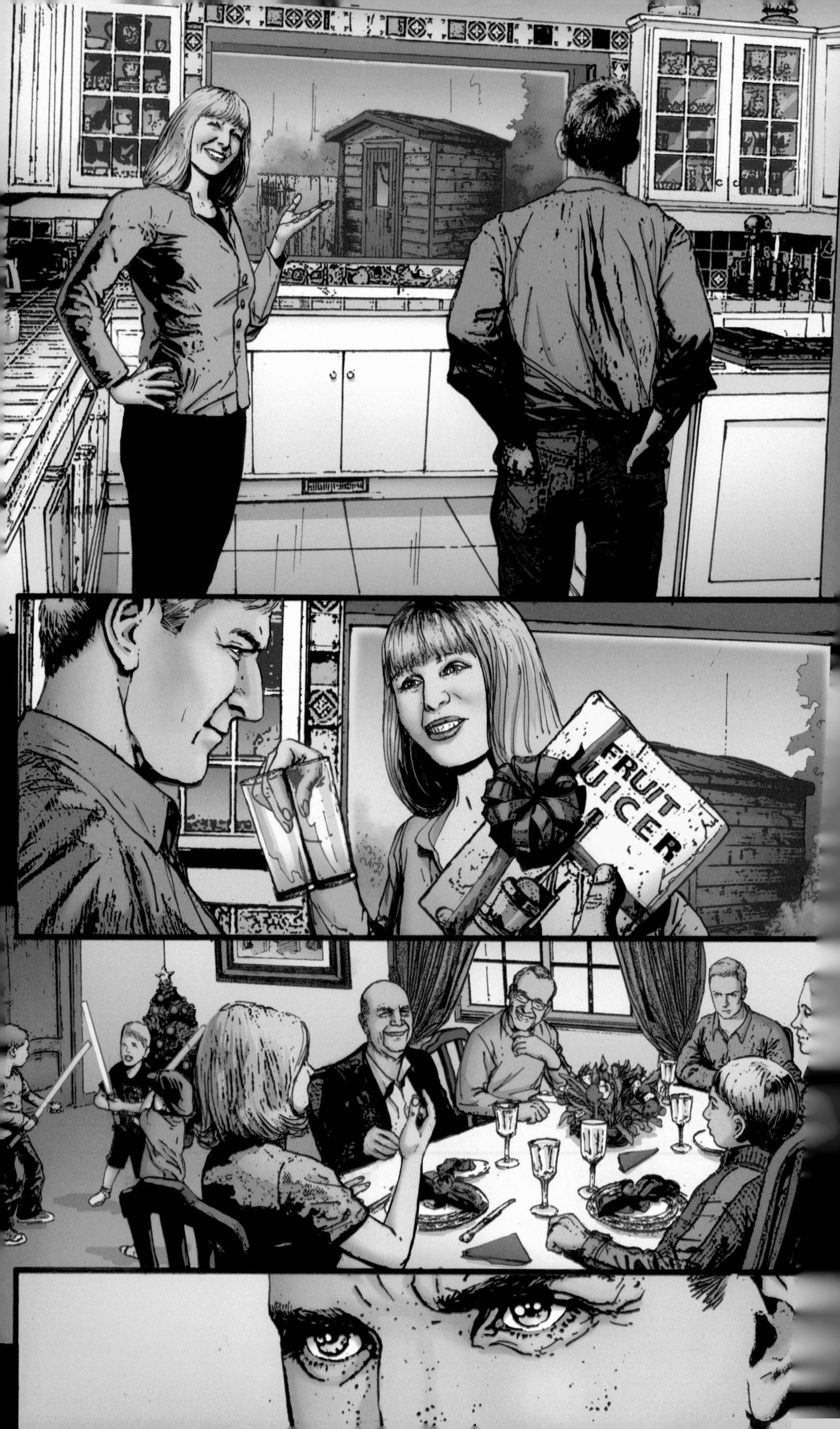
FRUIT
UICER

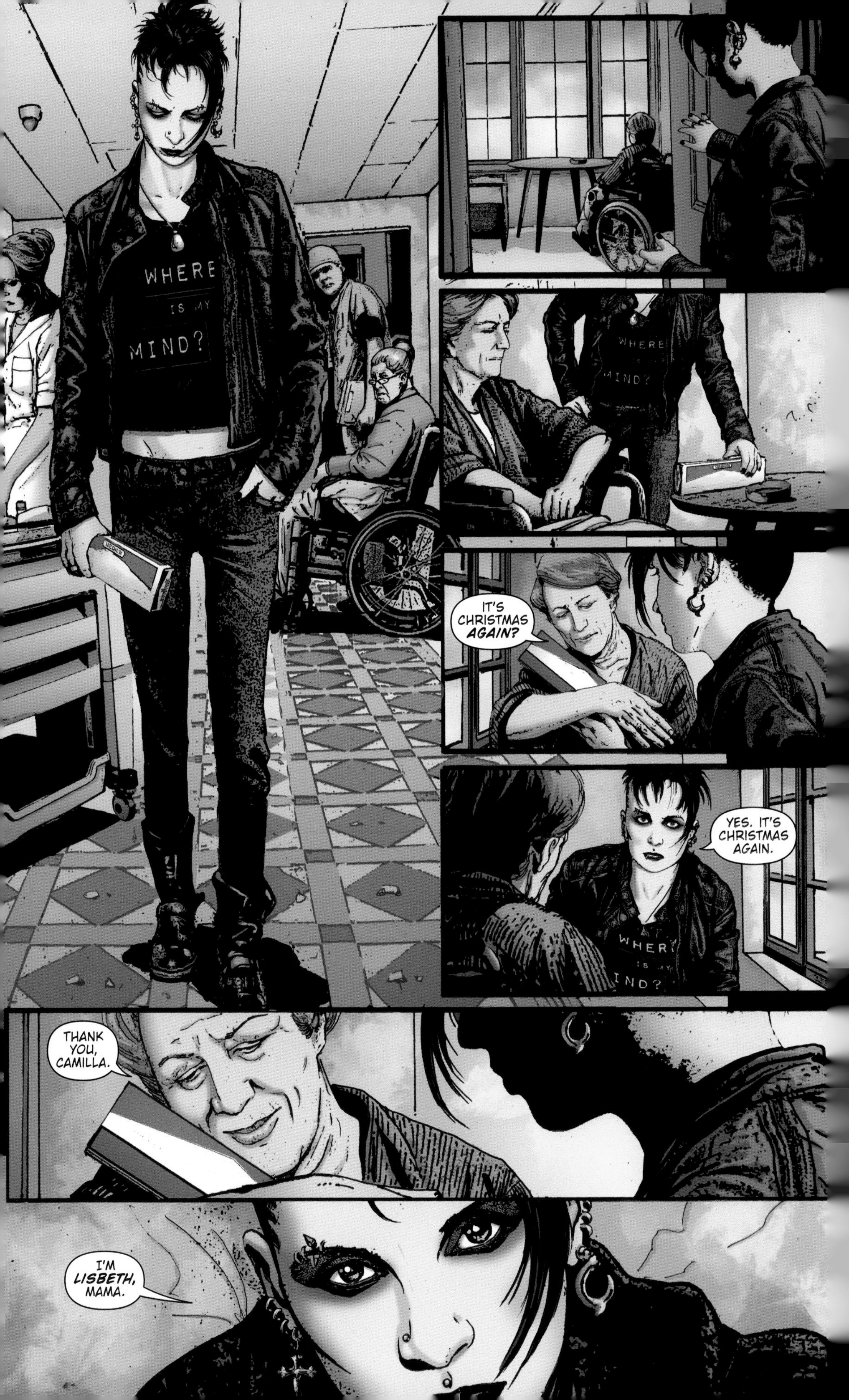
WHERE IS MY MIND?
IT'S CHRISTMAS *AGAIN?*
YES. IT'S CHRISTMAS AGAIN.
THANK YOU, CAMILLA.
I'M *LISBETH,* MAMA.

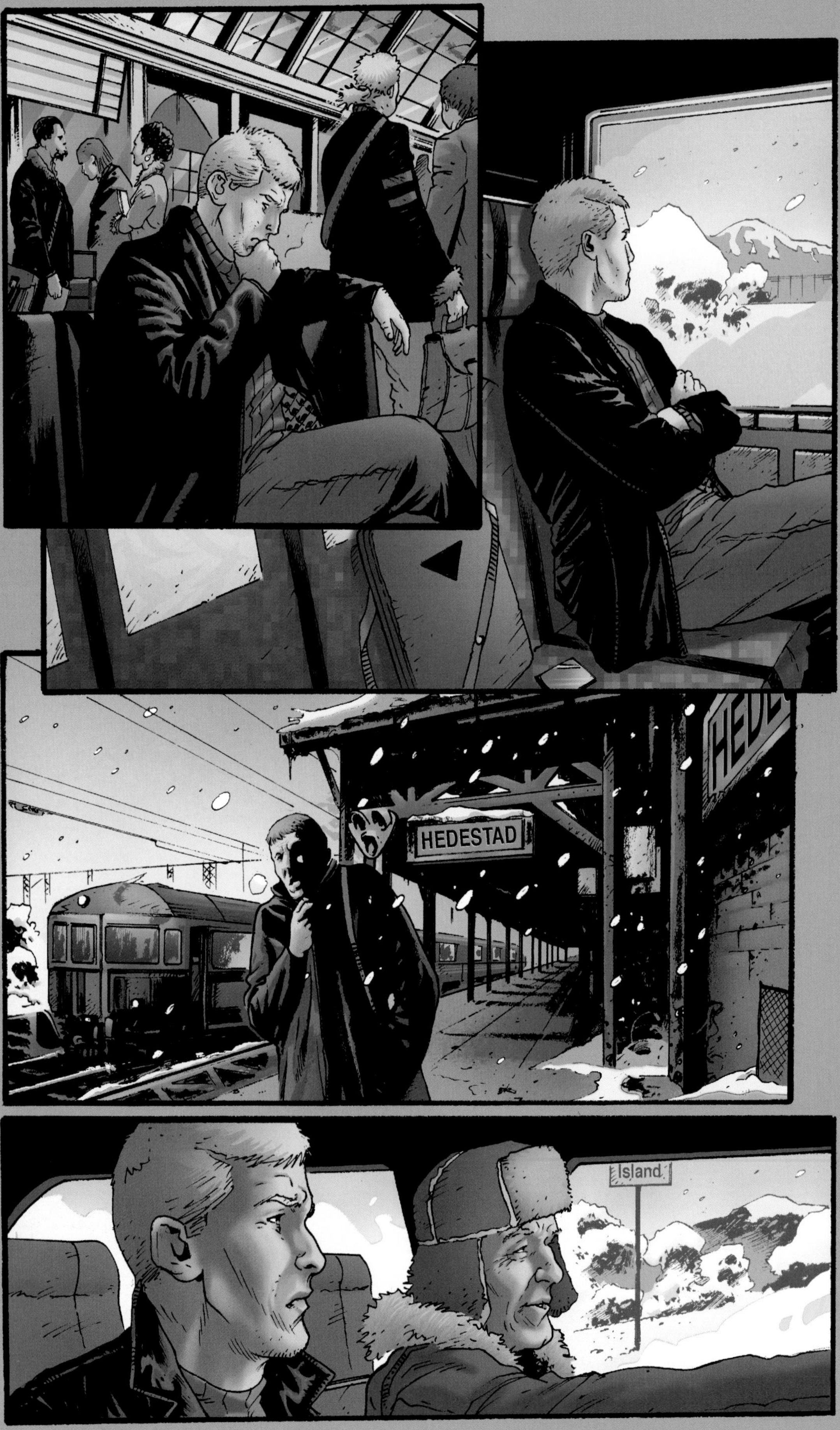

HEDESTAD
Island

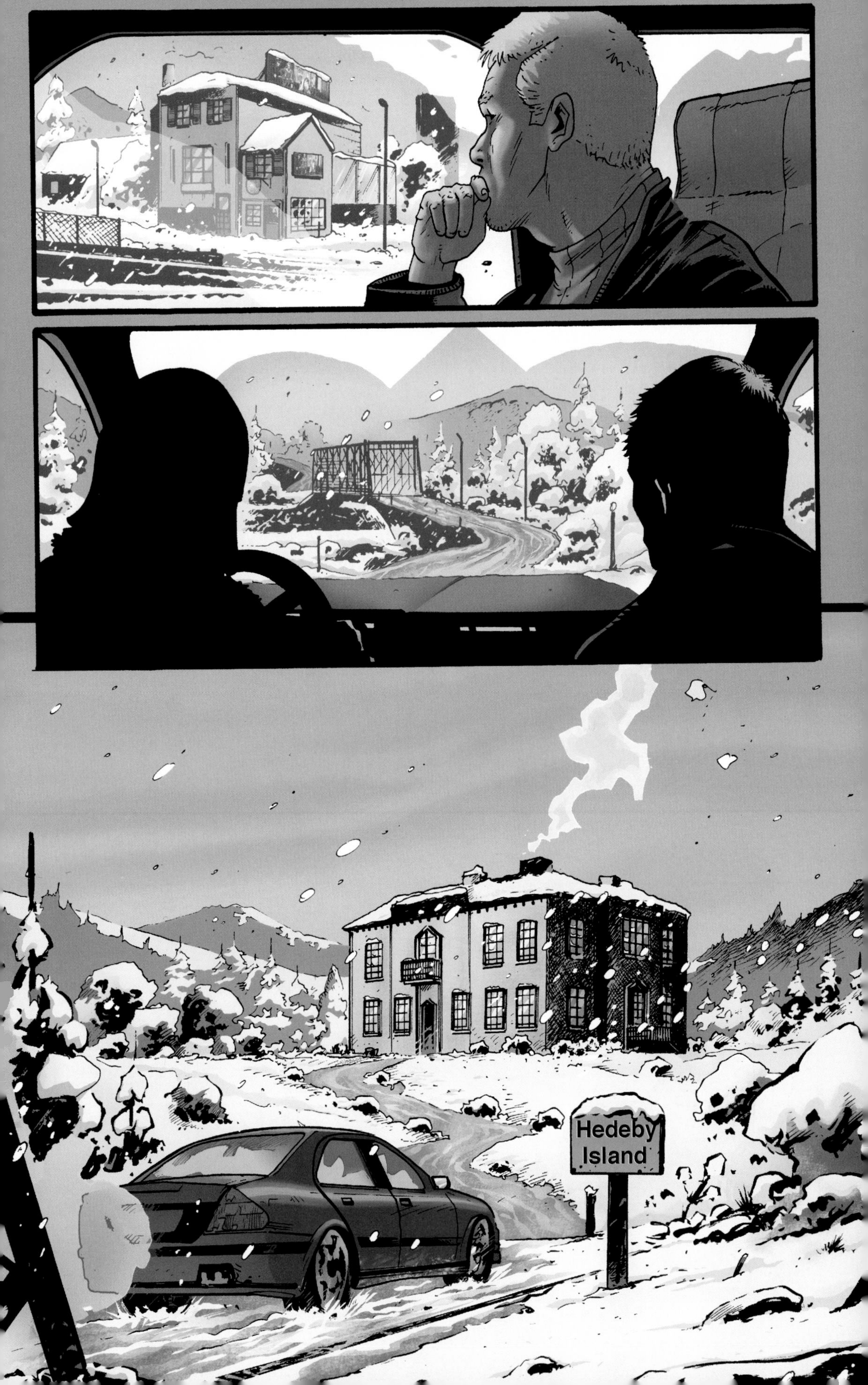
Hedeby Island

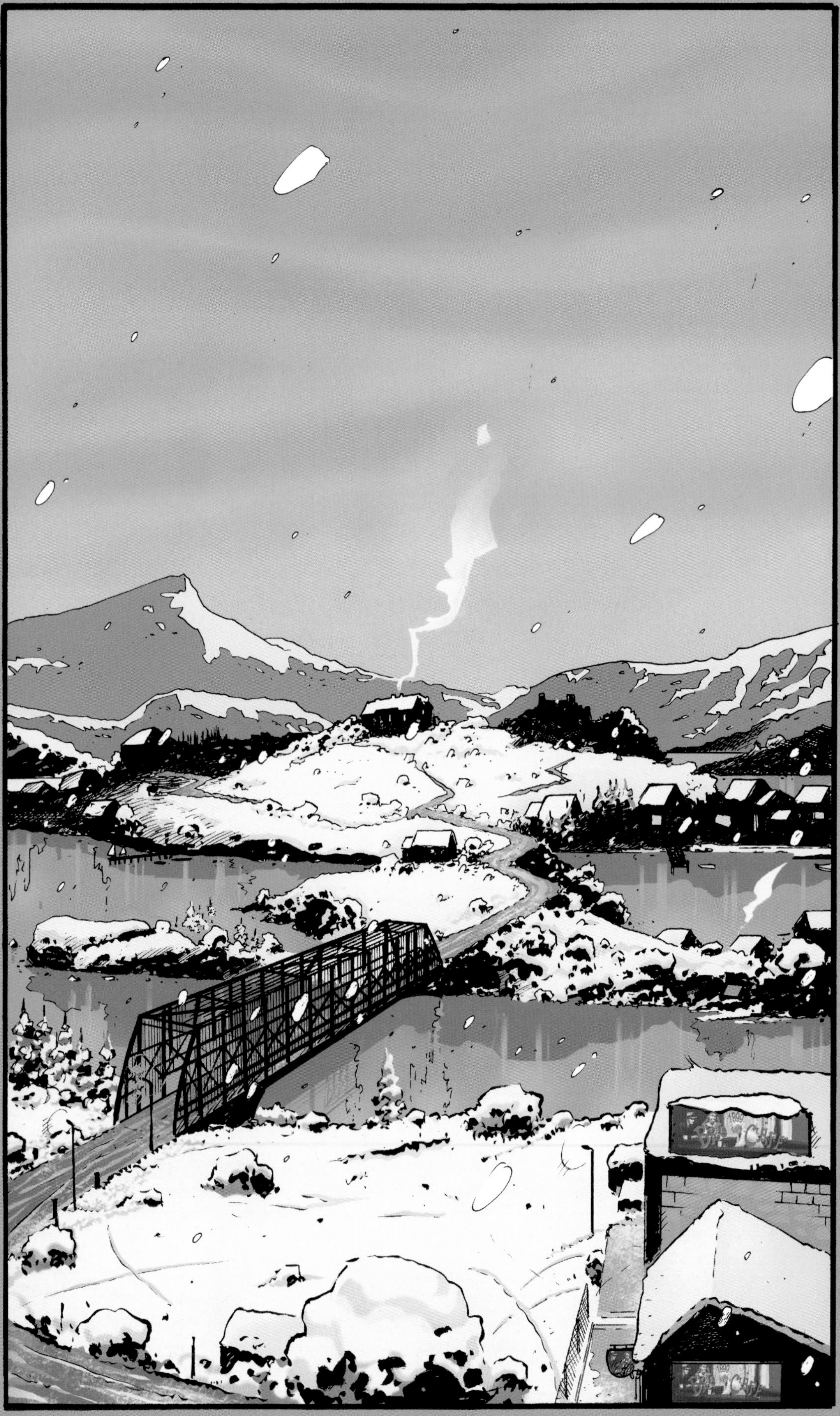

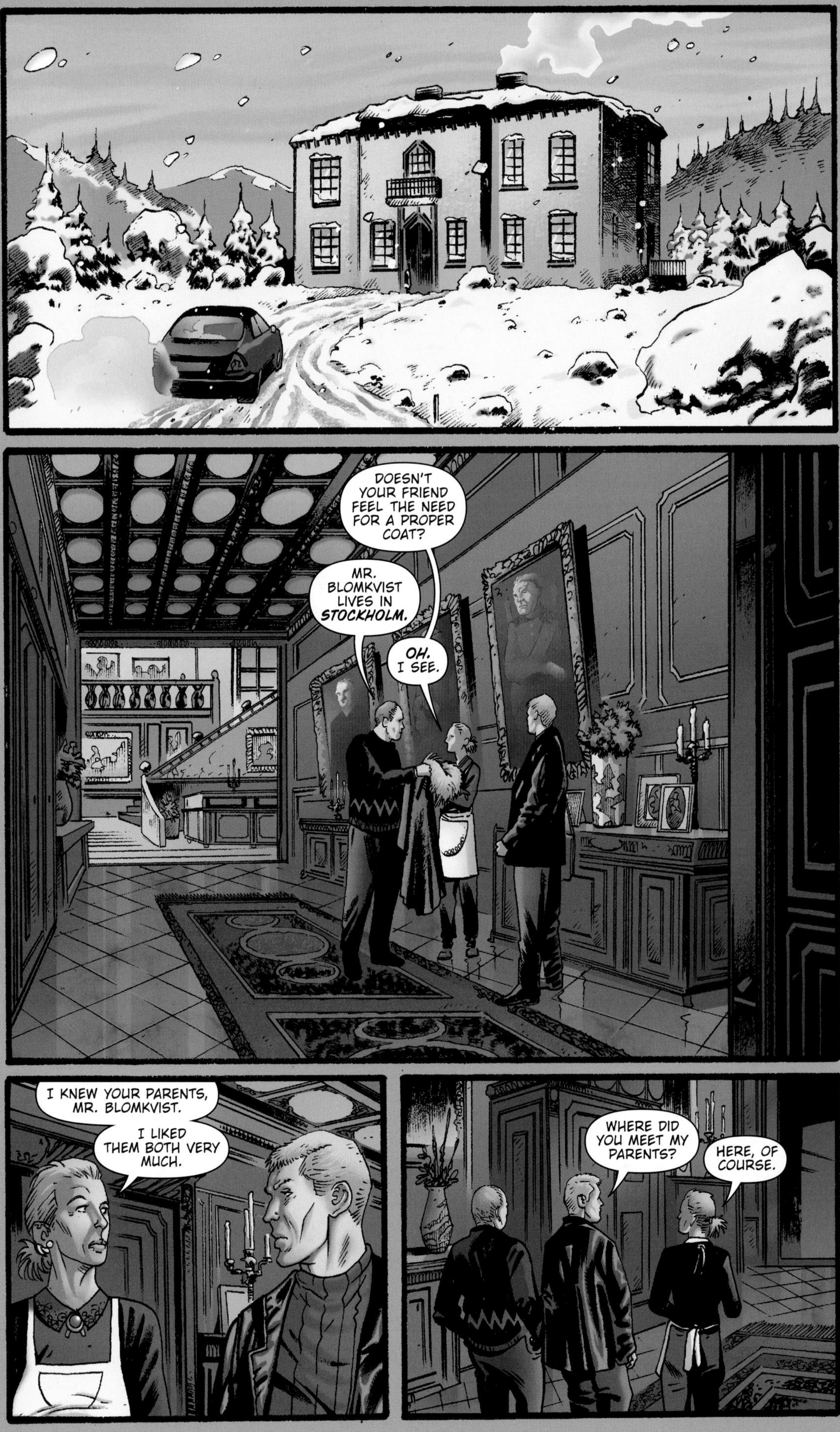
DOESN'T YOUR FRIEND FEEL THE NEED FOR A PROPER COAT?
MR. BLOMKVIST LIVES IN STOCKHOLM.
OH. I SEE.
I KNEW YOUR PARENTS, MR. BLOMKVIST.
I LIKED THEM BOTH VERY MUCH.
WHERE DID YOU MEET MY PARENTS?
HERE, OF COURSE.

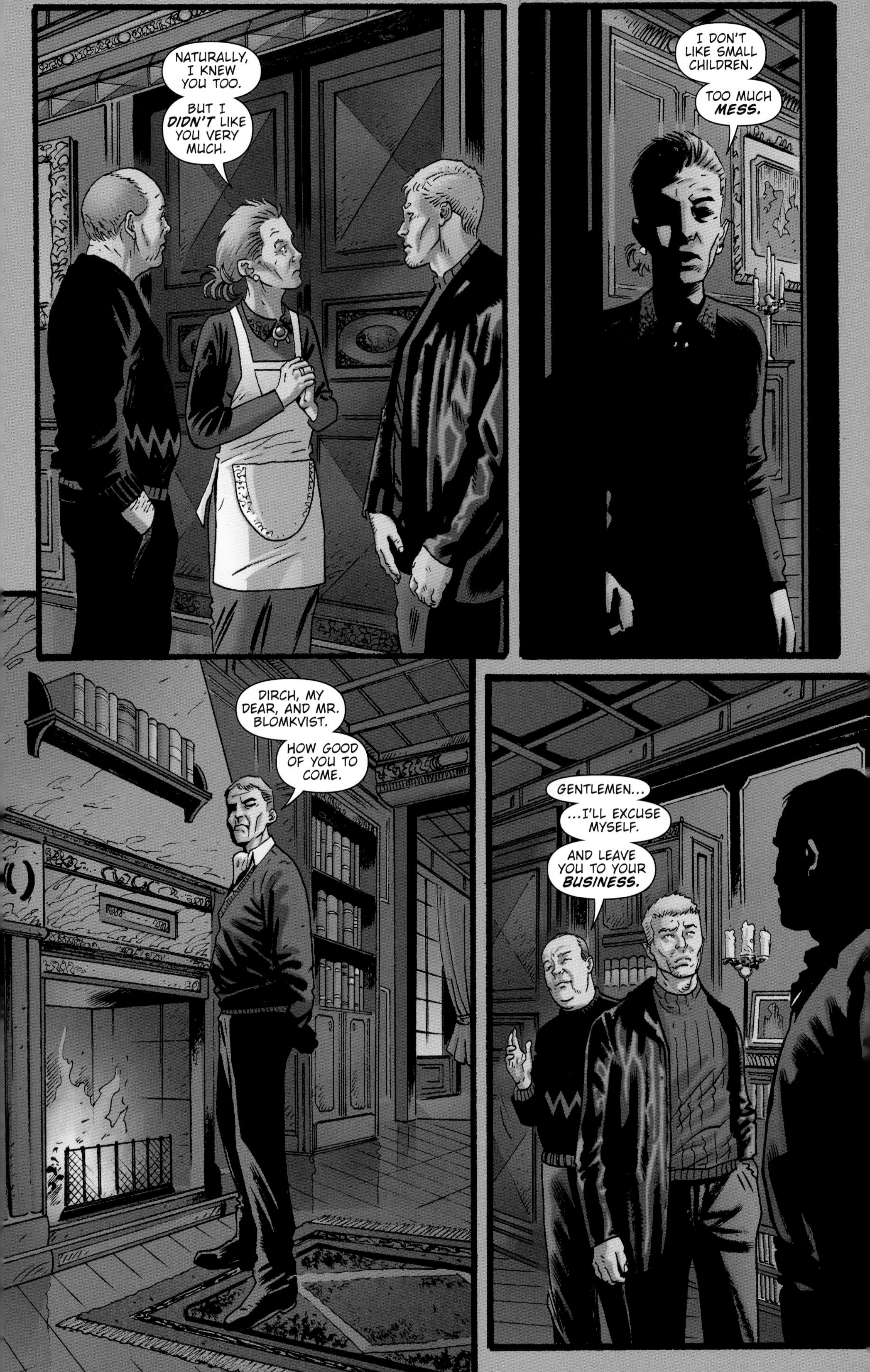
NATURALLY, I KNEW YOU TOO.
BUT I *DIDN'T* LIKE YOU VERY MUCH.
I DON'T LIKE SMALL CHILDREN.
TOO MUCH **MESS.**
DIRCH, MY DEAR, AND MR. BLOMKVIST.
HOW GOOD OF YOU TO COME.
GENTLEMEN...
...I'LL EXCUSE MYSELF.
AND LEAVE YOU TO YOUR **BUSINESS.**

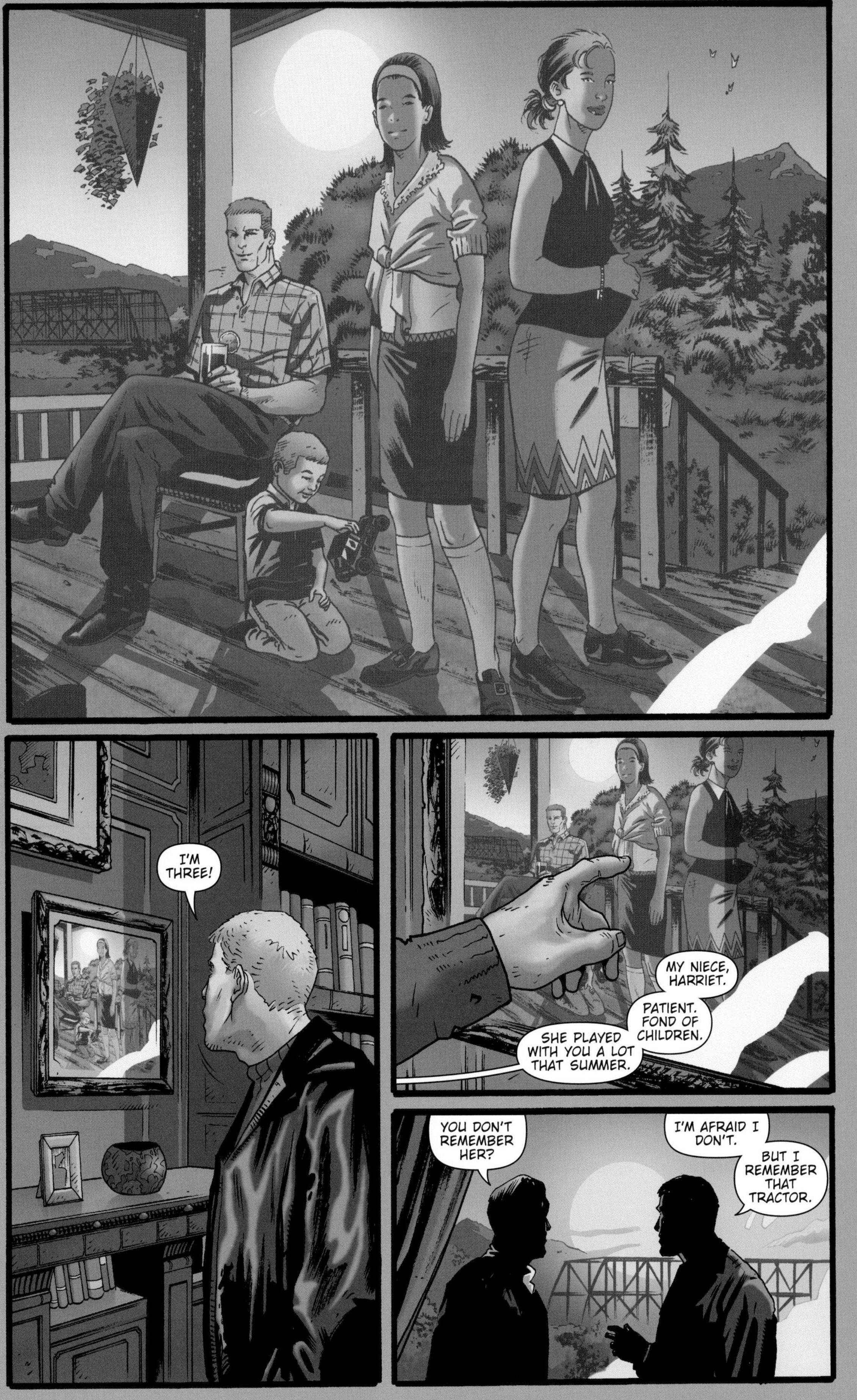
I'M THREE!
MY NIECE, HARRIET.
PATIENT. FOND OF CHILDREN.
SHE PLAYED WITH YOU A LOT THAT SUMMER.
YOU DON'T REMEMBER HER?
I'M AFRAID I DON'T.
BUT I REMEMBER THAT TRACTOR.

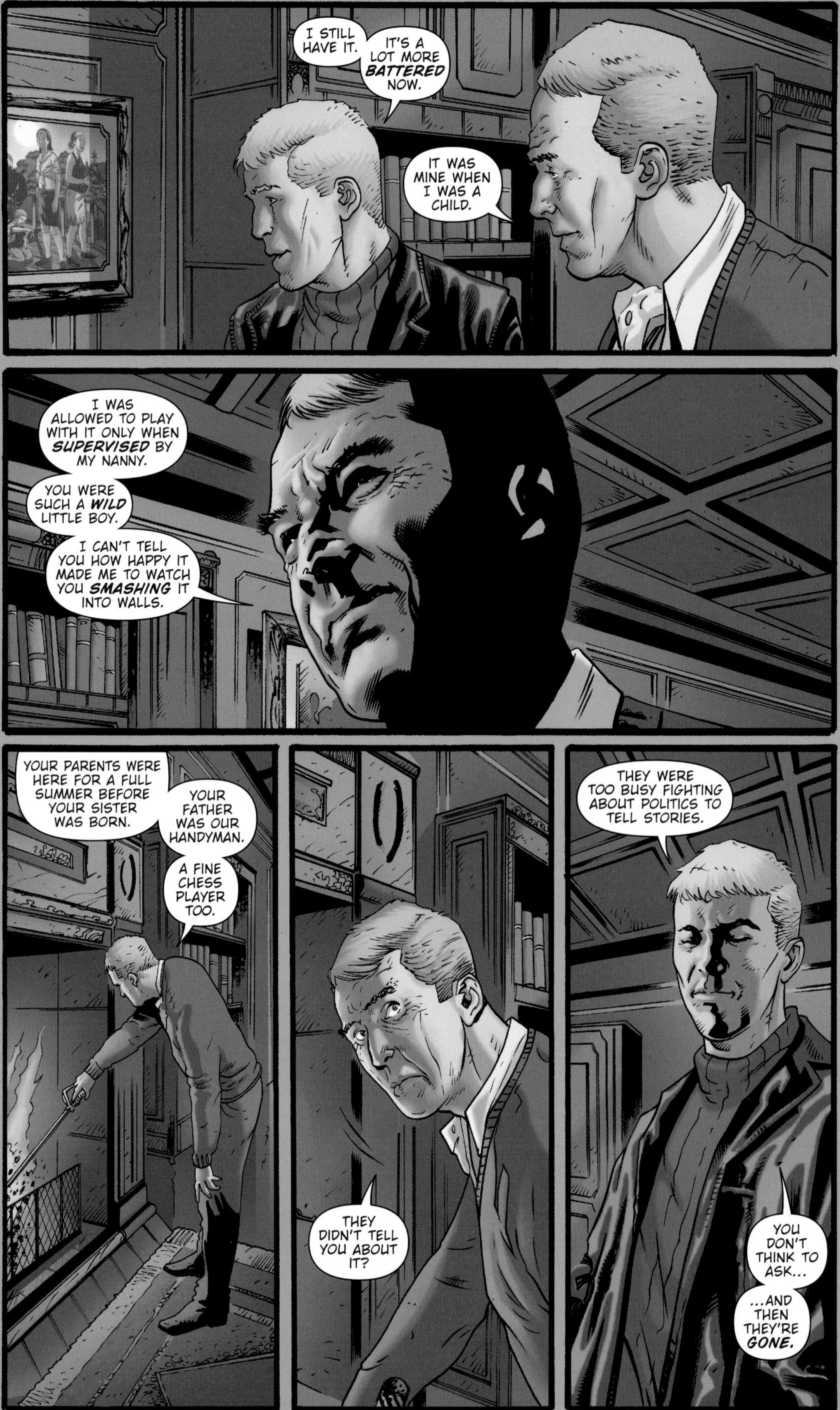
I STILL HAVE IT.
IT'S A LOT MORE BATTERED NOW.
IT WAS MINE WHEN I WAS A CHILD.
I WAS ALLOWED TO PLAY WITH IT ONLY WHEN SUPERVISED BY MY NANNY.
YOU WERE SUCH A WILD LITTLE BOY.
I CAN'T TELL YOU HOW HAPPY IT MADE ME TO WATCH YOU SMASHING IT INTO WALLS.
YOUR PARENTS WERE HERE FOR A FULL SUMMER BEFORE YOUR SISTER WAS BORN.
YOUR FATHER WAS OUR HANDYMAN.
A FINE CHESS PLAYER TOO.
THEY DIDN'T TELL YOU ABOUT IT?
THEY WERE TOO BUSY FIGHTING ABOUT POLITICS TO TELL STORIES.
YOU DON'T THINK TO ASK...
...AND THEN THEY'RE GONE.

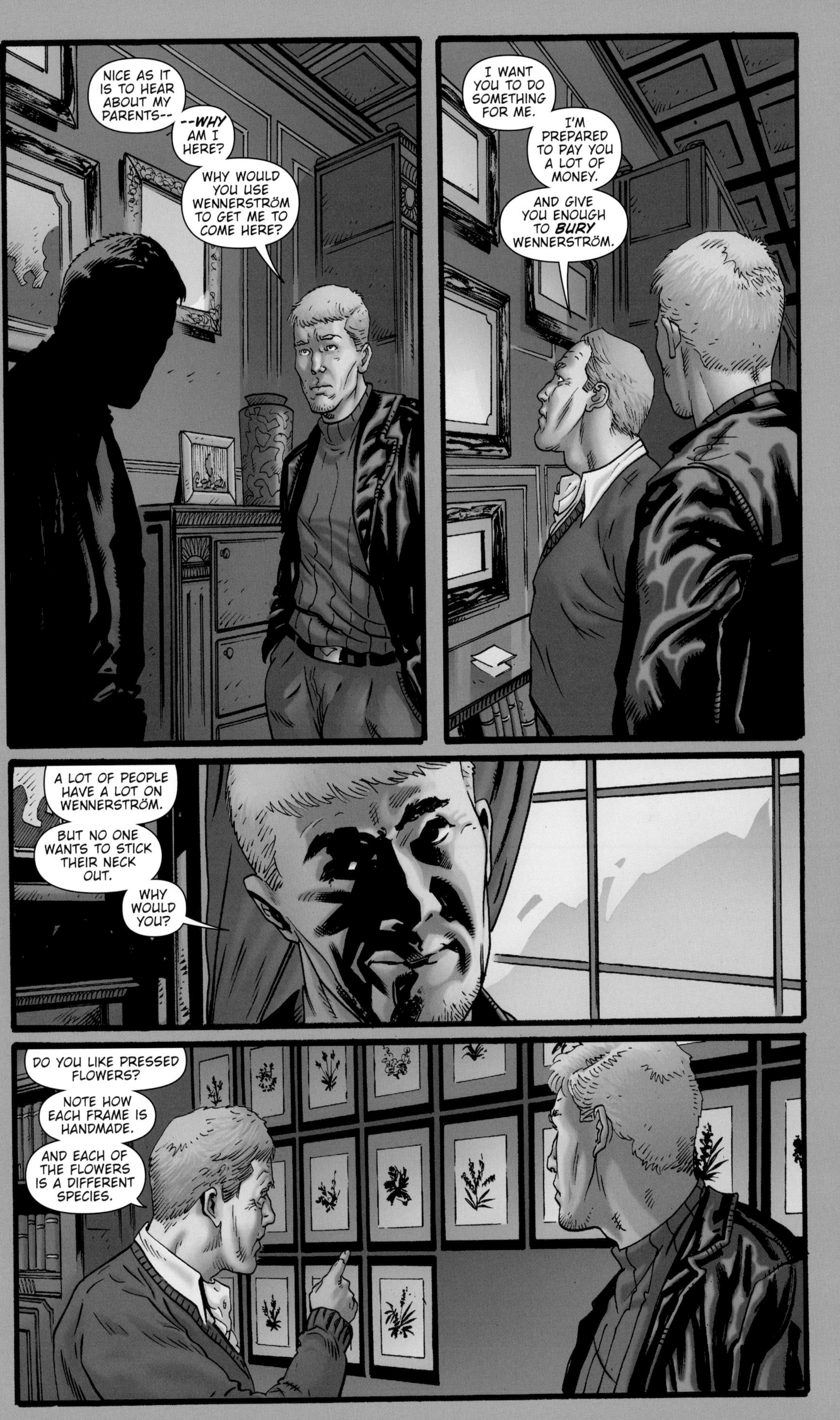
NICE AS IT IS TO HEAR ABOUT MY PARENTS--
--WHY AM I HERE?
WHY WOULD YOU USE WENNERSTRÖM TO GET ME TO COME HERE?
I WANT YOU TO DO SOMETHING FOR ME.
I'M PREPARED TO PAY YOU A LOT OF MONEY.
AND GIVE YOU ENOUGH TO BURY WENNERSTRÖM.
A LOT OF PEOPLE HAVE A LOT ON WENNERSTRÖM.
BUT NO ONE WANTS TO STICK THEIR NECK OUT.
WHY WOULD YOU?
DO YOU LIKE PRESSED FLOWERS?
NOTE HOW EACH FRAME IS HANDMADE.
AND EACH OF THE FLOWERS IS A DIFFERENT SPECIES.

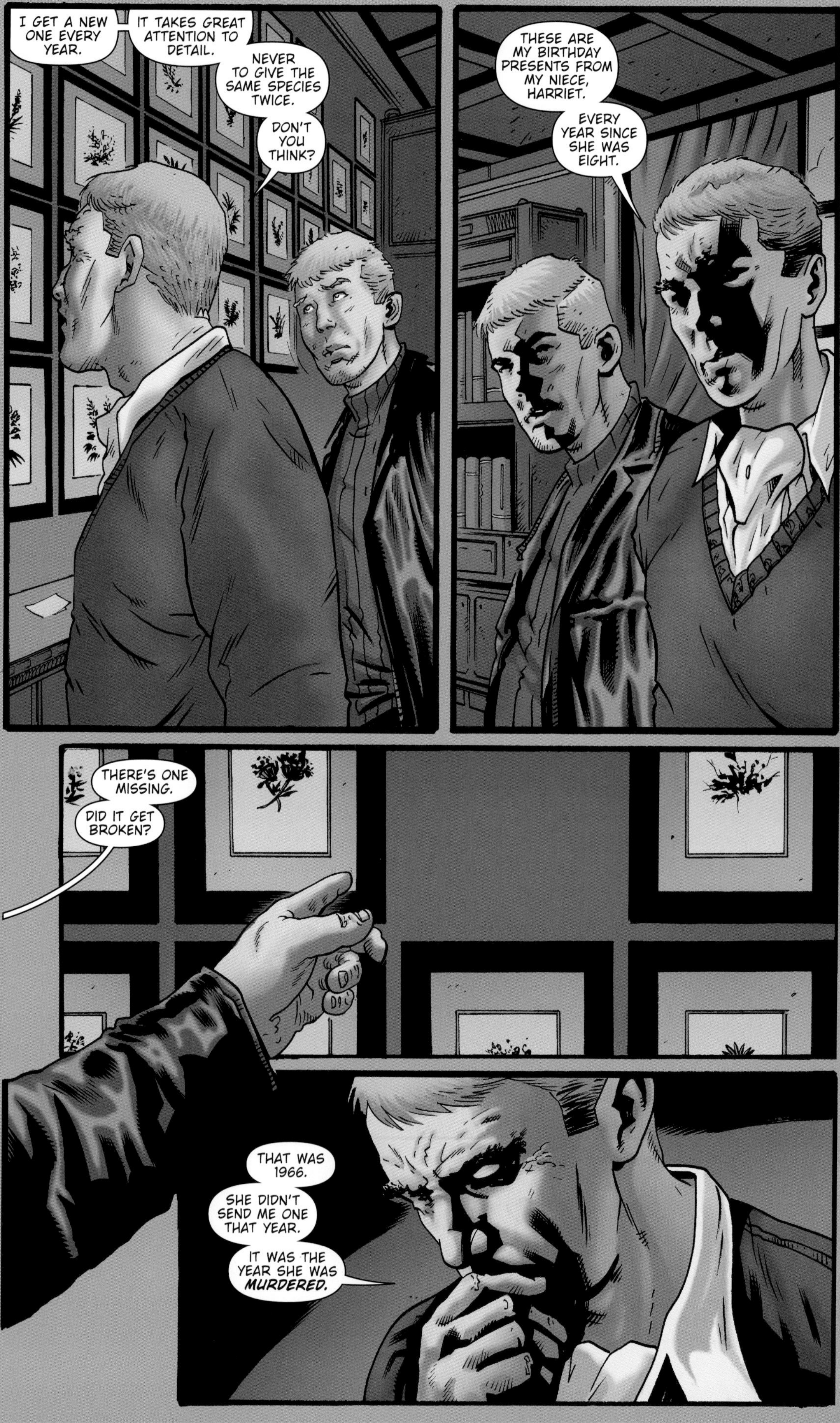

I GET A NEW ONE EVERY YEAR.
IT TAKES GREAT ATTENTION TO DETAIL.
NEVER TO GIVE THE SAME SPECIES TWICE.
DON'T YOU THINK?
THESE ARE MY BIRTHDAY PRESENTS FROM MY NIECE, HARRIET.
EVERY YEAR SINCE SHE WAS EIGHT.
THERE'S ONE MISSING.
DID IT GET BROKEN?
THAT WAS 1966.
SHE DIDN'T SEND ME ONE THAT YEAR.
IT WAS THE YEAR SHE WAS *MURDERED.*

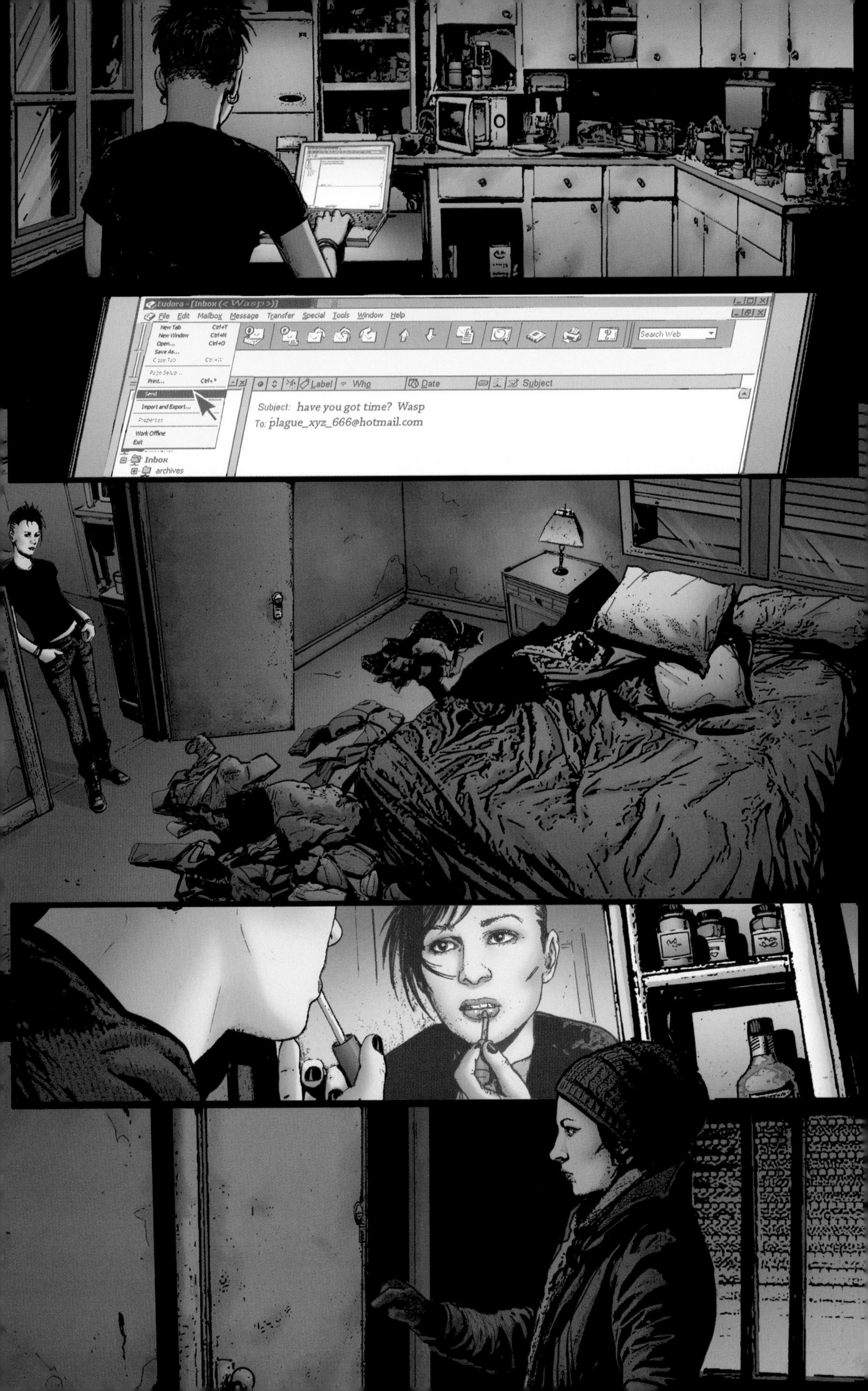
Eudora - [Inbox (< Wasp >)]
File Edit Mailbox Message Transfer Special Tools Window Help
New Tab Ctrl+T
New Window Ctrl+N
Open... Ctrl+O
Save As...
Print...
Send
Import and Export...
Work Offline
Exit
Search Web
Label Who Date Subject
Subject: have you got time? Wasp
To: plague_xyz_666@hotmail.com
Inbox
archives

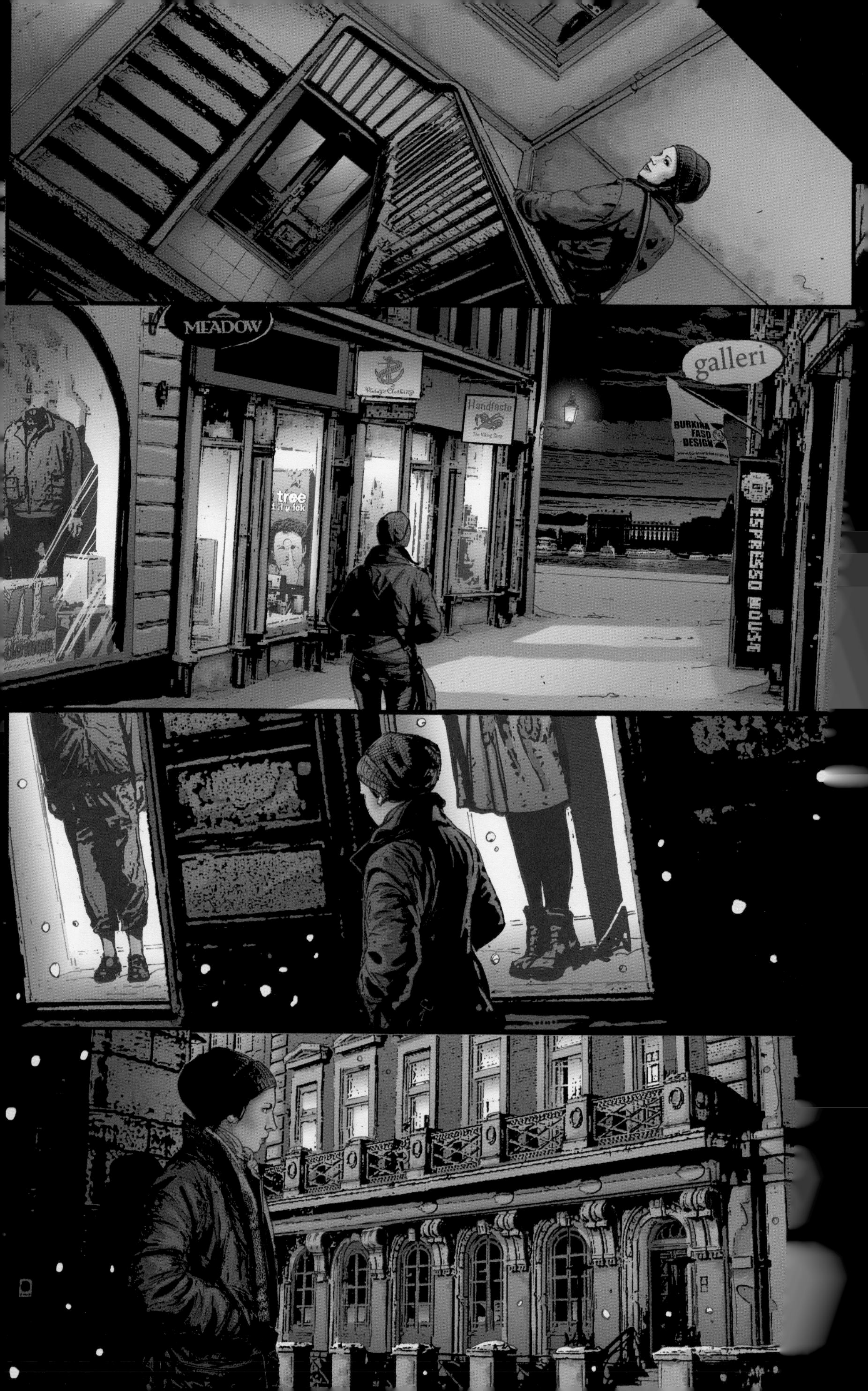
MEADOW
Handfaste
The Viking Shop
galleri
BURKINA FASO DESIGN
tree
ESPRESSO HOUSE

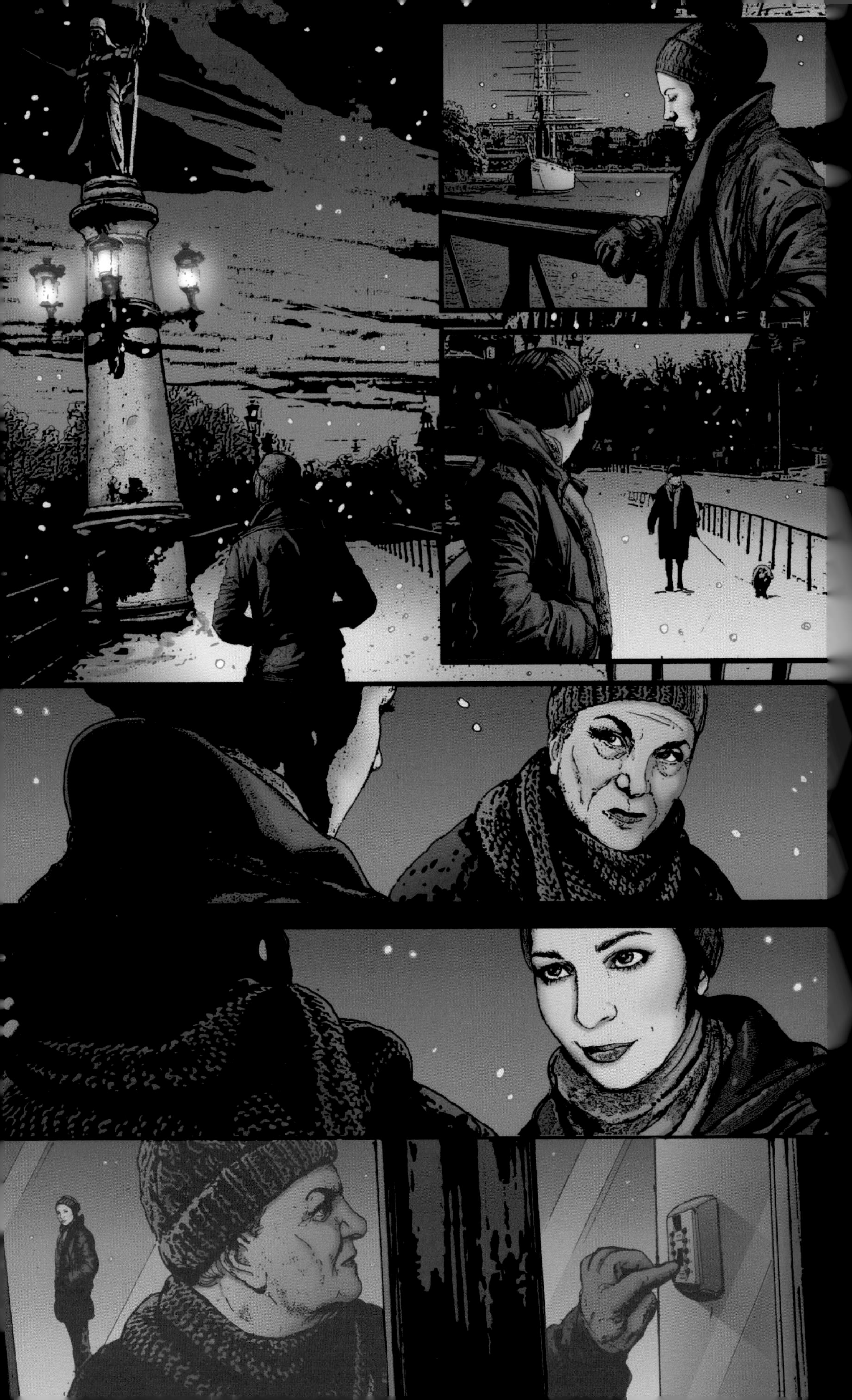

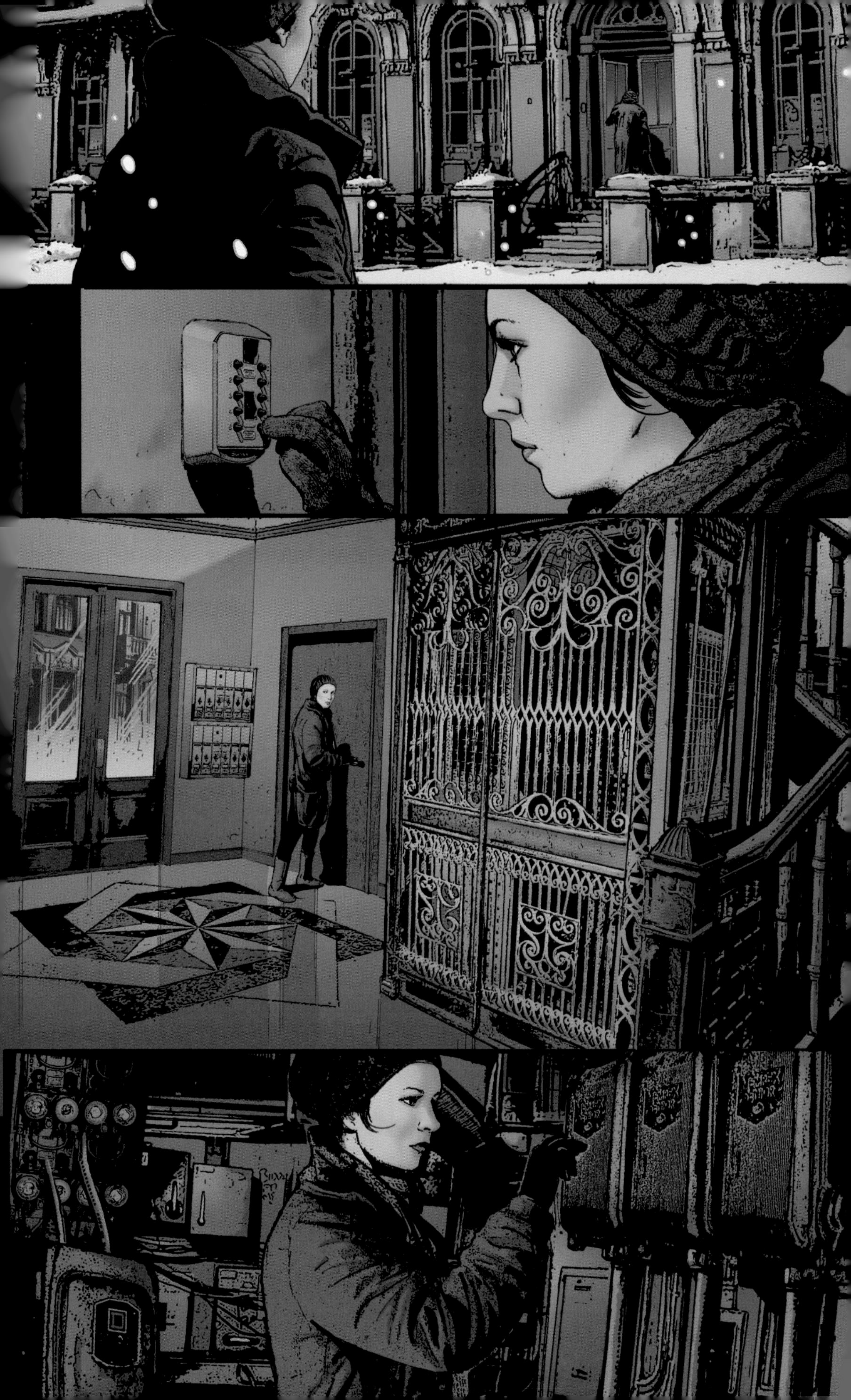

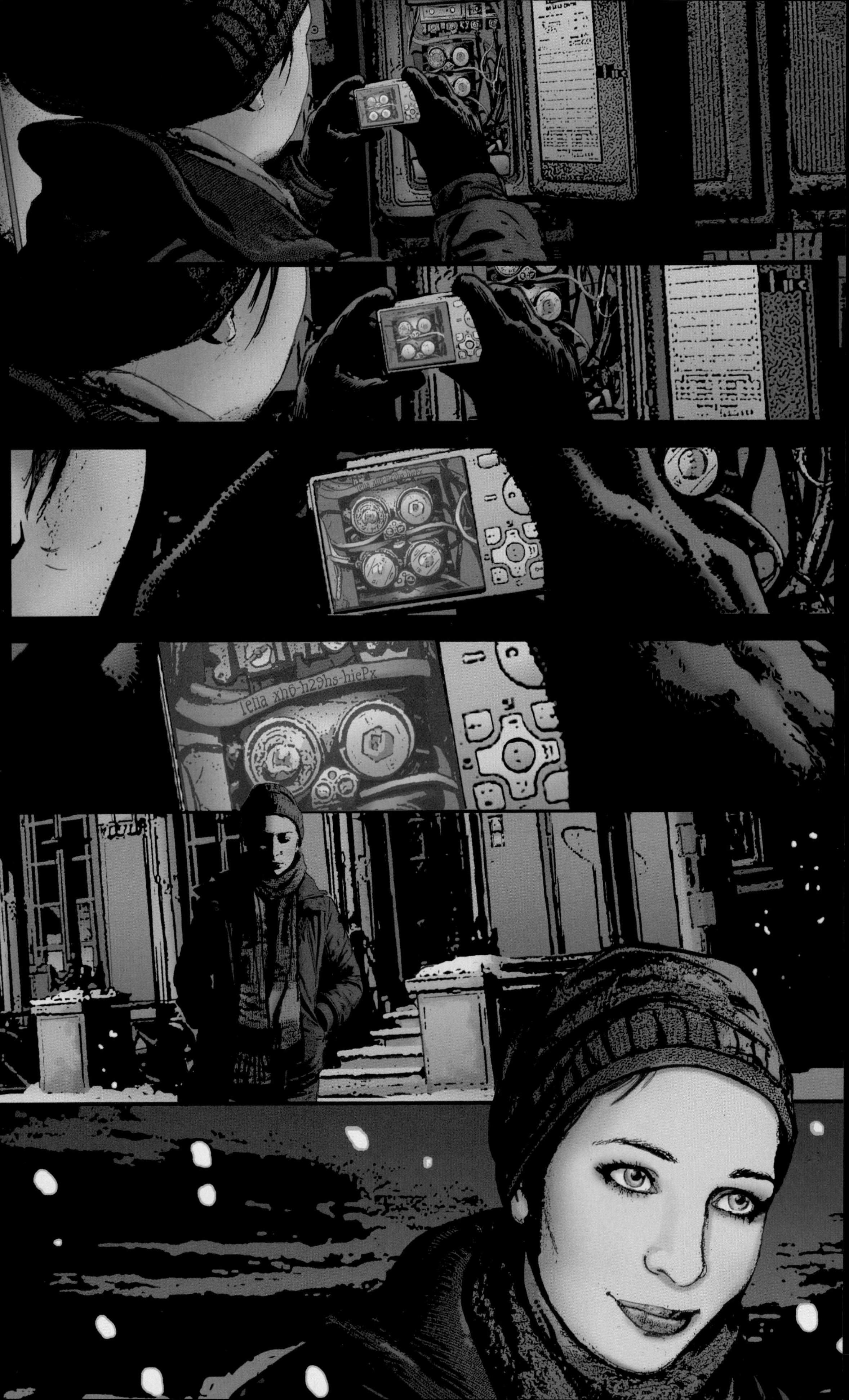
Telia xh6-h29hs-hiePx

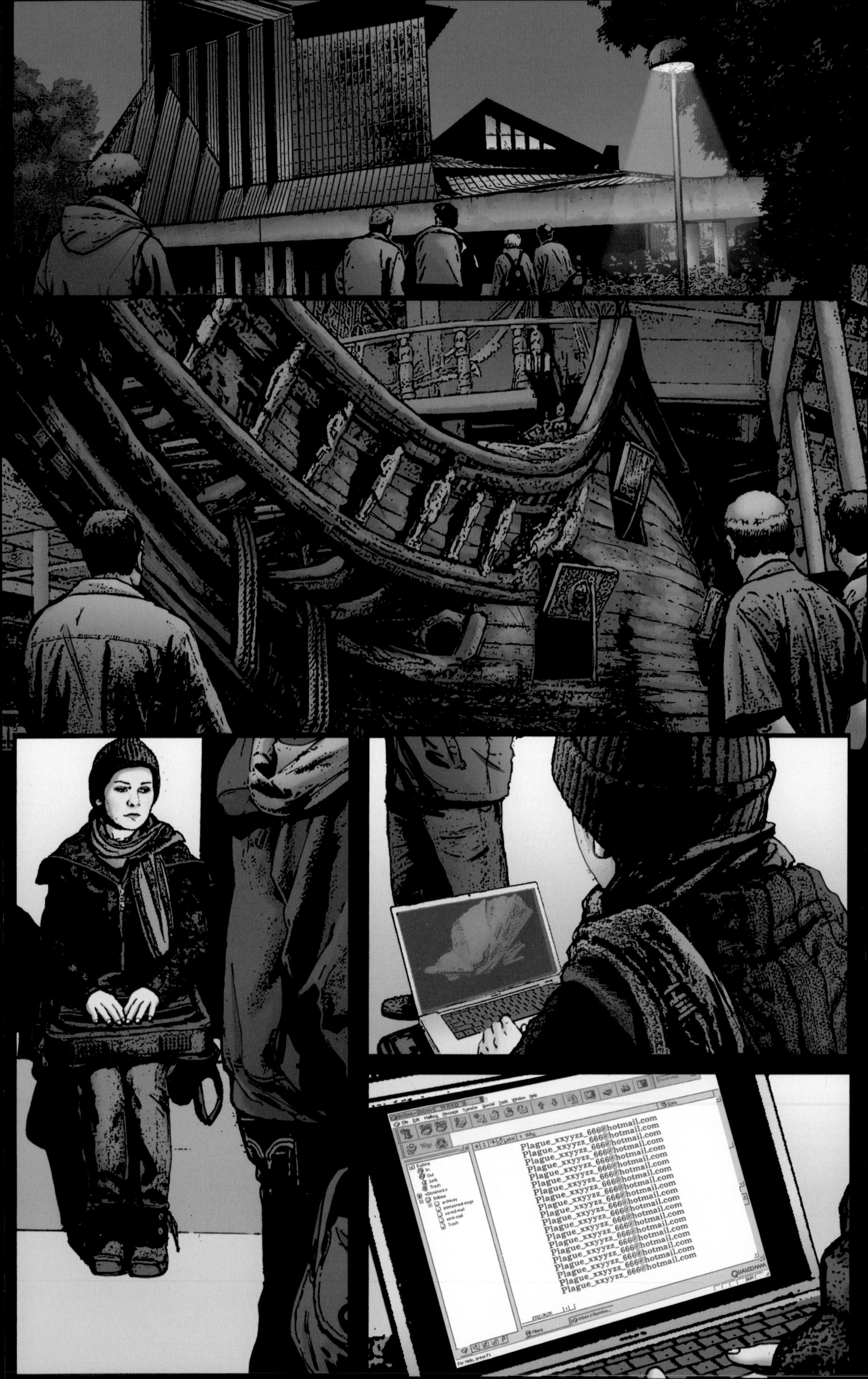

File Edit Mailbox Message Transfer Special Tools Window Help
Label
Who
Date
Eudora
In
Out
Junk
Trash
Inbox
archives
postponed-msgs
saved-mail
sent-mail
Trash
hotmail.com
Plague_xxyyzz_666@hotmail.com
Plague_xxyyzz_666@hotmail.com
Plague_xxyyzz_666@hotmail.com
Plague_xxyyzz_666@hotmail.com
Plague_xxyyzz_666@hotmail.com
Plague_xxyyzz_666@hotmail.com
Plague_xxyyzz_666@hotmail.com
Plague_xxyyzz_666@hotmail.com
Plague_xxyyzz_666@hotmail.com
Plague_xxyyzz_666@hotmail.com
Plague_xxyyzz_666@hotmail.com
Plague_xxyyzz_666@hotmail.com
Plague_xxyyzz_666@hotmail.com
Plague_xxyyzz_666@hotmail.com
Plague_xxyyzz_666@hotmail.com
Plague_xxyyzz_666@hotmail.com
Plague_xxyyzz_666@hotmail.com
Plague_xxyyzz_666@hotmail.com
QUALCOMM

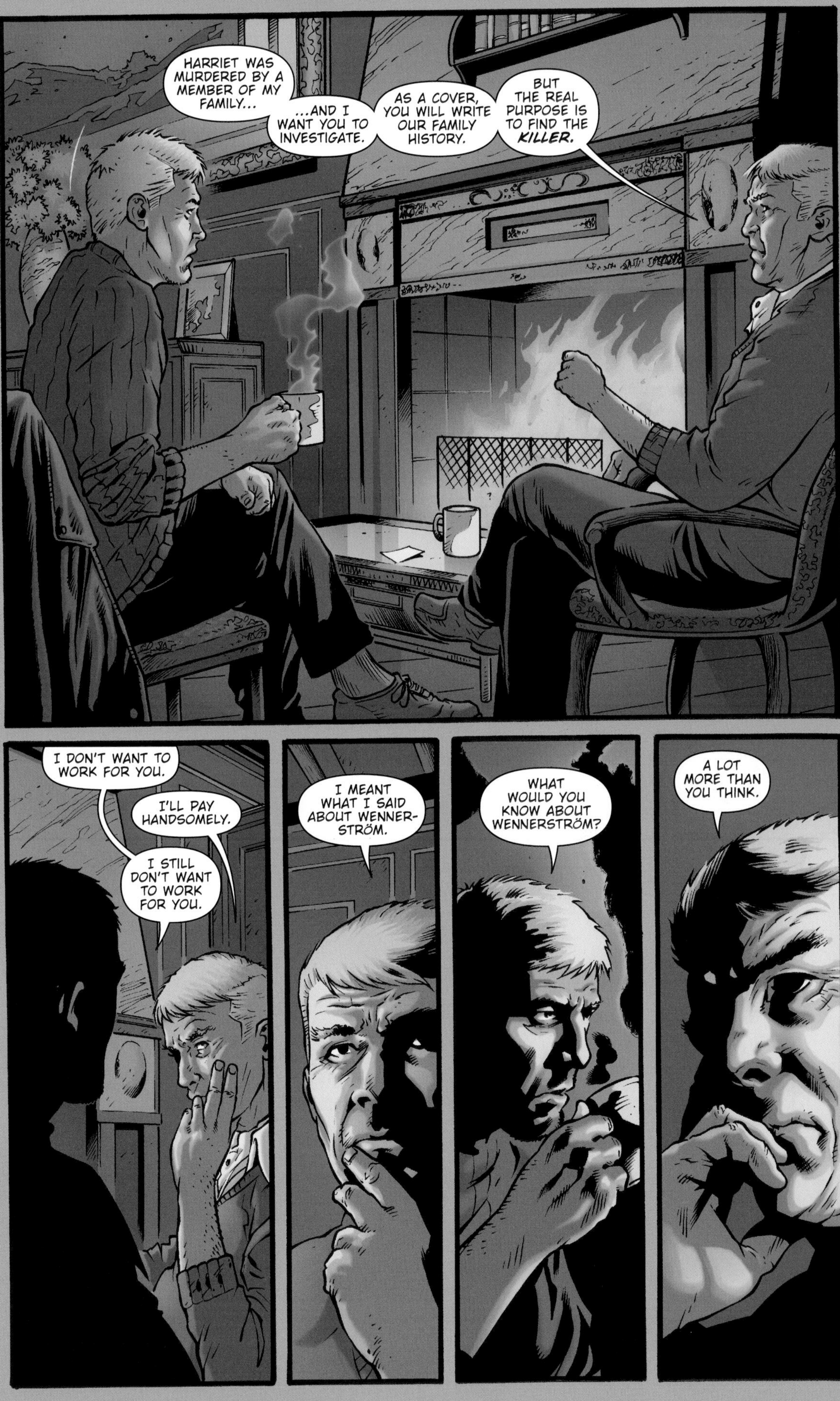
HARRIET WAS MURDERED BY A MEMBER OF MY FAMILY...
...AND I WANT YOU TO INVESTIGATE.
AS A COVER, YOU WILL WRITE OUR FAMILY HISTORY.
BUT THE REAL PURPOSE IS TO FIND THE *KILLER.*
I DON'T WANT TO WORK FOR YOU.
I'LL PAY HANDSOMELY.
I STILL DON'T WANT TO WORK FOR YOU.
I MEANT WHAT I SAID ABOUT WENNERSTRÖM.
WHAT WOULD YOU KNOW ABOUT WENNERSTRÖM?
A LOT MORE THAN YOU THINK.

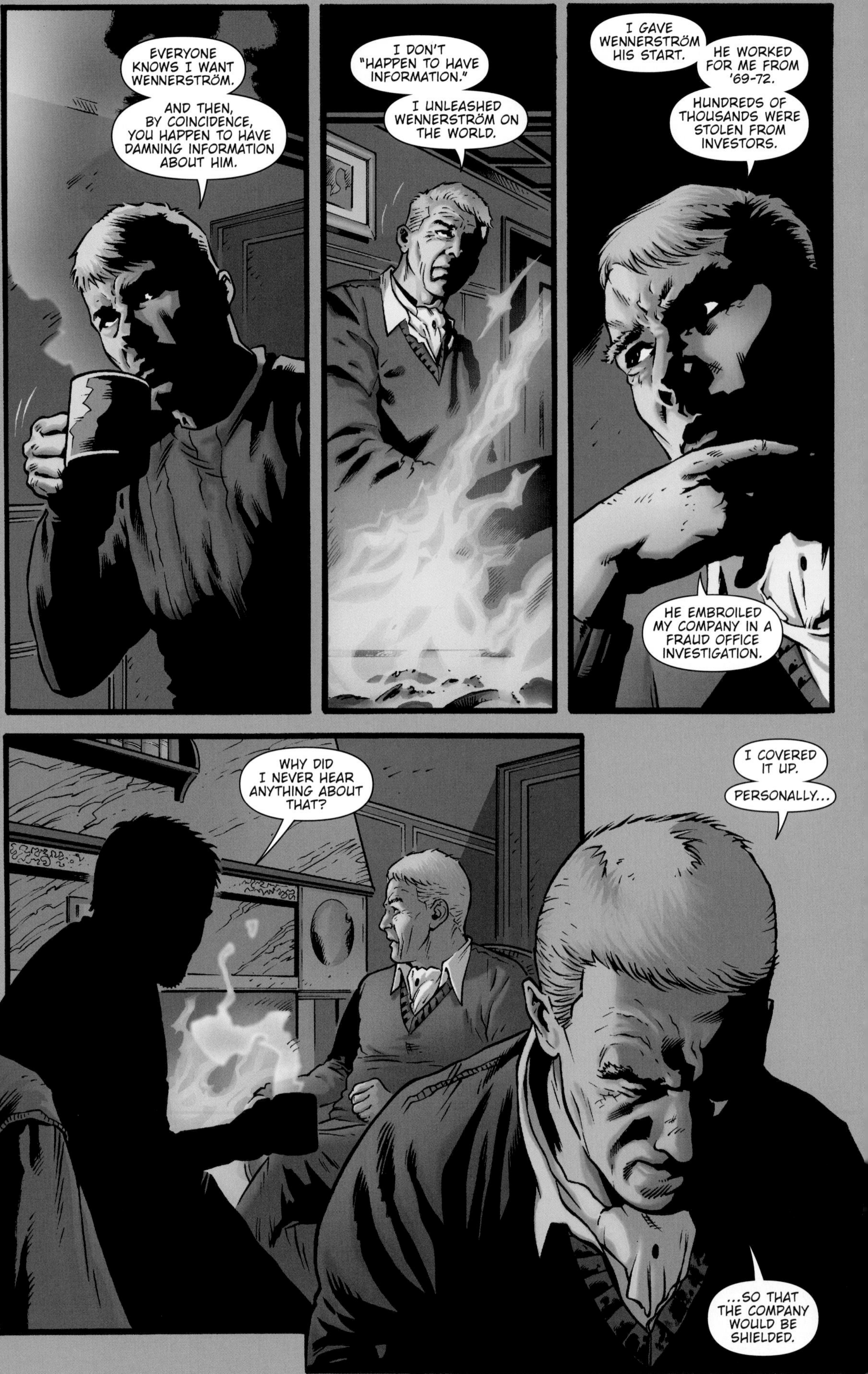
EVERYONE KNOWS I WANT WENNERSTRÖM.
AND THEN, BY COINCIDENCE, YOU HAPPEN TO HAVE DAMNING INFORMATION ABOUT HIM.
I DON'T "HAPPEN TO HAVE INFORMATION."
I UNLEASHED WENNERSTRÖM ON THE WORLD.
I GAVE WENNERSTRÖM HIS START.
HE WORKED FOR ME FROM '69-72.
HUNDREDS OF THOUSANDS WERE STOLEN FROM INVESTORS.
HE EMBROILED MY COMPANY IN A FRAUD OFFICE INVESTIGATION.
WHY DID I NEVER HEAR ANYTHING ABOUT THAT?
I COVERED IT UP.
PERSONALLY...
...SO THAT THE COMPANY WOULD BE SHIELDED.

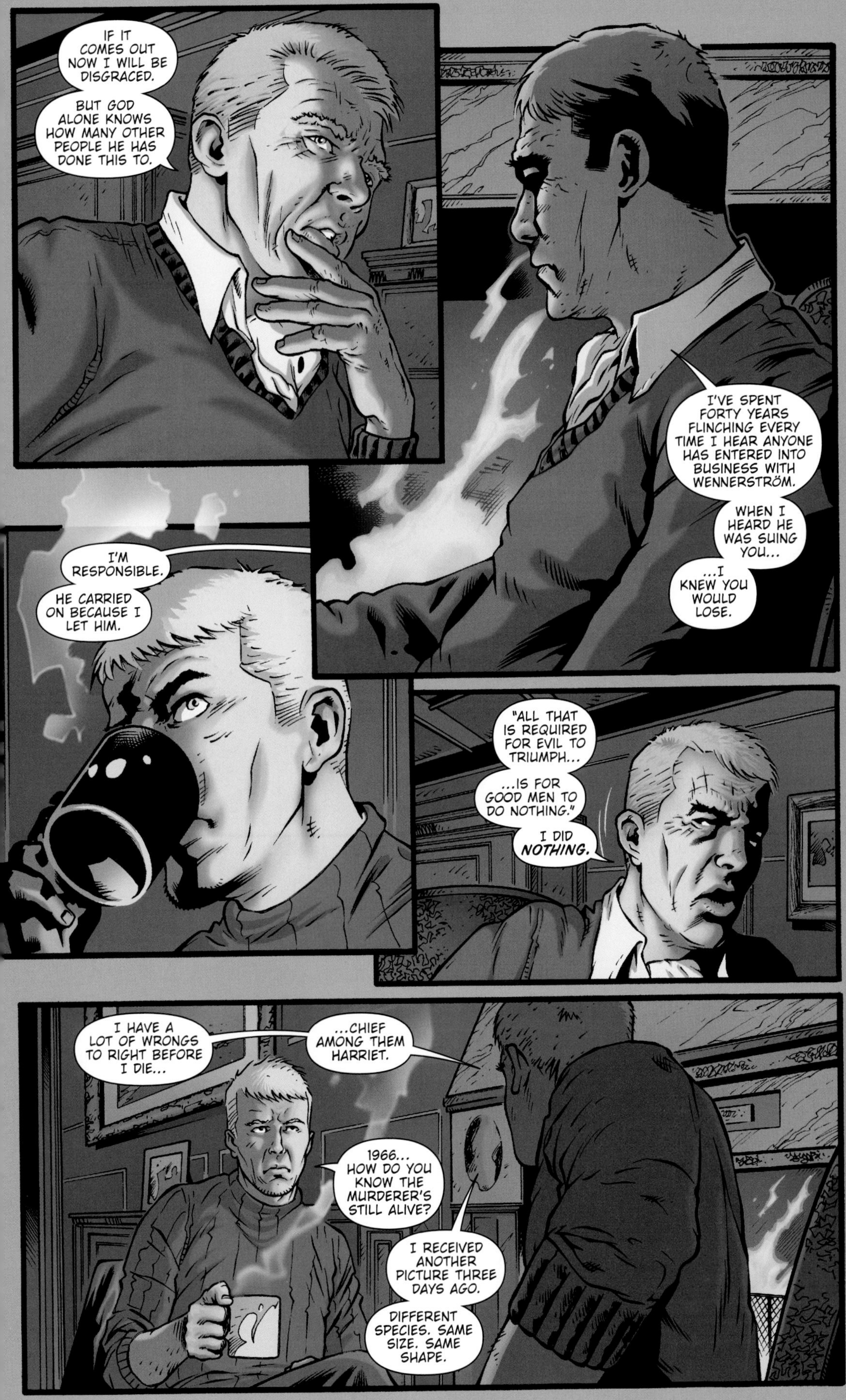
IF IT COMES OUT NOW I WILL BE DISGRACED.
BUT GOD ALONE KNOWS HOW MANY OTHER PEOPLE HE HAS DONE THIS TO.
I'VE SPENT FORTY YEARS FLINCHING EVERY TIME I HEAR ANYONE HAS ENTERED INTO BUSINESS WITH WENNERSTRÖM.
WHEN I HEARD HE WAS SUING YOU...
...I KNEW YOU WOULD LOSE.
I'M RESPONSIBLE.
HE CARRIED ON BECAUSE I LET HIM.
"ALL THAT IS REQUIRED FOR EVIL TO TRIUMPH...
...IS FOR GOOD MEN TO DO NOTHING."
I DID ***NOTHING.***
I HAVE A LOT OF WRONGS TO RIGHT BEFORE I DIE...
...CHIEF AMONG THEM HARRIET.
1966... HOW DO YOU KNOW THE MURDERER'S STILL ALIVE?
I RECEIVED ANOTHER PICTURE THREE DAYS AGO.
DIFFERENT SPECIES. SAME SIZE. SAME SHAPE.

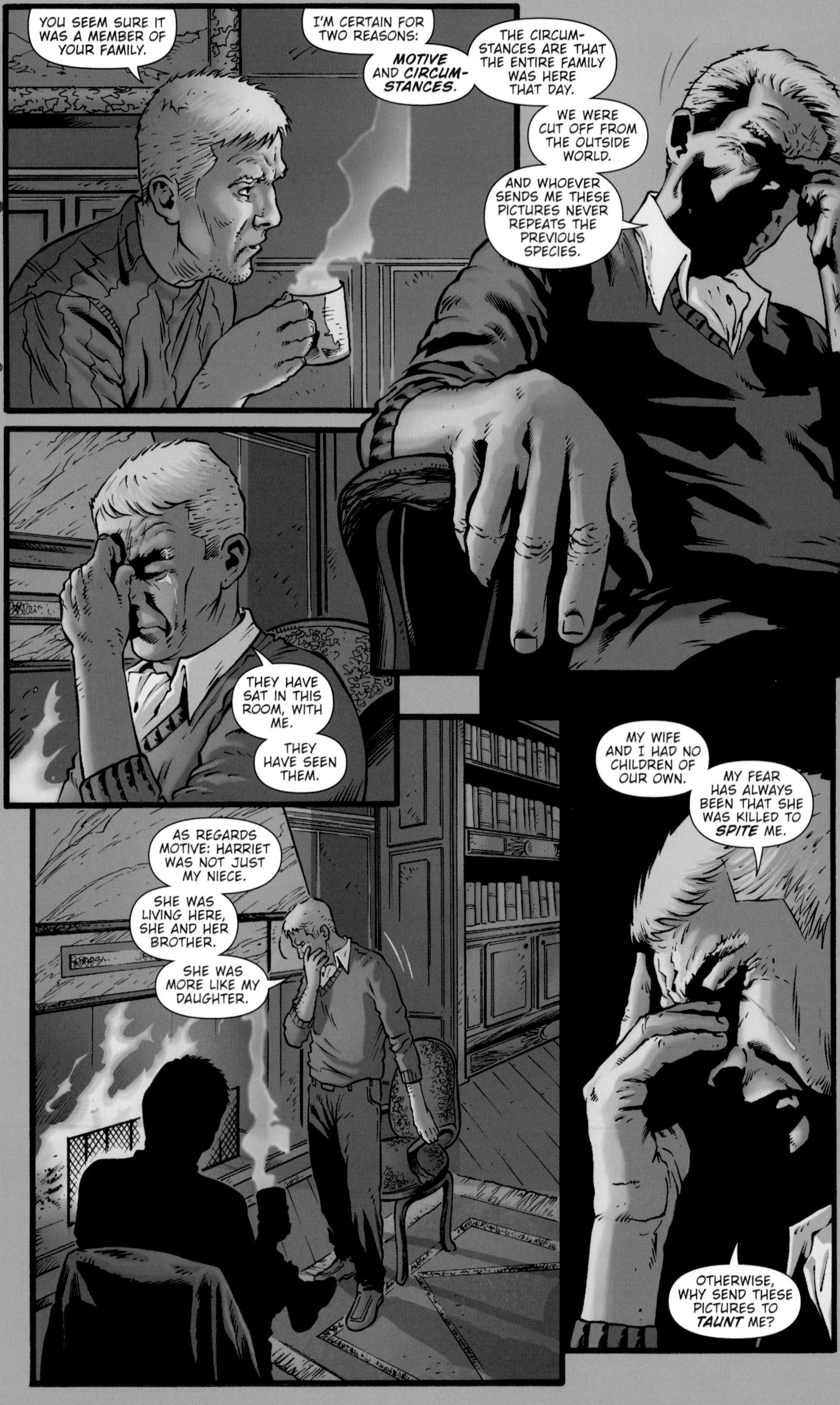
YOU SEEM SURE IT WAS A MEMBER OF YOUR FAMILY.
I'M CERTAIN FOR TWO REASONS: MOTIVE AND CIRCUMSTANCES.
THE CIRCUMSTANCES ARE THAT THE ENTIRE FAMILY WAS HERE THAT DAY.
WE WERE CUT OFF FROM THE OUTSIDE WORLD.
AND WHOEVER SENDS ME THESE PICTURES NEVER REPEATS THE PREVIOUS SPECIES.
THEY HAVE SAT IN THIS ROOM, WITH ME.
THEY HAVE SEEN THEM.
AS REGARDS MOTIVE: HARRIET WAS NOT JUST MY NIECE.
SHE WAS LIVING HERE, SHE AND HER BROTHER.
SHE WAS MORE LIKE MY DAUGHTER.
MY WIFE AND I HAD NO CHILDREN OF OUR OWN.
MY FEAR HAS ALWAYS BEEN THAT SHE WAS KILLED TO SPITE ME.
OTHERWISE, WHY SEND THESE PICTURES TO TAUNT ME?

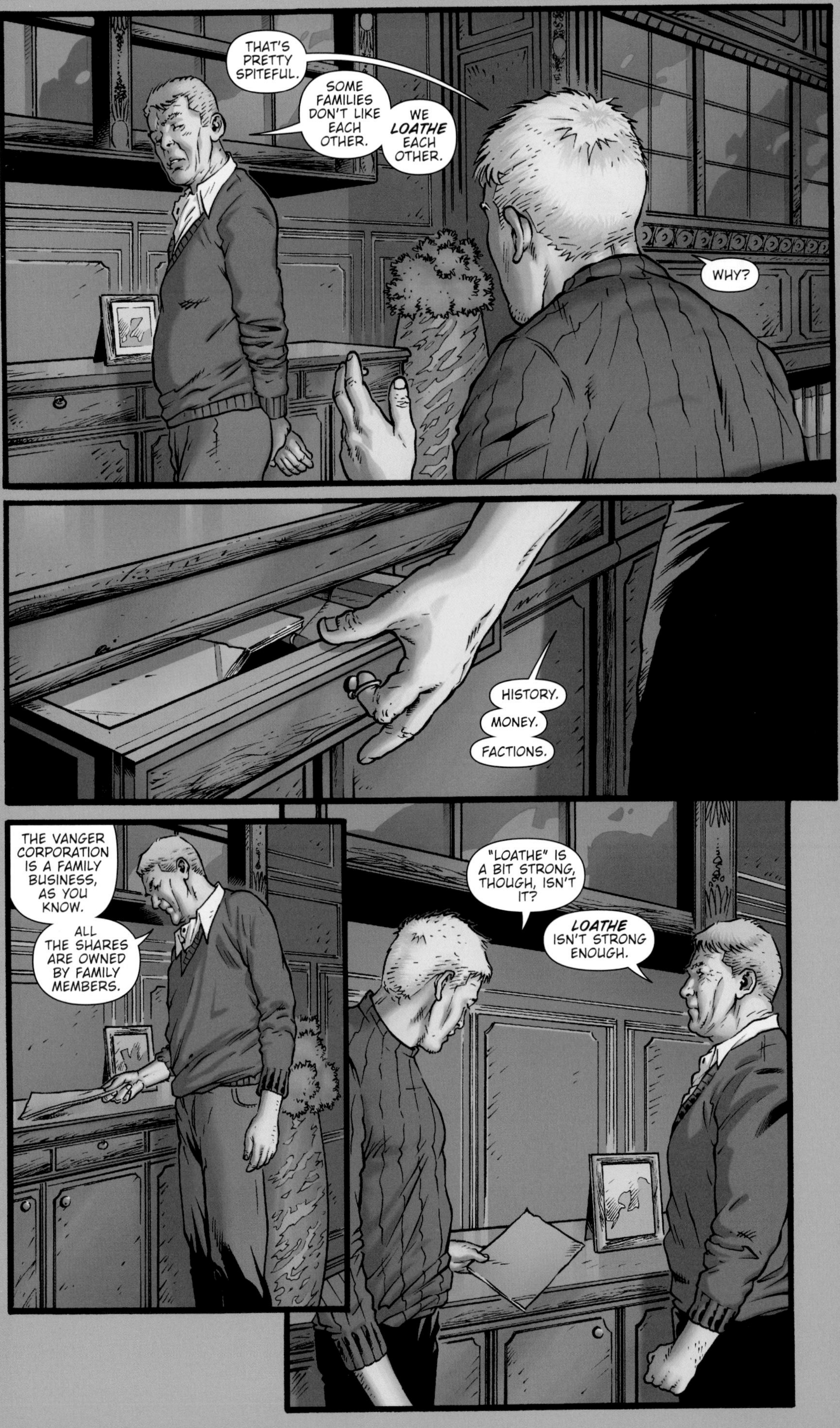

THAT'S PRETTY SPITEFUL.
SOME FAMILIES DON'T LIKE EACH OTHER.
WE LOATHE EACH OTHER.
WHY?
HISTORY.
MONEY.
FACTIONS.
THE VANGER CORPORATION IS A FAMILY BUSINESS, AS YOU KNOW.
ALL THE SHARES ARE OWNED BY FAMILY MEMBERS.
"LOATHE" IS A BIT STRONG, THOUGH, ISN'T IT?
LOATHE ISN'T STRONG ENOUGH.

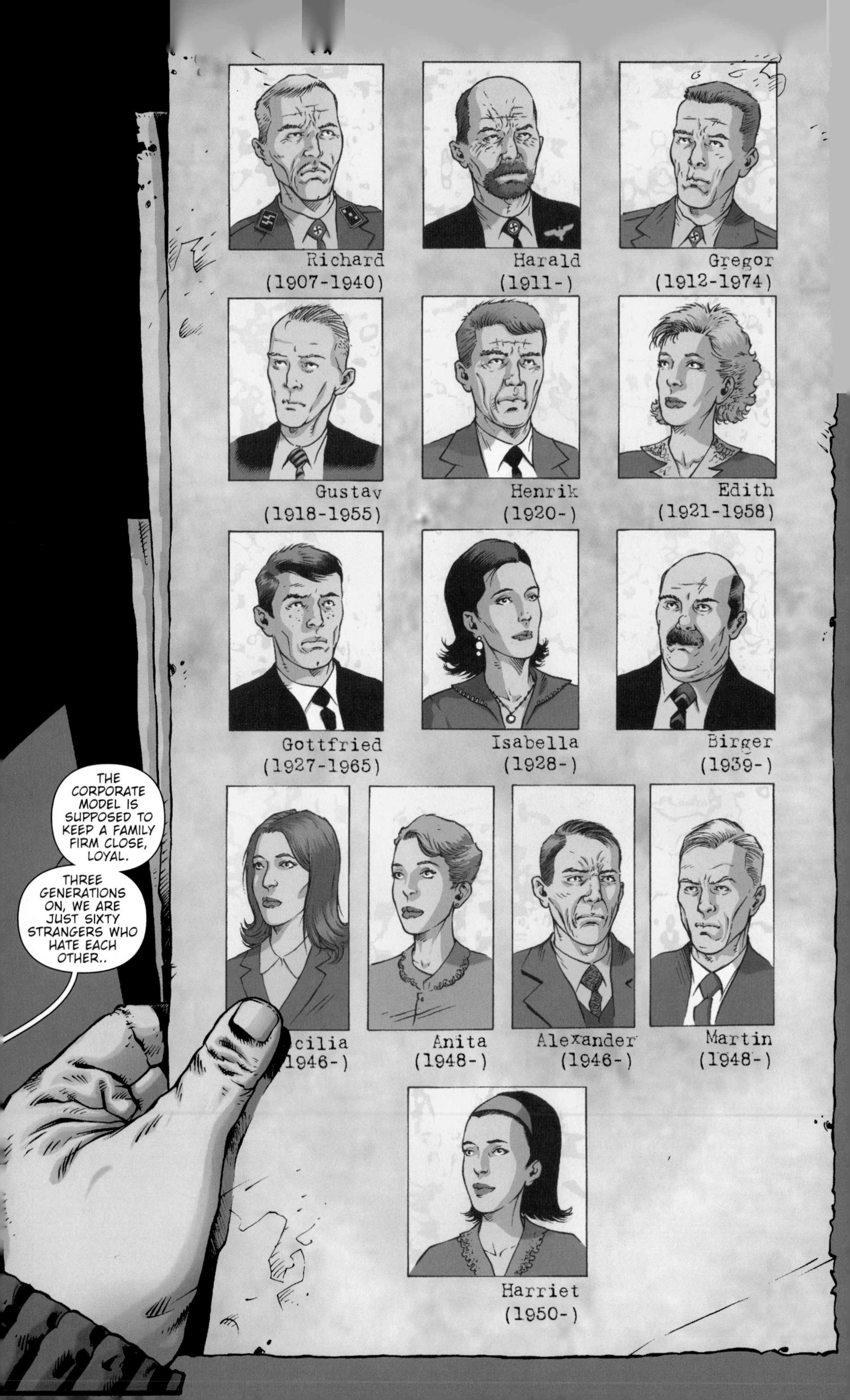

Richard
(1907-1940)
Harald
(1911-)
Gregor
(1912-1974)
Gustav
(1918-1955)
Henrik
(1920-)
Edith
(1921-1958)
Gottfried
(1927-1965)
Isabella
(1928-)
Birger
(1939-)
THE CORPORATE MODEL IS SUPPOSED TO KEEP A FAMILY FIRM CLOSE, LOYAL.
THREE GENERATIONS ON, WE ARE JUST SIXTY STRANGERS WHO HATE EACH OTHER..
(1946-)
Anita
(1948-)
Alexander
(1946-)
Martin
(1948-)
Harriet
(1950-)

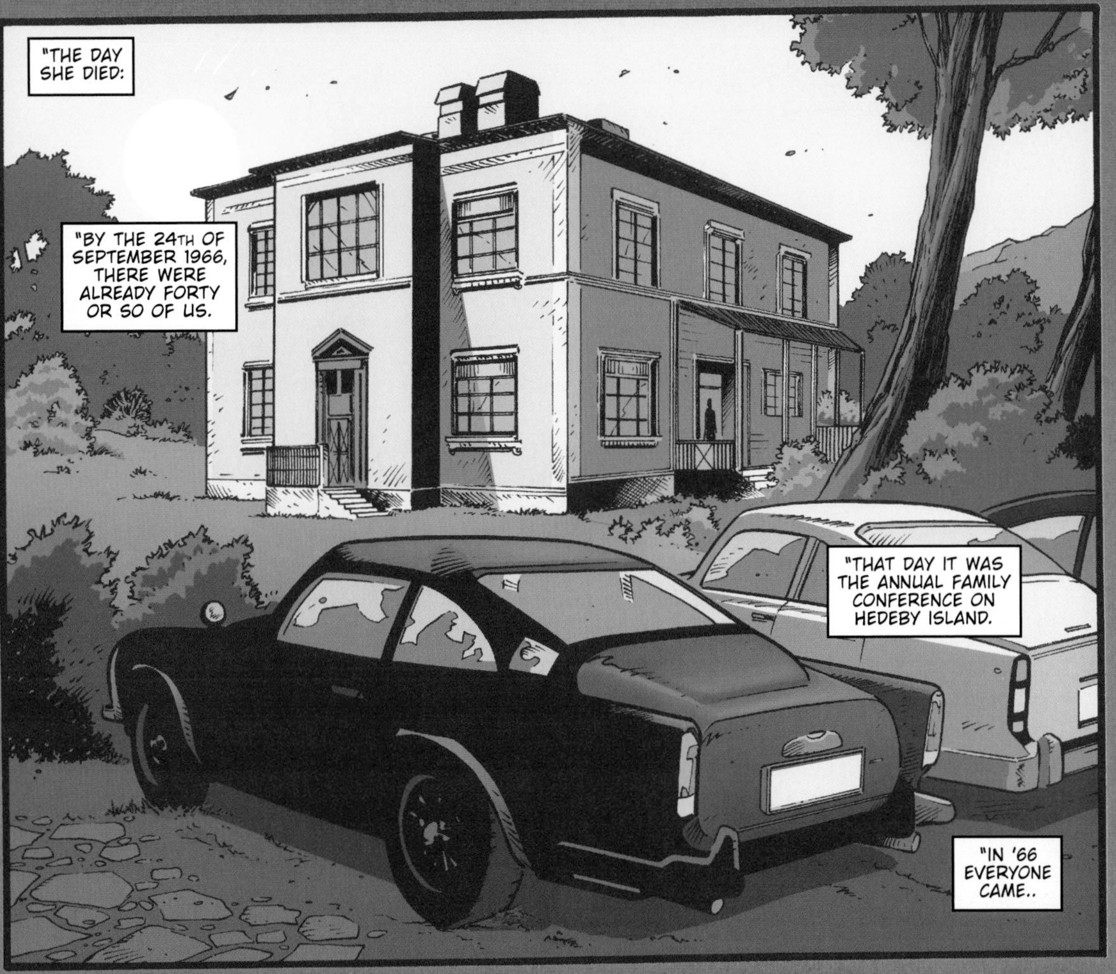
"THE DAY SHE DIED:
"BY THE 24TH OF SEPTEMBER 1966, THERE WERE ALREADY FORTY OR SO OF US.
"THAT DAY IT WAS THE ANNUAL FAMILY CONFERENCE ON HEDEBY ISLAND.
"IN '66 EVERYONE CAME..

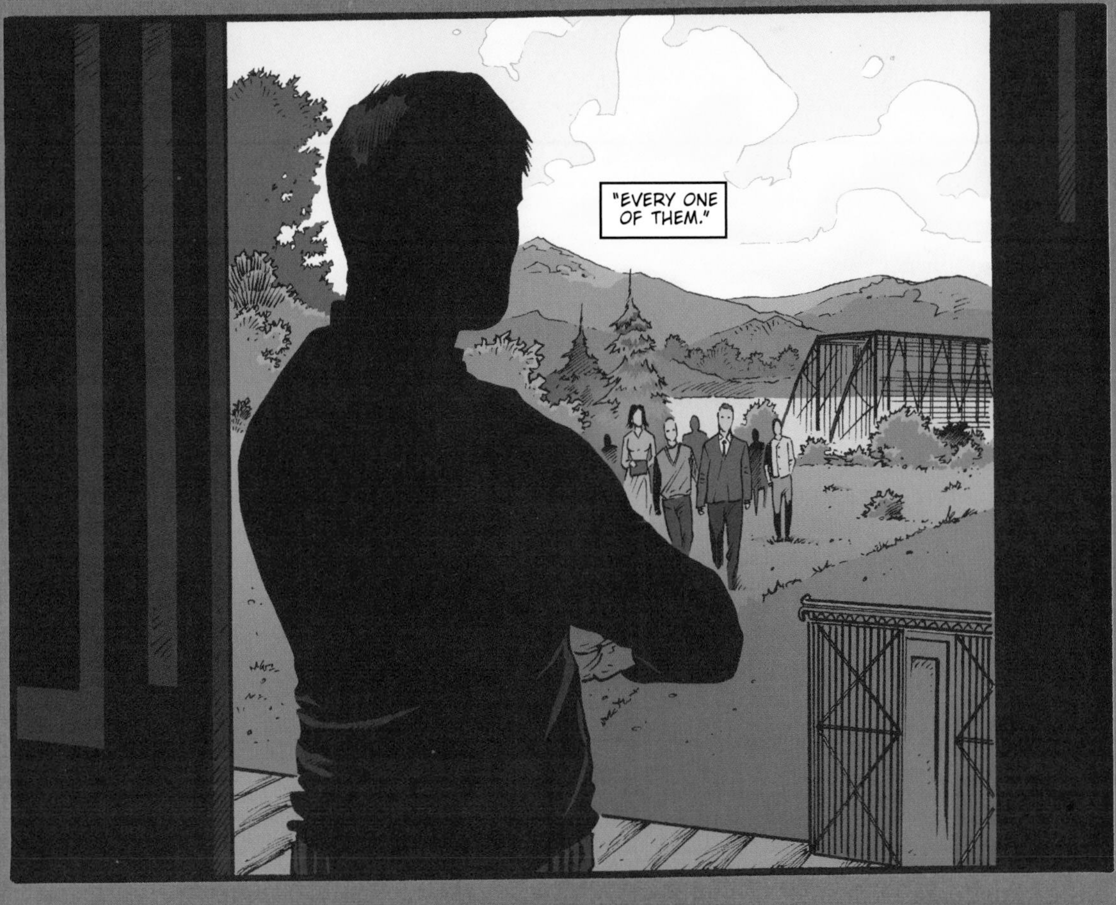
"EVERY ONE OF THEM."

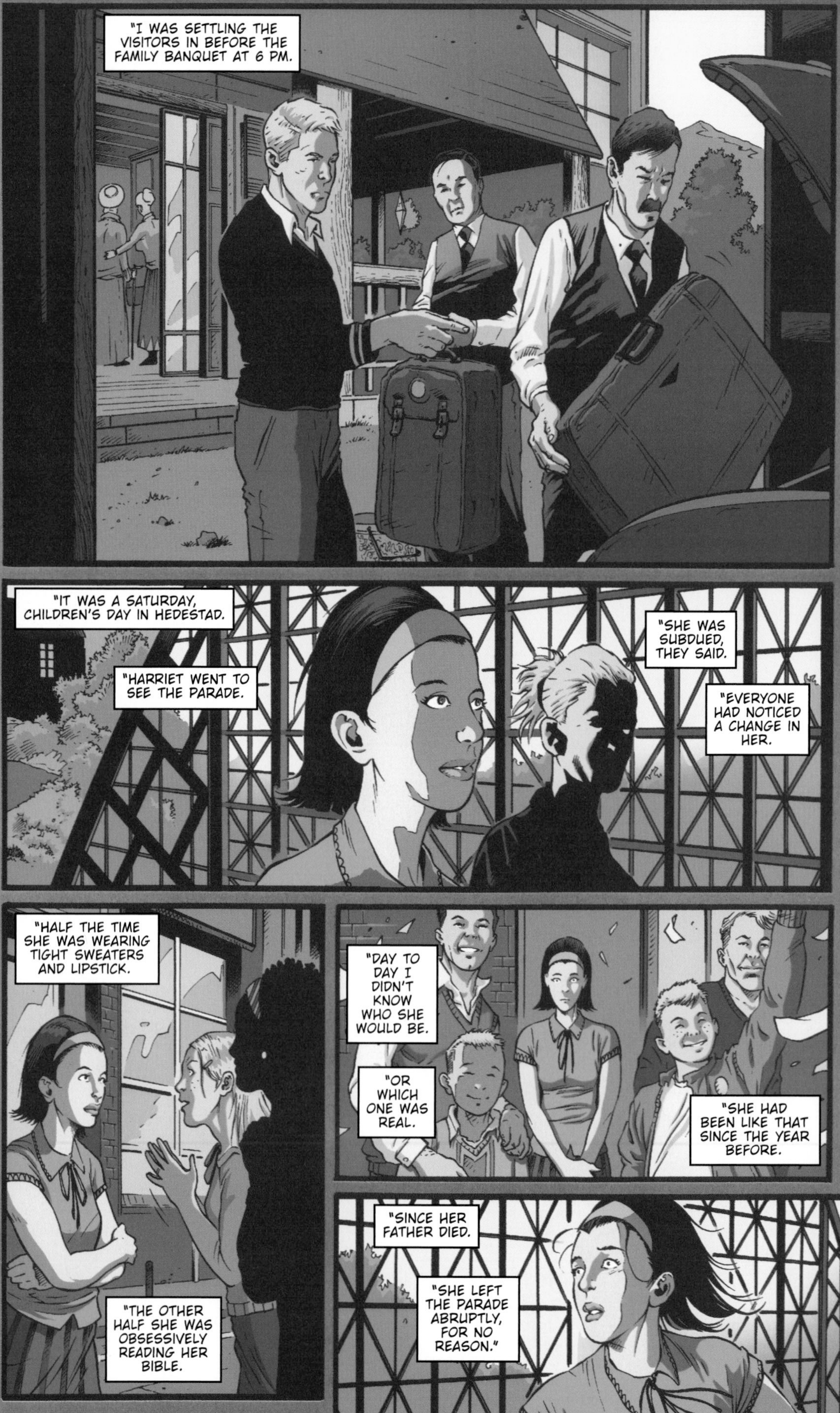
"I WAS SETTLING THE VISITORS IN BEFORE THE FAMILY BANQUET AT 6 PM.
"IT WAS A SATURDAY, CHILDREN'S DAY IN HEDESTAD.
"HARRIET WENT TO SEE THE PARADE.
"SHE WAS SUBDUED, THEY SAID.
"EVERYONE HAD NOTICED A CHANGE IN HER.
"HALF THE TIME SHE WAS WEARING TIGHT SWEATERS AND LIPSTICK.
"THE OTHER HALF SHE WAS OBSESSIVELY READING HER BIBLE.
"DAY TO DAY I DIDN'T KNOW WHO SHE WOULD BE.
"OR WHICH ONE WAS REAL.
"SHE HAD BEEN LIKE THAT SINCE THE YEAR BEFORE.
"SINCE HER FATHER DIED.
"SHE LEFT THE PARADE ABRUPTLY, FOR NO REASON."

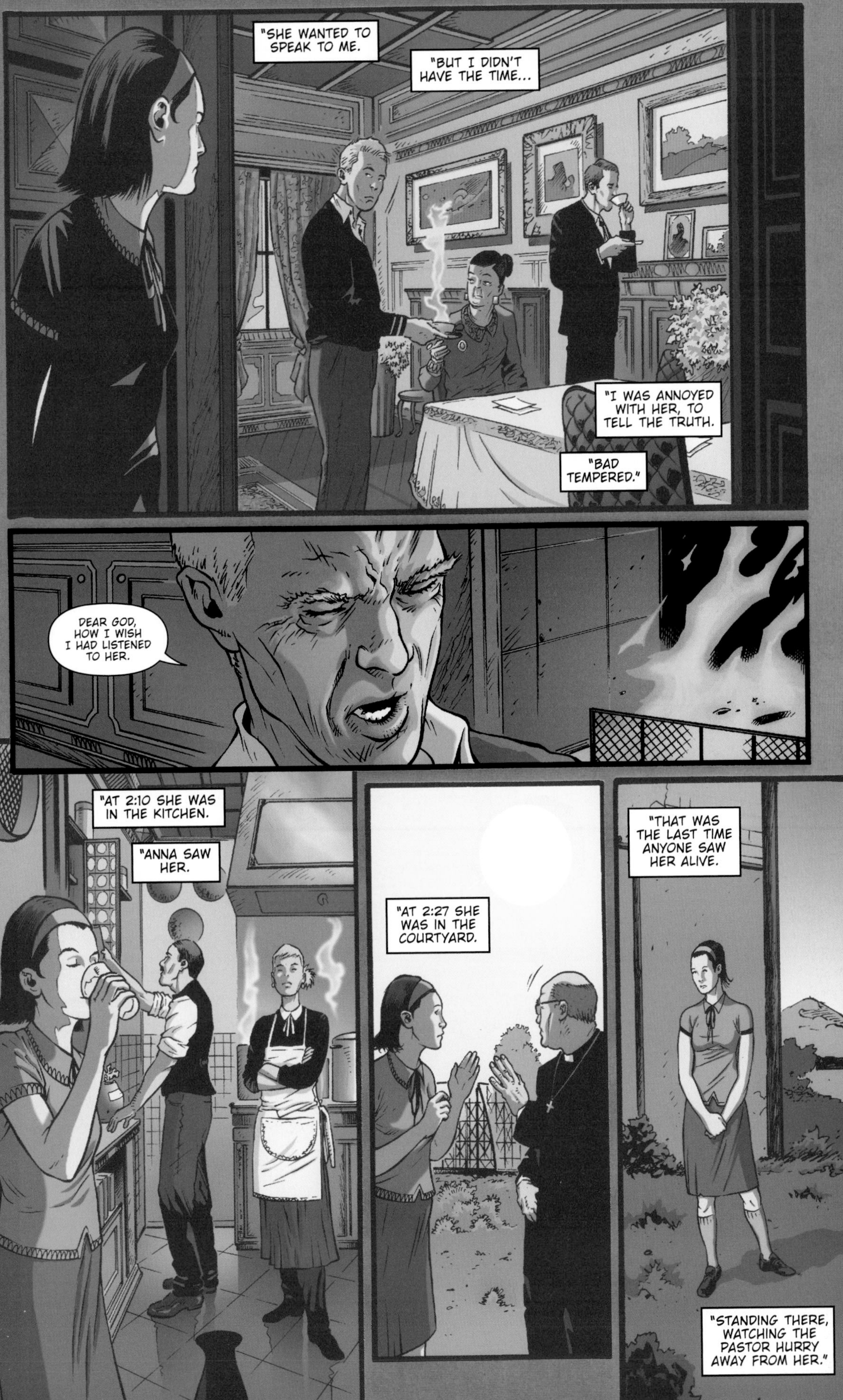
"SHE WANTED TO SPEAK TO ME.
"BUT I DIDN'T HAVE THE TIME...
"I WAS ANNOYED WITH HER, TO TELL THE TRUTH.
"BAD TEMPERED."
DEAR GOD, HOW I WISH I HAD LISTENED TO HER.
"AT 2:10 SHE WAS IN THE KITCHEN.
"ANNA SAW HER.
"AT 2:27 SHE WAS IN THE COURTYARD.
"THAT WAS THE LAST TIME ANYONE SAW HER ALIVE.
"STANDING THERE, WATCHING THE PASTOR HURRY AWAY FROM HER."

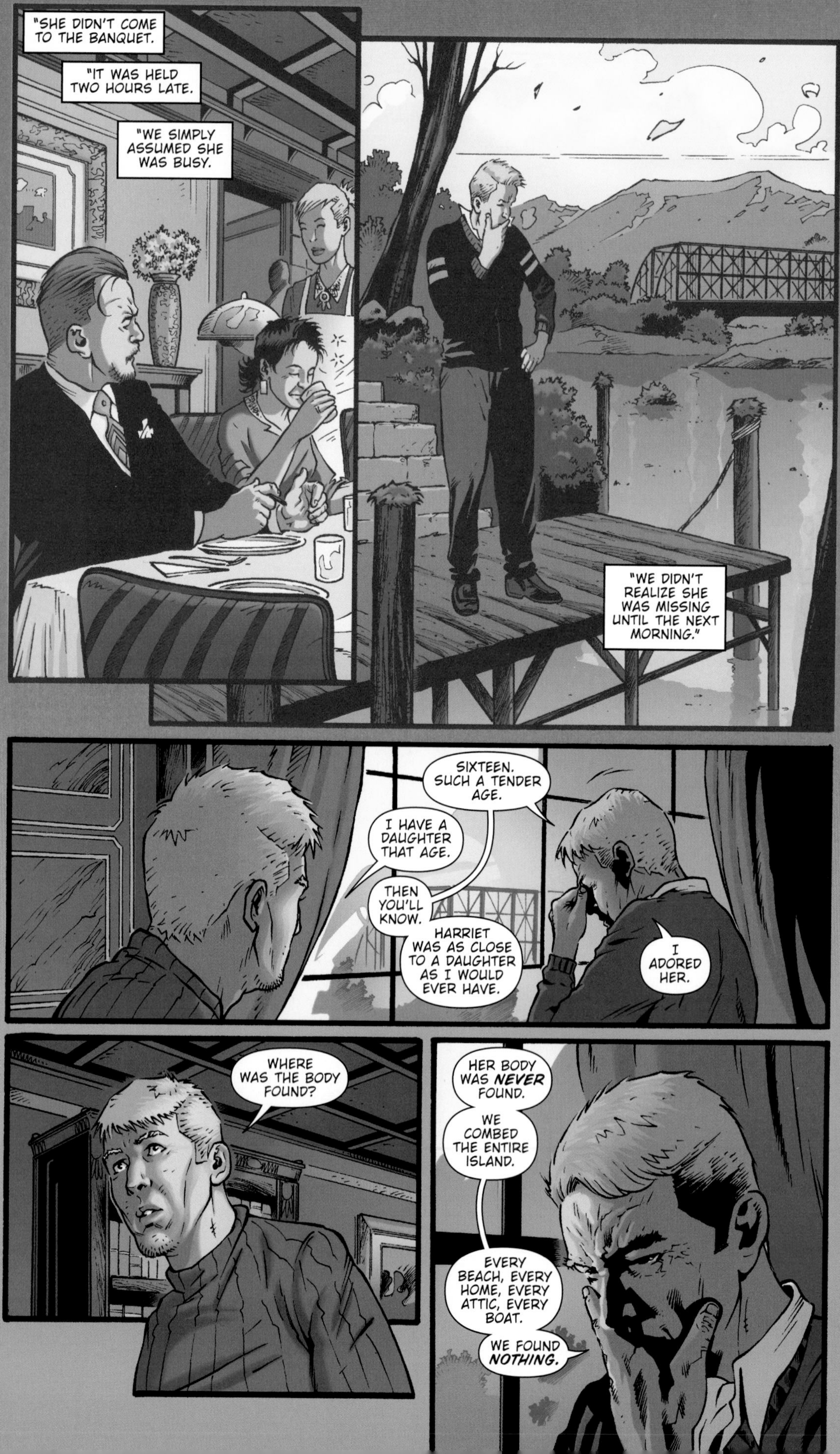
"SHE DIDN'T COME TO THE BANQUET.
"IT WAS HELD TWO HOURS LATE.
"WE SIMPLY ASSUMED SHE WAS BUSY.
"WE DIDN'T REALIZE SHE WAS MISSING UNTIL THE NEXT MORNING."
SIXTEEN. SUCH A TENDER AGE.
I HAVE A DAUGHTER THAT AGE.
THEN YOU'LL KNOW.
HARRIET WAS AS CLOSE TO A DAUGHTER AS I WOULD EVER HAVE.
I ADORED HER.
WHERE WAS THE BODY FOUND?
HER BODY WAS *NEVER* FOUND.
WE COMBED THE ENTIRE ISLAND.
EVERY BEACH, EVERY HOME, EVERY ATTIC, EVERY BOAT.
WE FOUND *NOTHING.*

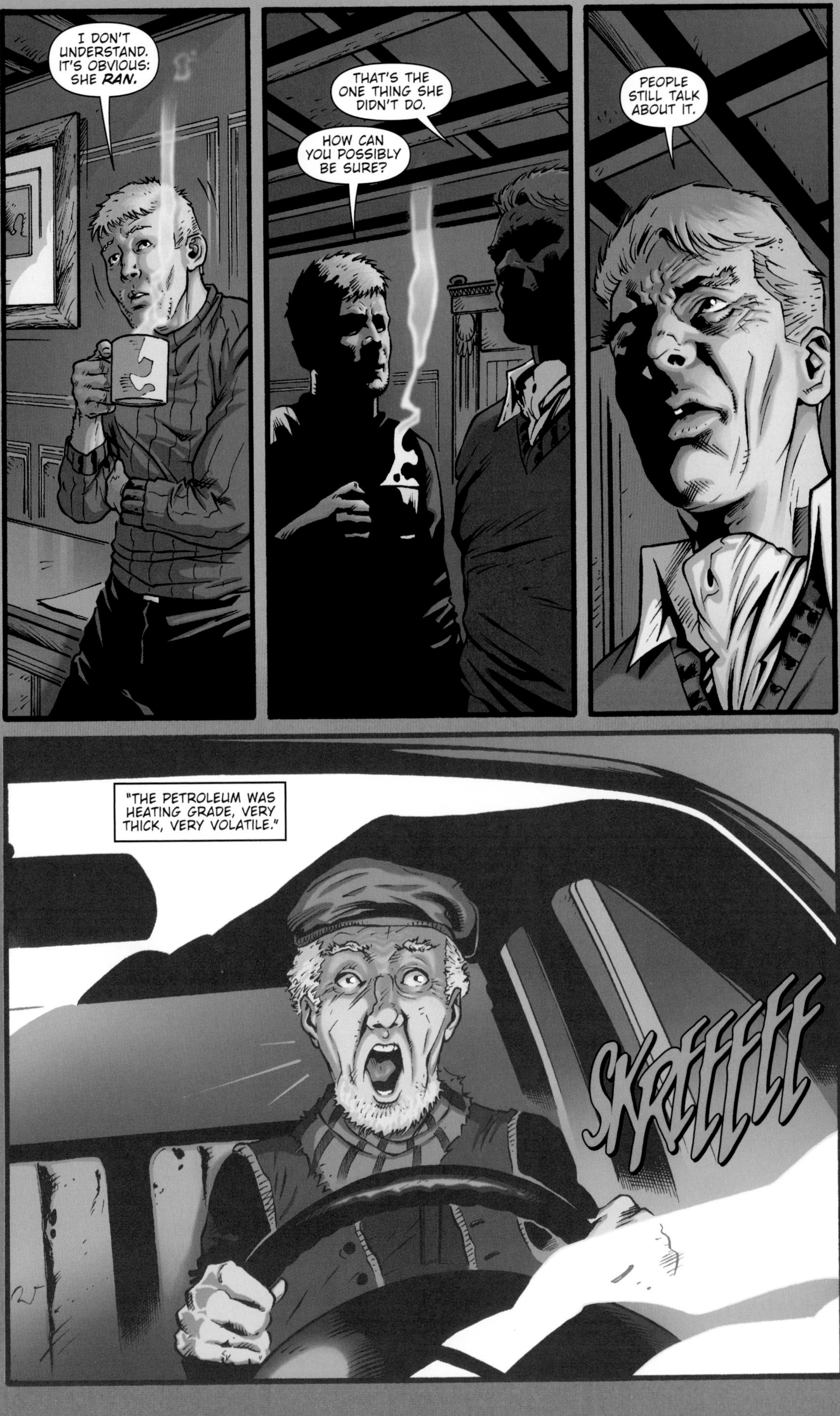
I DON'T UNDERSTAND. IT'S OBVIOUS: SHE *RAN.*
THAT'S THE ONE THING SHE DIDN'T DO.
HOW CAN YOU POSSIBLY BE SURE?
PEOPLE STILL TALK ABOUT IT.
"THE PETROLEUM WAS HEATING GRADE, VERY THICK, VERY VOLATILE."
SKREEEEE

"WE ALL SAW WHAT COULD HAPPEN IF THE PETROLEUM CAUGHT A SPARK:
"BOATS, HOUSES, FORESTS ON BOTH SHORES, EVERY-THING WOULD BE AFLAME.
"EVERYONE RUSHED TO THE BRIDGE AND SHORE, BOTH SIDES.
"ON THE BRIDGE WE HAD TO TRY TO PARE THE DRIVERS FROM THE WRECKAGE WITHOUT CAUSING A SPARK.
"PEOPLE WATCHED THE SHORE FOR THE SLIGHTEST FLAME.
"AND EVERYONE WAS LOOKING FOR THEIR OWN PEOPLE.
"READING FACES...
"...VIGILANT...
"...WATCHING..."

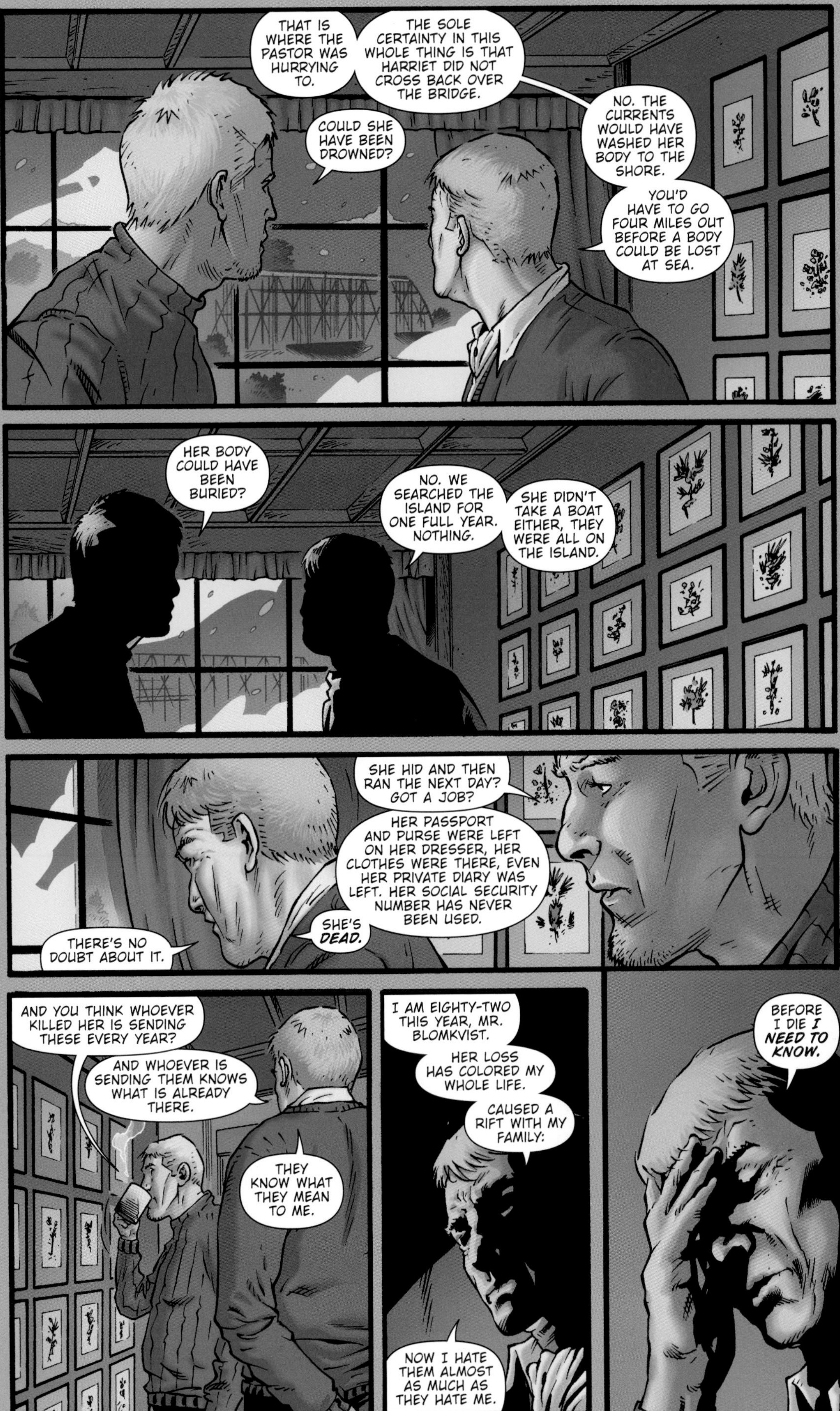

THAT IS WHERE THE PASTOR WAS HURRYING TO.
THE SOLE CERTAINTY IN THIS WHOLE THING IS THAT HARRIET DID NOT CROSS BACK OVER THE BRIDGE.
COULD SHE HAVE BEEN DROWNED?
NO. THE CURRENTS WOULD HAVE WASHED HER BODY TO THE SHORE.
YOU'D HAVE TO GO FOUR MILES OUT BEFORE A BODY COULD BE LOST AT SEA.
HER BODY COULD HAVE BEEN BURIED?
NO. WE SEARCHED THE ISLAND FOR ONE FULL YEAR. NOTHING.
SHE DIDN'T TAKE A BOAT EITHER, THEY WERE ALL ON THE ISLAND.
SHE HID AND THEN RAN THE NEXT DAY? GOT A JOB?
HER PASSPORT AND PURSE WERE LEFT ON HER DRESSER, HER CLOTHES WERE THERE, EVEN HER PRIVATE DIARY WAS LEFT. HER SOCIAL SECURITY NUMBER HAS NEVER BEEN USED.
SHE'S *DEAD.*
THERE'S NO DOUBT ABOUT IT.
AND YOU THINK WHOEVER KILLED HER IS SENDING THESE EVERY YEAR?
AND WHOEVER IS SENDING THEM KNOWS WHAT IS ALREADY THERE.
THEY KNOW WHAT THEY MEAN TO ME.
I AM EIGHTY-TWO THIS YEAR, MR. BLOMKVIST.
HER LOSS HAS COLORED MY WHOLE LIFE.
CAUSED A RIFT WITH MY FAMILY:
NOW I HATE THEM ALMOST AS MUCH AS THEY HATE ME.
BEFORE I DIE *I NEED TO KNOW.*

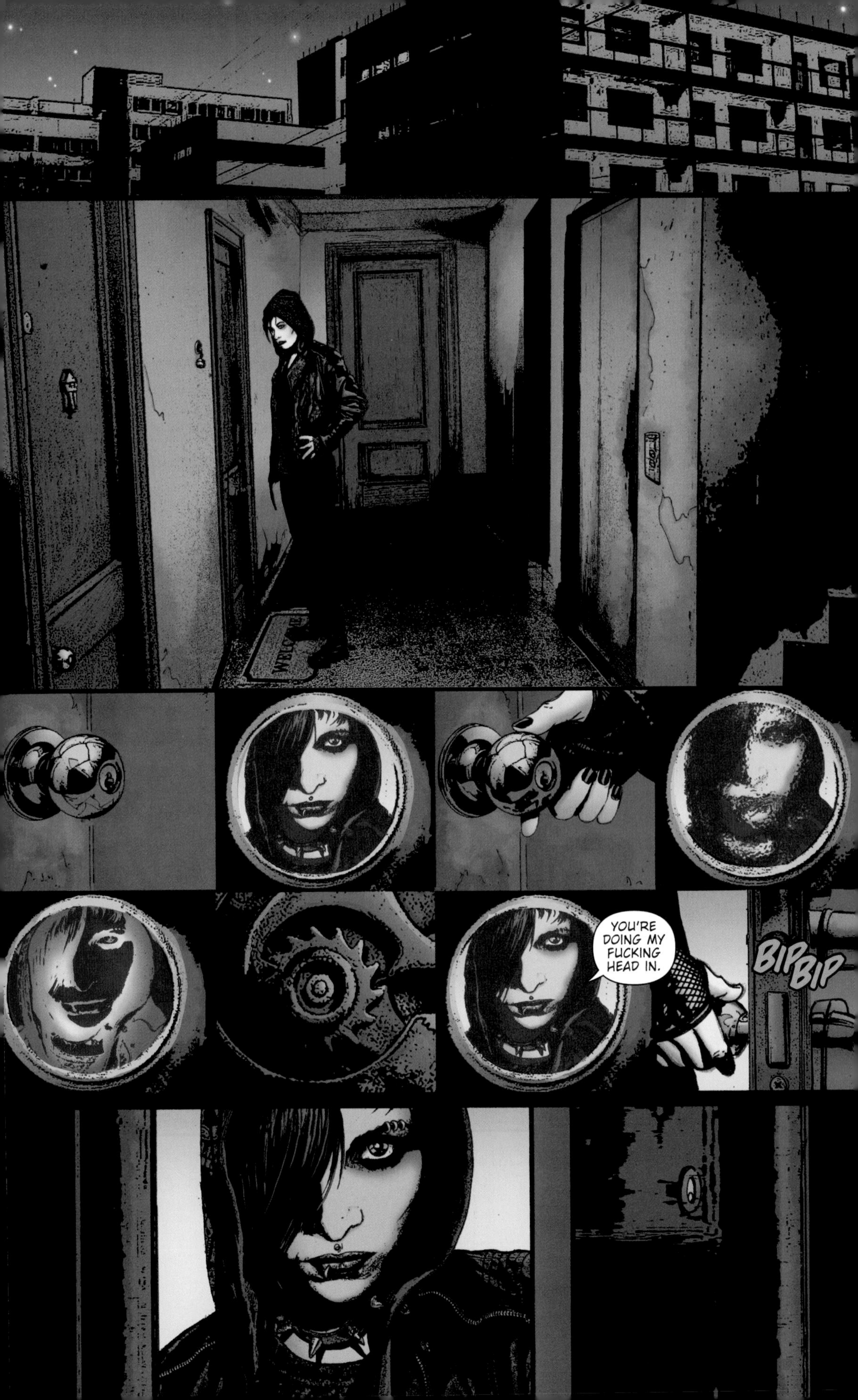

YOU'RE DOING MY FUCKING HEAD IN.
BIP BIP

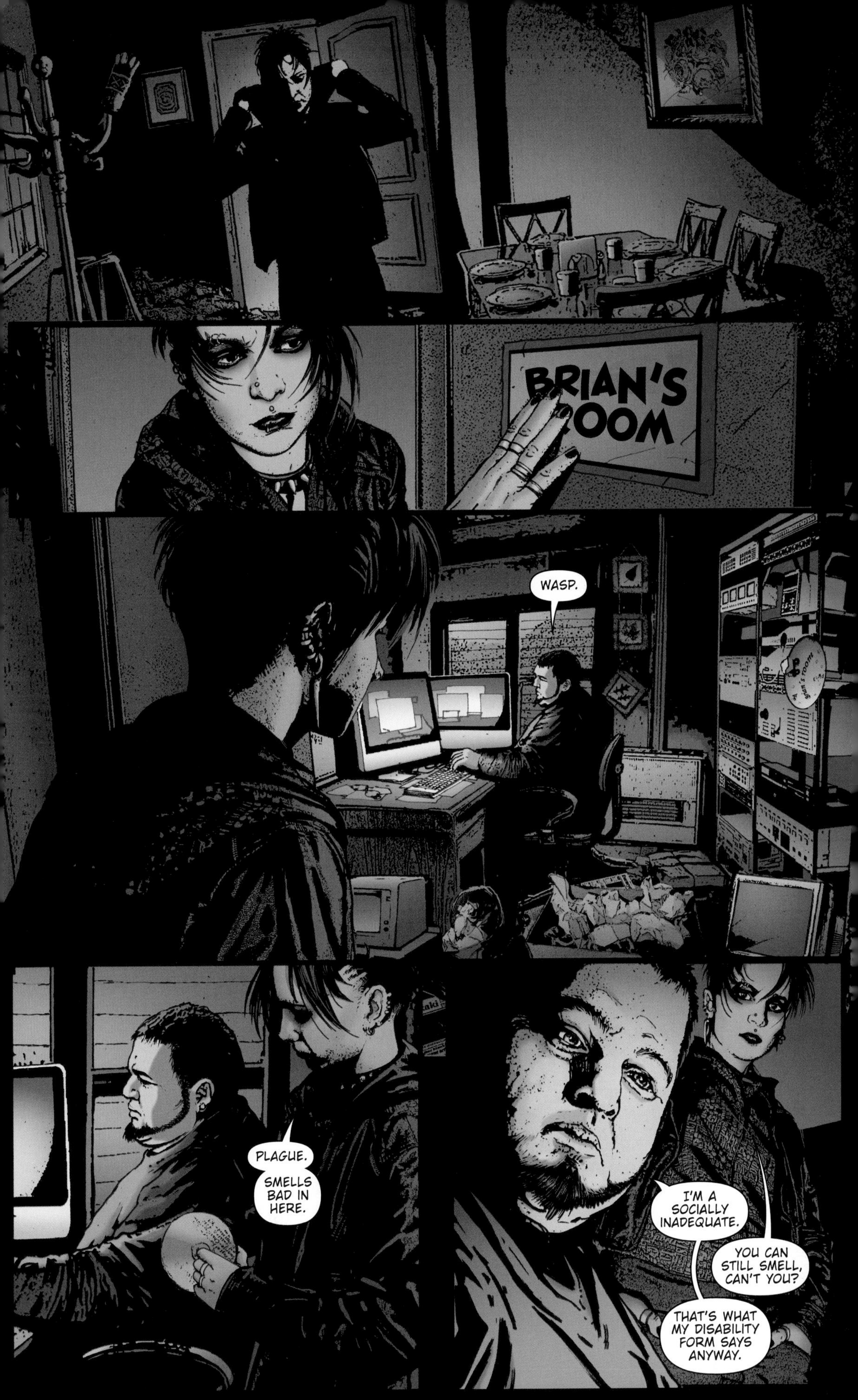
BRIAN'S ROOM
WASP.
PLAGUE.
SMELLS BAD IN HERE.
I'M A SOCIALLY INADEQUATE.
YOU CAN STILL SMELL, CAN'T YOU?
THAT'S WHAT MY DISABILITY FORM SAYS ANYWAY.

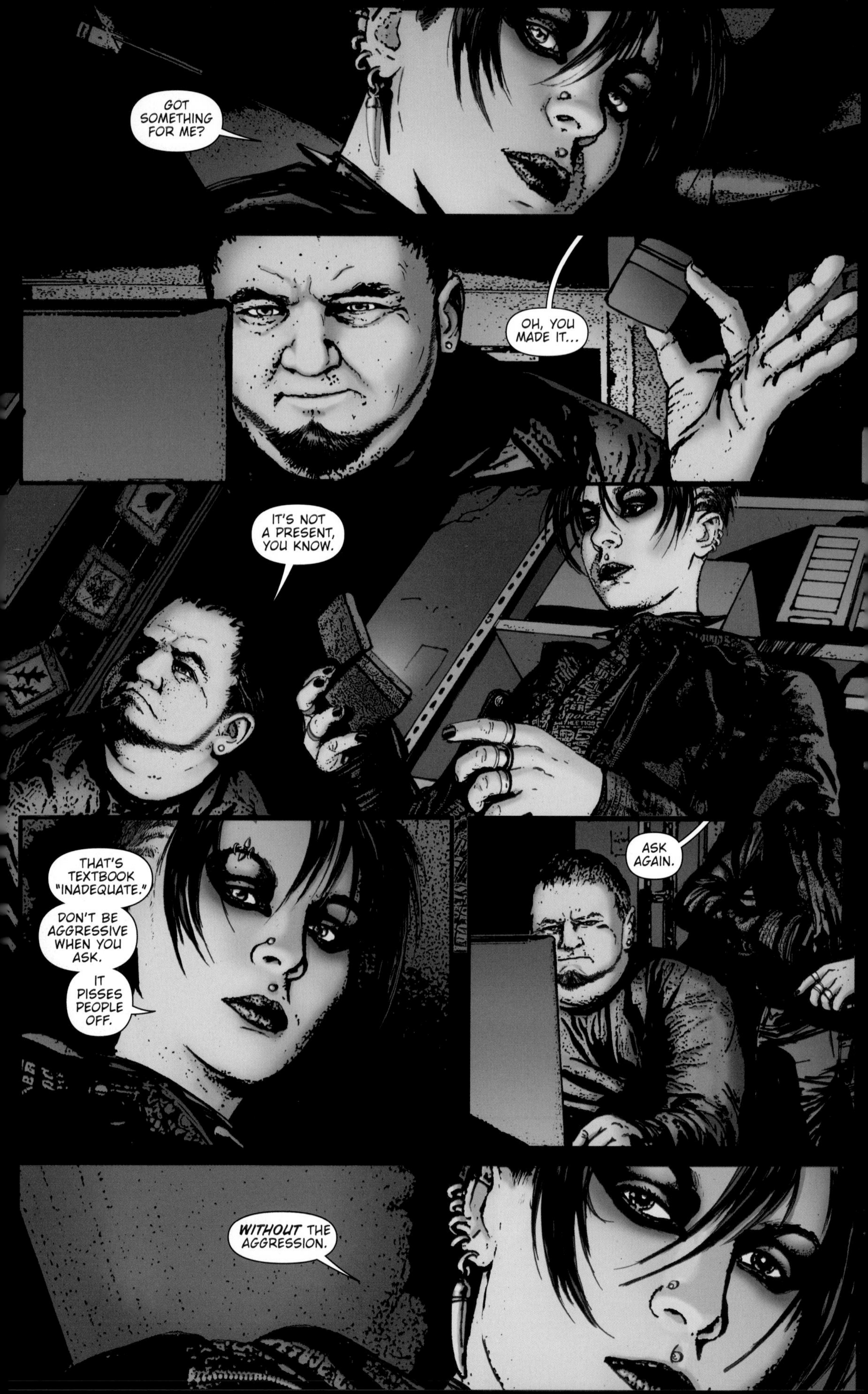
GOT SOMETHING FOR ME?
OH, YOU MADE IT...
IT'S NOT A PRESENT, YOU KNOW.
THAT'S TEXTBOOK "INADEQUATE."
DON'T BE AGGRESSIVE WHEN YOU ASK.
IT PISSES PEOPLE OFF.
ASK AGAIN.
WITHOUT THE AGGRESSION.

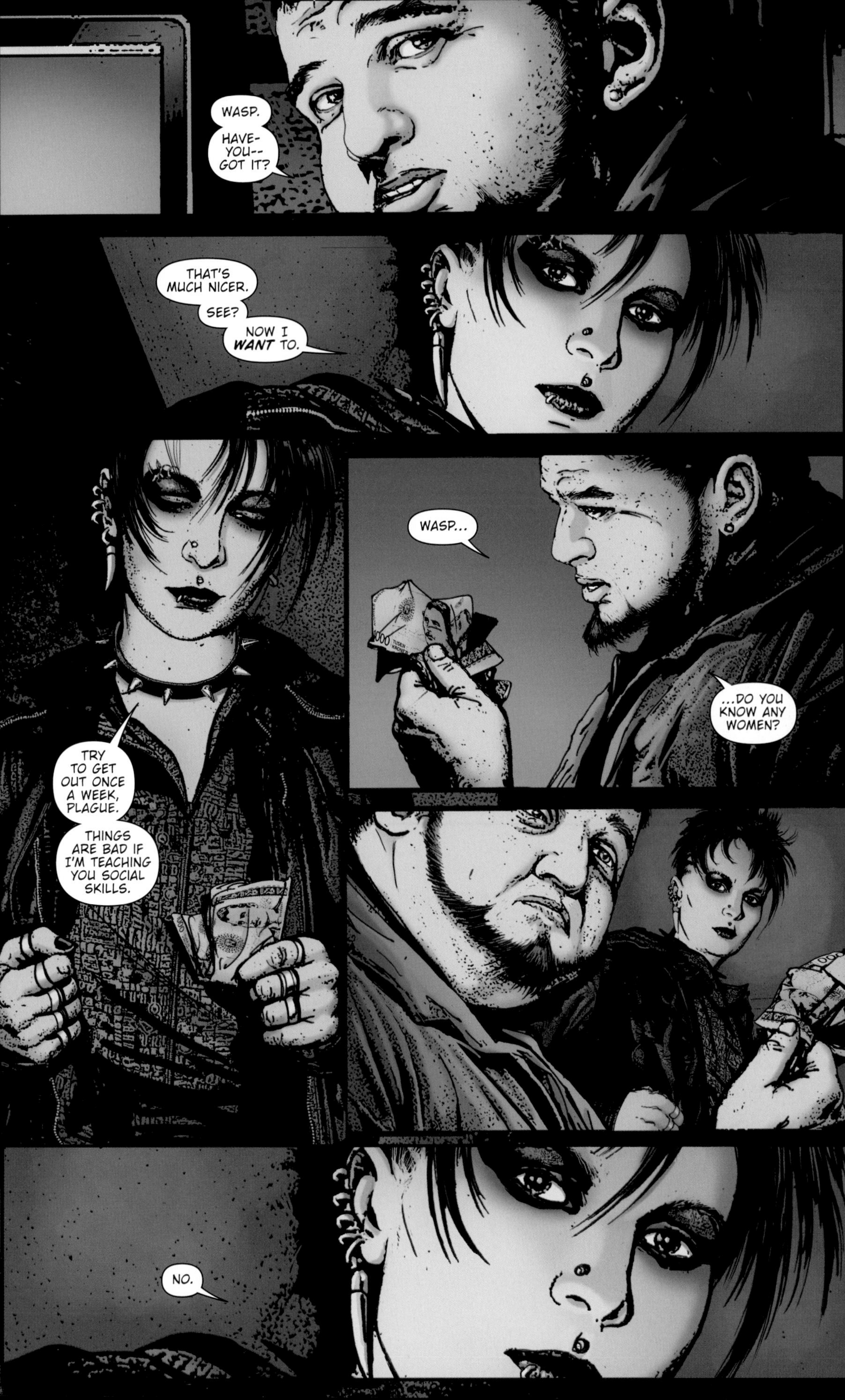
WASP.
HAVE- YOU-- GOT IT?
THAT'S MUCH NICER.
SEE?
NOW I **WANT** TO.
TRY TO GET OUT ONCE A WEEK, PLAGUE.
THINGS ARE BAD IF I'M TEACHING YOU SOCIAL SKILLS.
WASP...
...DO YOU KNOW ANY WOMEN?
NO.

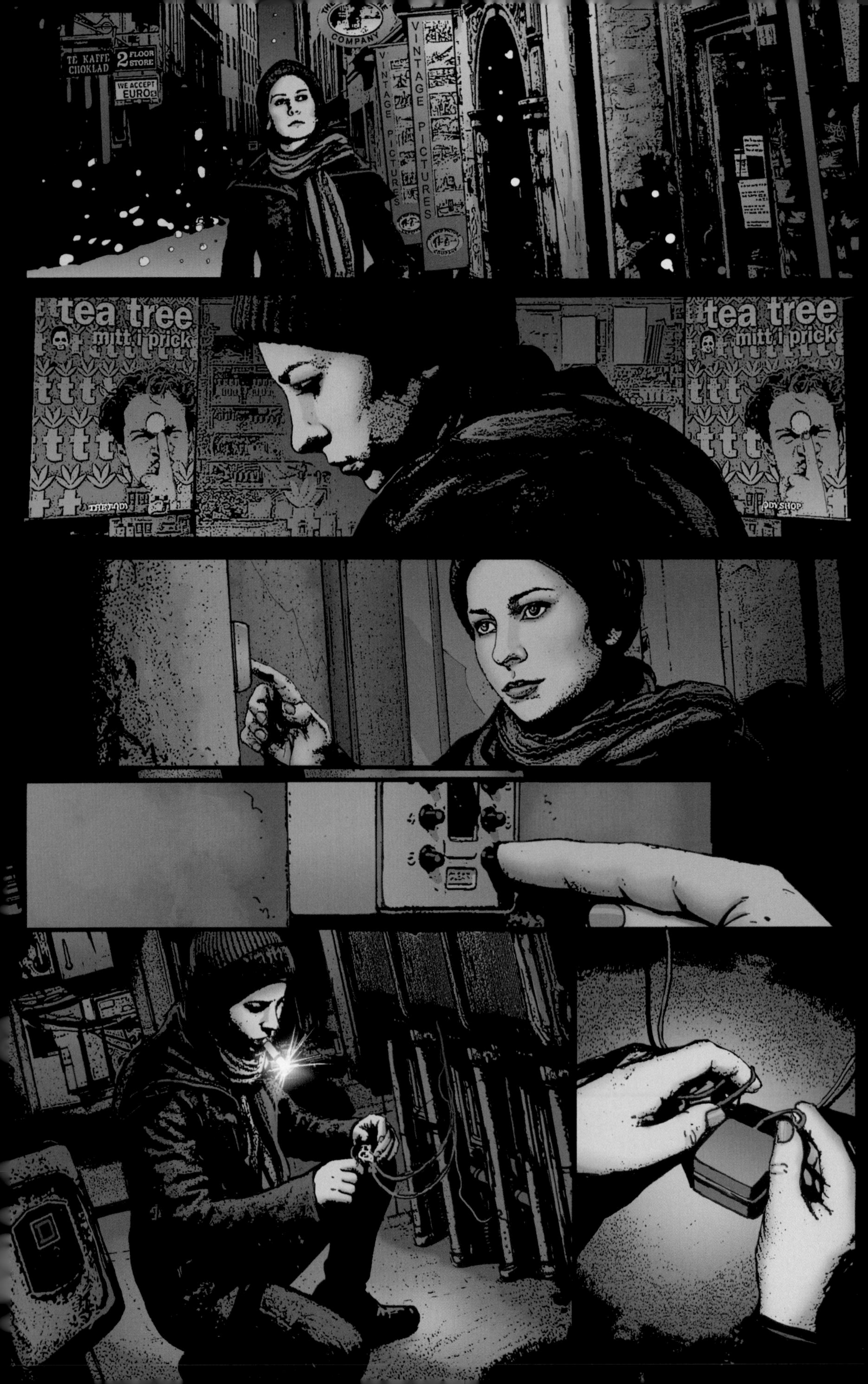

TE KAFFE CHOKLAD
2 FLOOR STORE
WE ACCEPT EURO
COMPANY
VINTAGE PICTURES
VINTAGE PICTURES
tea tree
mitt i prick
tea tree
mitt i prick

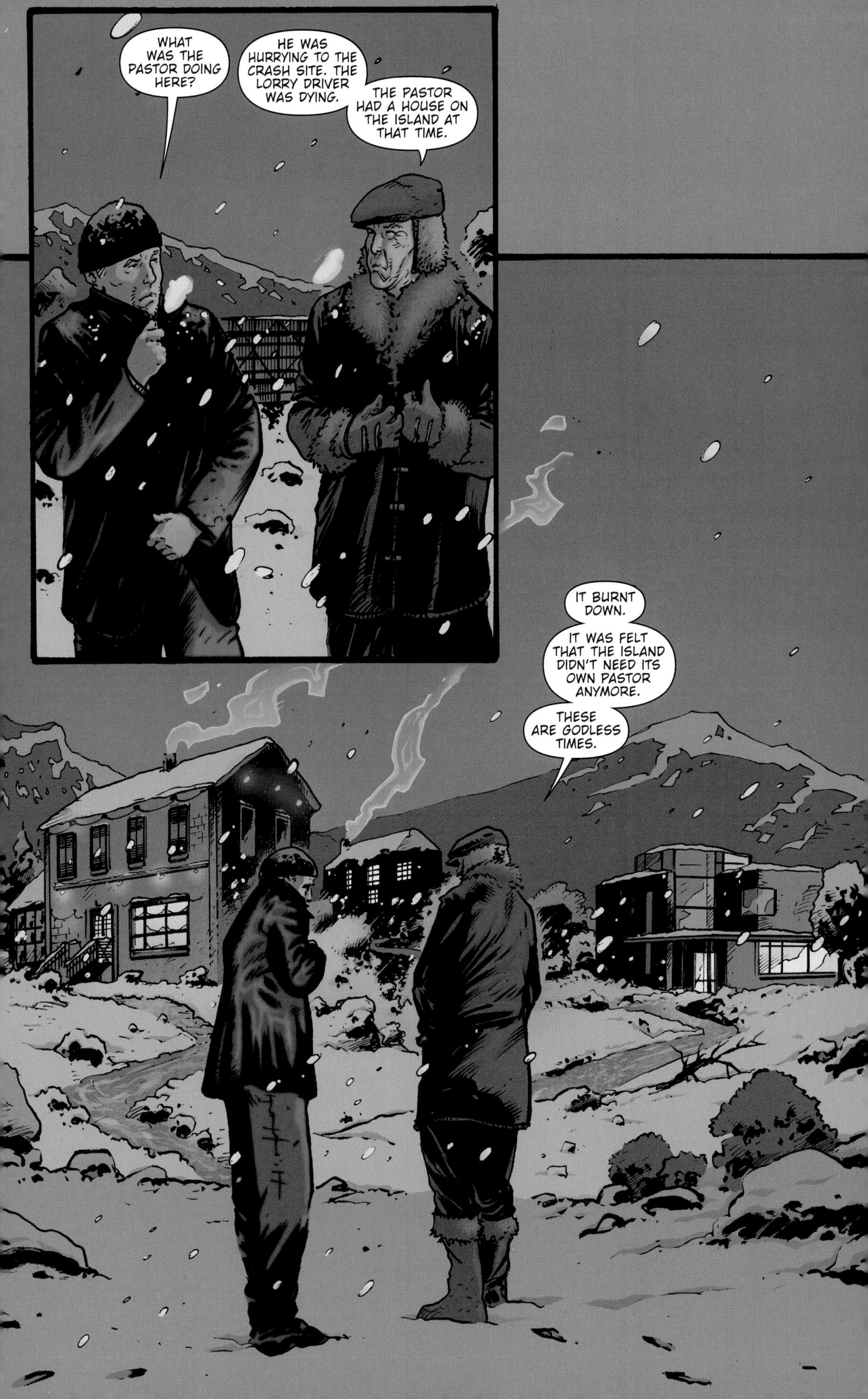
WHAT WAS THE PASTOR DOING HERE?
HE WAS HURRYING TO THE CRASH SITE. THE LORRY DRIVER WAS DYING.
THE PASTOR HAD A HOUSE ON THE ISLAND AT THAT TIME.
IT BURNT DOWN.
IT WAS FELT THAT THE ISLAND DIDN'T NEED ITS OWN PASTOR ANYMORE.
THESE ARE GODLESS TIMES.

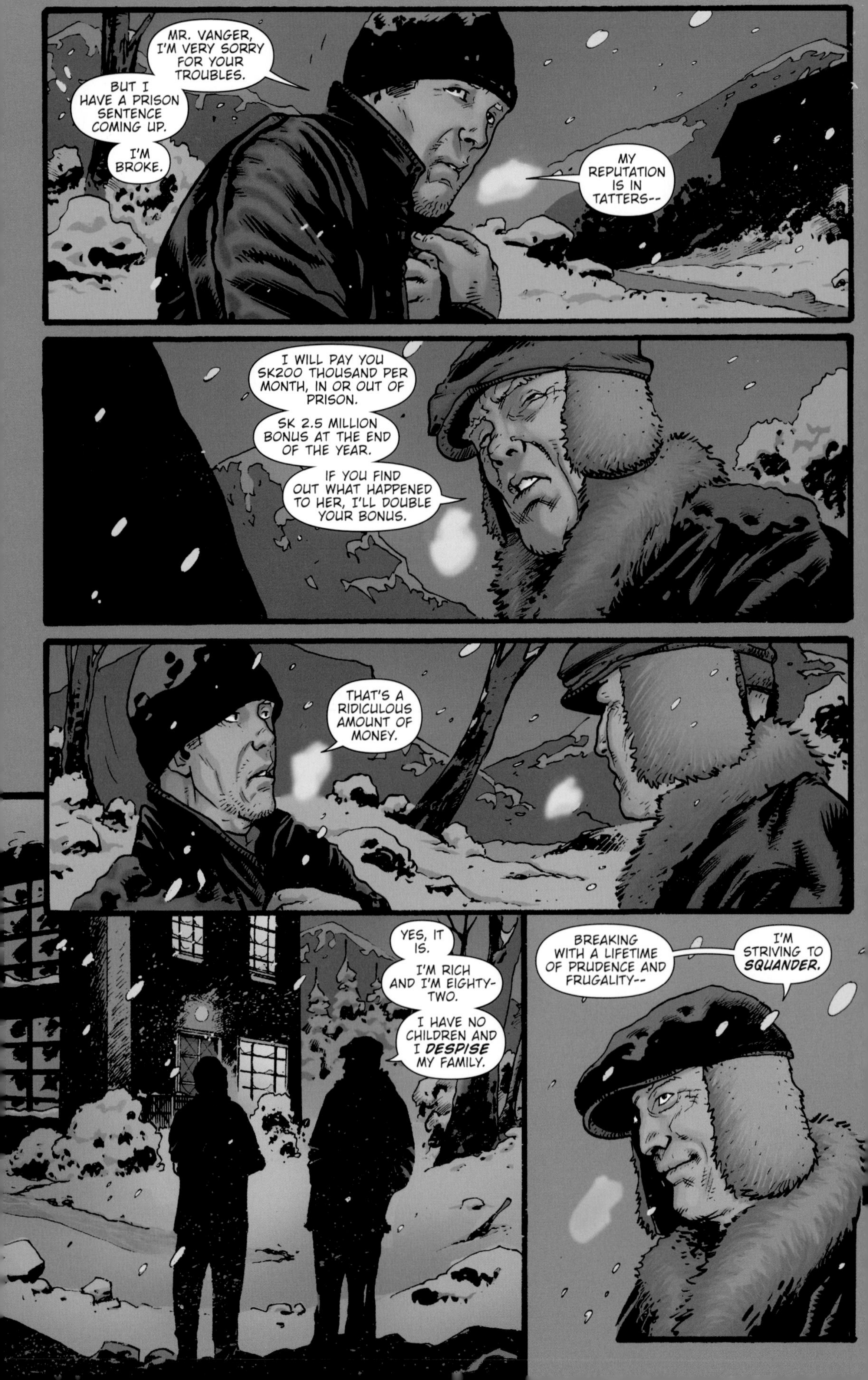
MR. VANGER, I'M VERY SORRY FOR YOUR TROUBLES.
BUT I HAVE A PRISON SENTENCE COMING UP.
I'M BROKE.
MY REPUTATION IS IN TATTERS--
I WILL PAY YOU SK200 THOUSAND PER MONTH, IN OR OUT OF PRISON.
SK 2.5 MILLION BONUS AT THE END OF THE YEAR.
IF YOU FIND OUT WHAT HAPPENED TO HER, I'LL DOUBLE YOUR BONUS.
THAT'S A RIDICULOUS AMOUNT OF MONEY.
YES, IT IS.
I'M RICH AND I'M EIGHTY-TWO.
I HAVE NO CHILDREN AND I DESPISE MY FAMILY.
BREAKING WITH A LIFETIME OF PRUDENCE AND FRUGALITY--
I'M STRIVING TO SQUANDER.

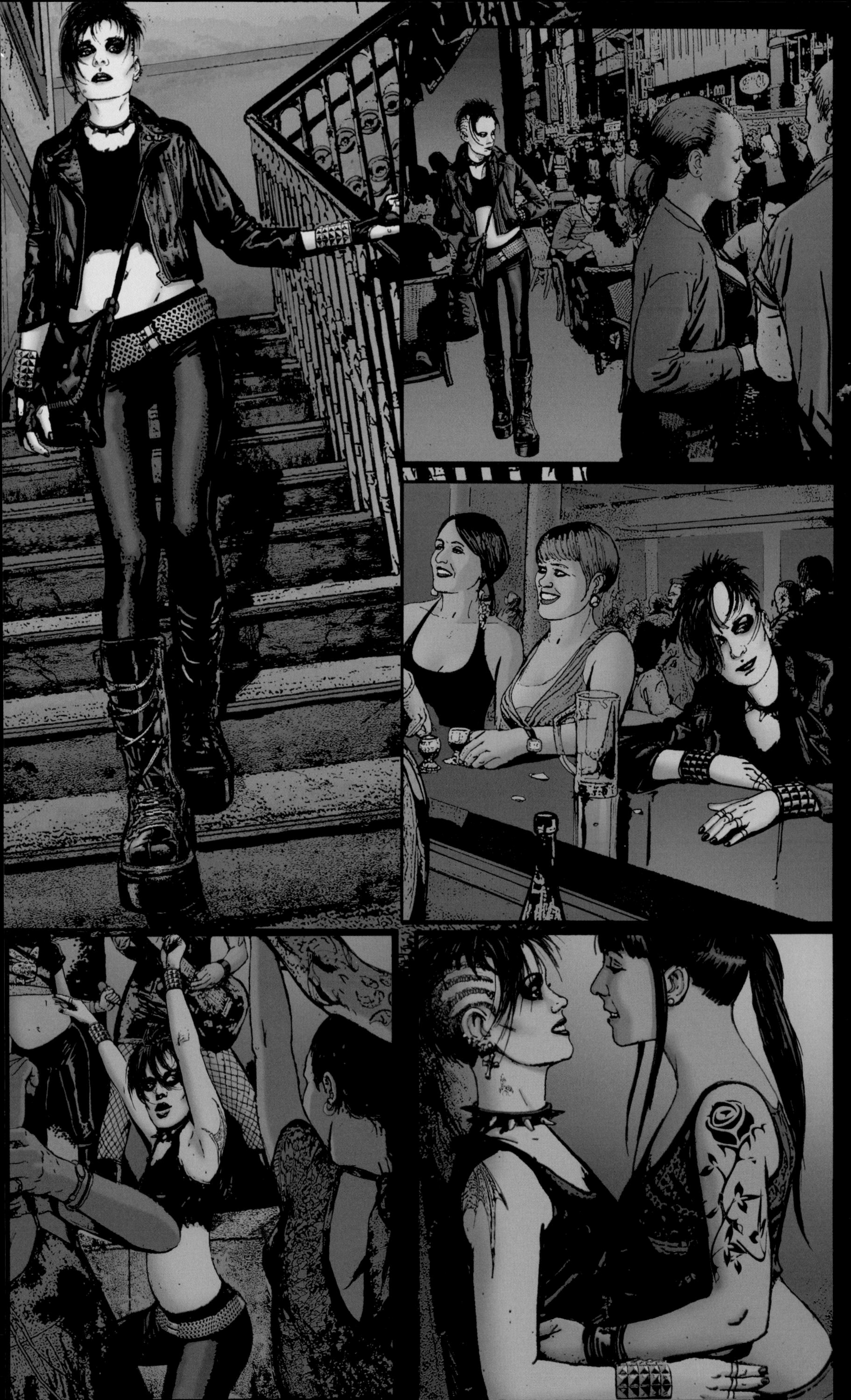

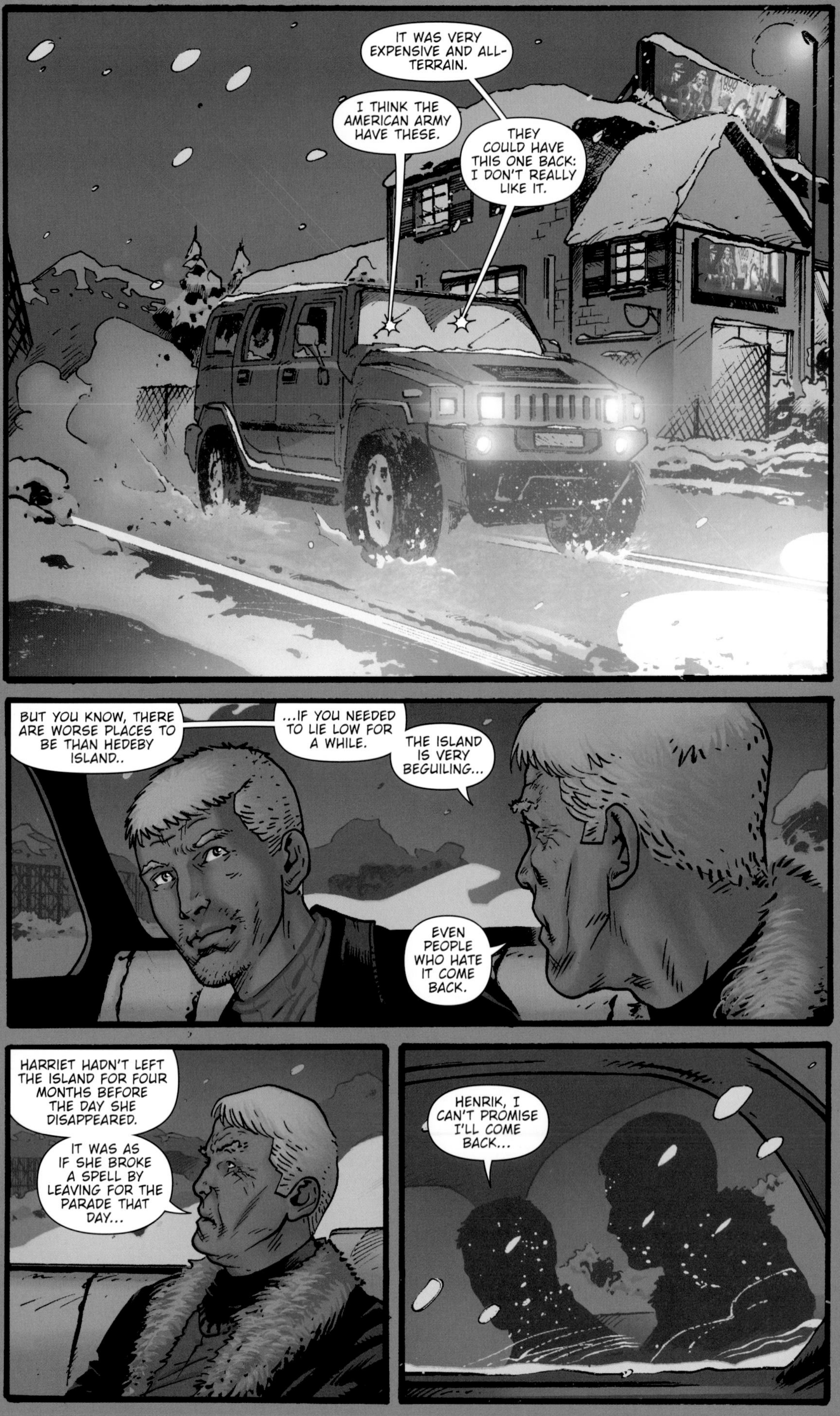
IT WAS VERY EXPENSIVE AND ALL-TERRAIN.
I THINK THE AMERICAN ARMY HAVE THESE.
THEY COULD HAVE THIS ONE BACK: I DON'T REALLY LIKE IT.
BUT YOU KNOW, THERE ARE WORSE PLACES TO BE THAN HEDEBY ISLAND..
...IF YOU NEEDED TO LIE LOW FOR A WHILE.
THE ISLAND IS VERY BEGUILING...
EVEN PEOPLE WHO HATE IT COME BACK.
HARRIET HADN'T LEFT THE ISLAND FOR FOUR MONTHS BEFORE THE DAY SHE DISAPPEARED.
IT WAS AS IF SHE BROKE A SPELL BY LEAVING FOR THE PARADE THAT DAY...
HENRIK, I CAN'T PROMISE I'LL COME BACK...

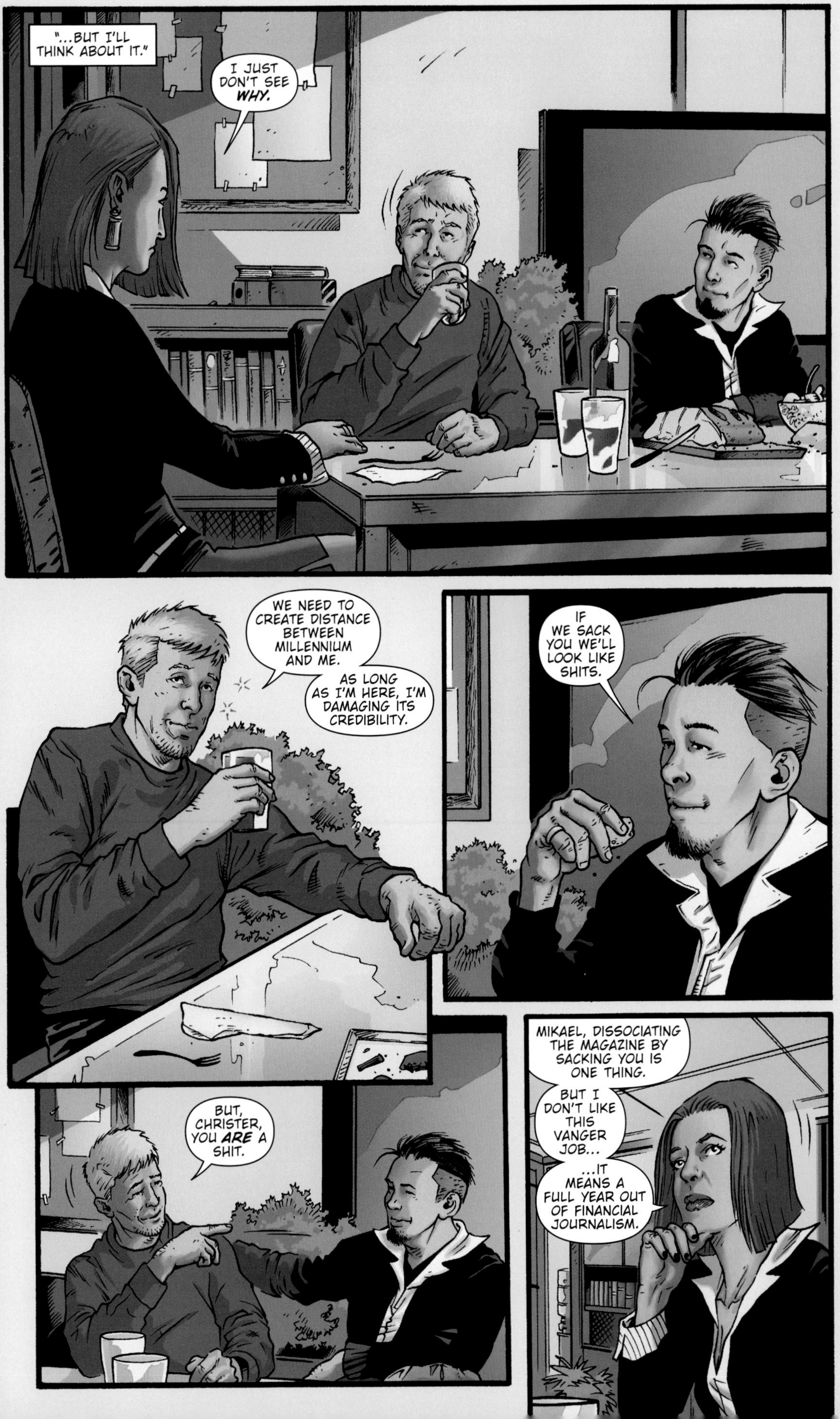
"...BUT I'LL THINK ABOUT IT."
I JUST DON'T SEE WHY.
WE NEED TO CREATE DISTANCE BETWEEN MILLENNIUM AND ME.
AS LONG AS I'M HERE, I'M DAMAGING ITS CREDIBILITY.
IF WE SACK YOU WE'LL LOOK LIKE SHITS.
BUT, CHRISTER, YOU ARE A SHIT.
MIKAEL, DISSOCIATING THE MAGAZINE BY SACKING YOU IS ONE THING.
BUT I DON'T LIKE THIS VANGER JOB...
...IT MEANS A FULL YEAR OUT OF FINANCIAL JOURNALISM.

WHEN WE OPENED, WE EACH PUT IN OUR STAKE.

I'VE COST THE MAGAZINE HUNDREDS OF THOUSANDS OVER THIS WENNERSTRÖM CASE.

I NEED THIS JOB TO MAKE IT RIGHT.

FOR GOD'S SAKE, MIKAEL, IT'S THE BUSINESS WE'RE IN.

WE SHARE THE RISK.

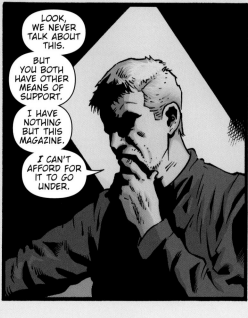

LOOK, WE NEVER TALK ABOUT THIS.

BUT YOU BOTH HAVE OTHER MEANS OF SUPPORT.

I HAVE NOTHING BUT THIS MAGAZINE.

I CAN'T AFFORD FOR IT TO GO UNDER.

GET OUT THE FUCKING VIOLINS!

AS A BOARD MEMBER I RECOMMEND SACKING ME.

I'M A LIABILITY.

I'M DRAGGING DOWN THE BRAND.

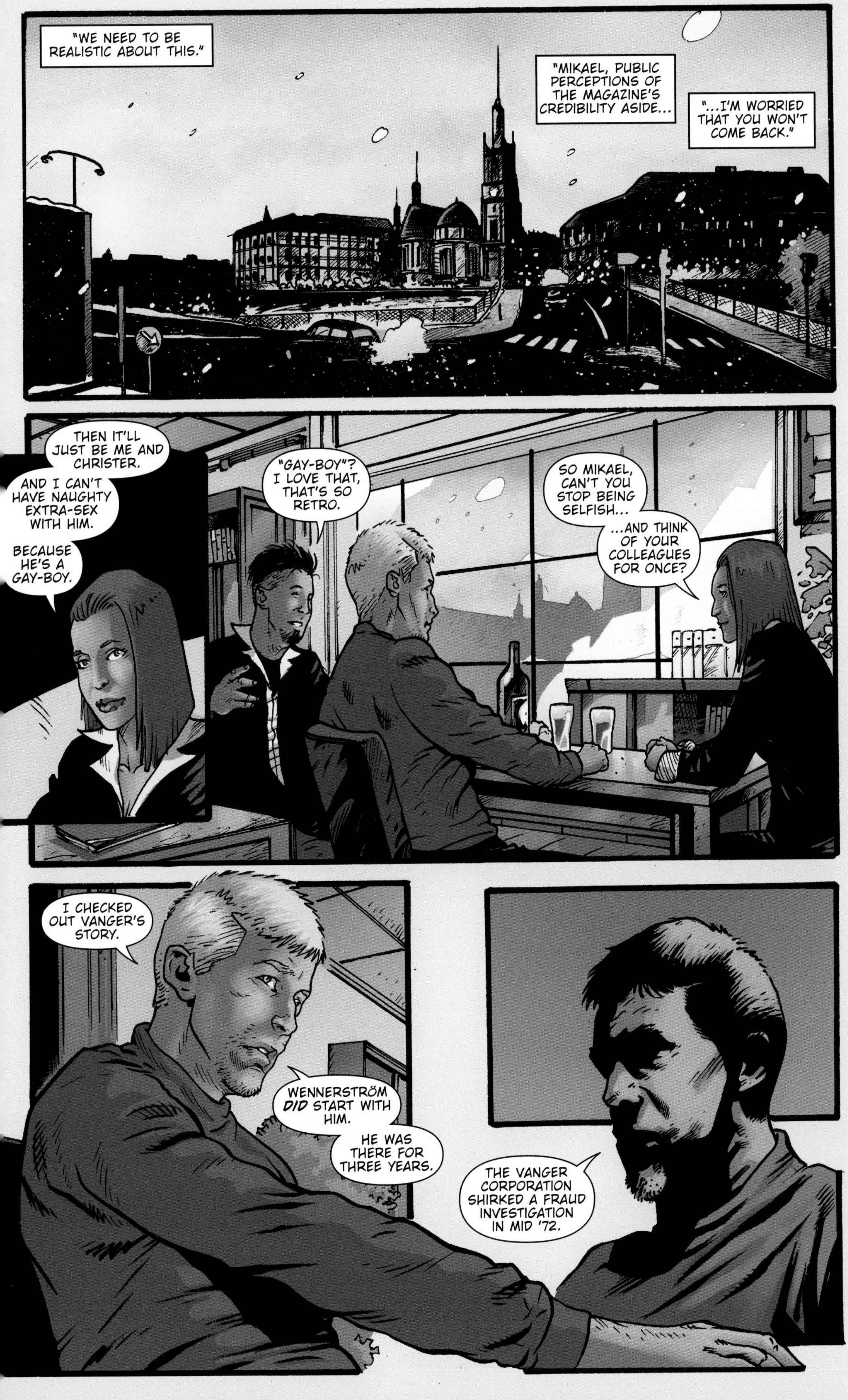
"WE NEED TO BE REALISTIC ABOUT THIS."
"MIKAEL, PUBLIC PERCEPTIONS OF THE MAGAZINE'S CREDIBILITY ASIDE...
"...I'M WORRIED THAT YOU WON'T COME BACK."
THEN IT'LL JUST BE ME AND CHRISTER.
AND I CAN'T HAVE NAUGHTY EXTRA-SEX WITH HIM.
BECAUSE HE'S A GAY-BOY.
"GAY-BOY"? I LOVE THAT, THAT'S SO RETRO.
SO MIKAEL, CAN'T YOU STOP BEING SELFISH...
...AND THINK OF YOUR COLLEAGUES FOR ONCE?
I CHECKED OUT VANGER'S STORY.
WENNERSTRÖM *DID* START WITH HIM.
HE WAS THERE FOR THREE YEARS.
THE VANGER CORPORATION SHIRKED A FRAUD INVESTIGATION IN MID '72.

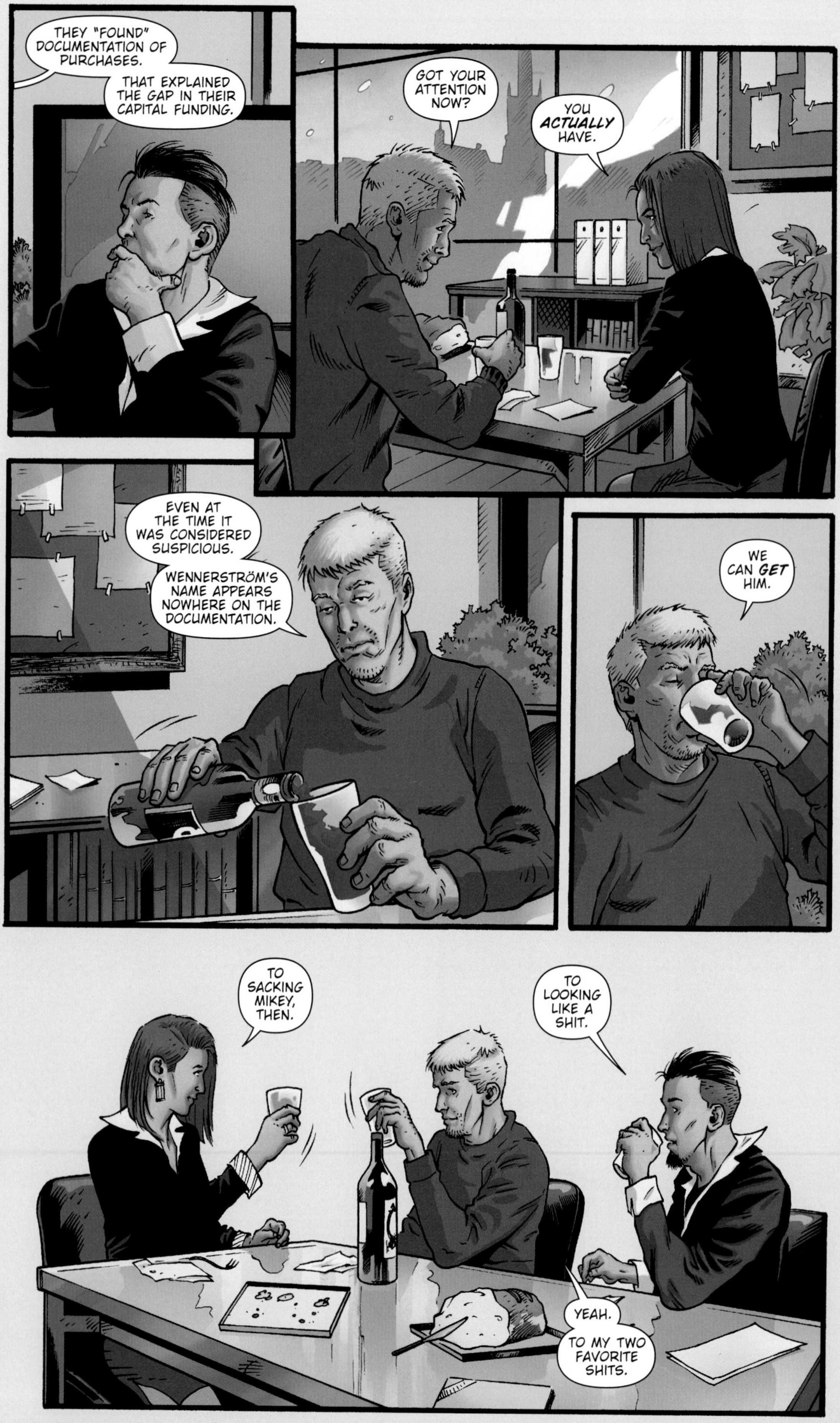
THEY "FOUND" DOCUMENTATION OF PURCHASES.
THAT EXPLAINED THE GAP IN THEIR CAPITAL FUNDING.
GOT YOUR ATTENTION NOW?
YOU **ACTUALLY** HAVE.
EVEN AT THE TIME IT WAS CONSIDERED SUSPICIOUS.
WENNERSTRÖM'S NAME APPEARS NOWHERE ON THE DOCUMENTATION.
WE CAN **GET** HIM.
TO SACKING MIKEY, THEN.
TO LOOKING LIKE A SHIT.
YEAH.
TO MY TWO FAVORITE SHITS.

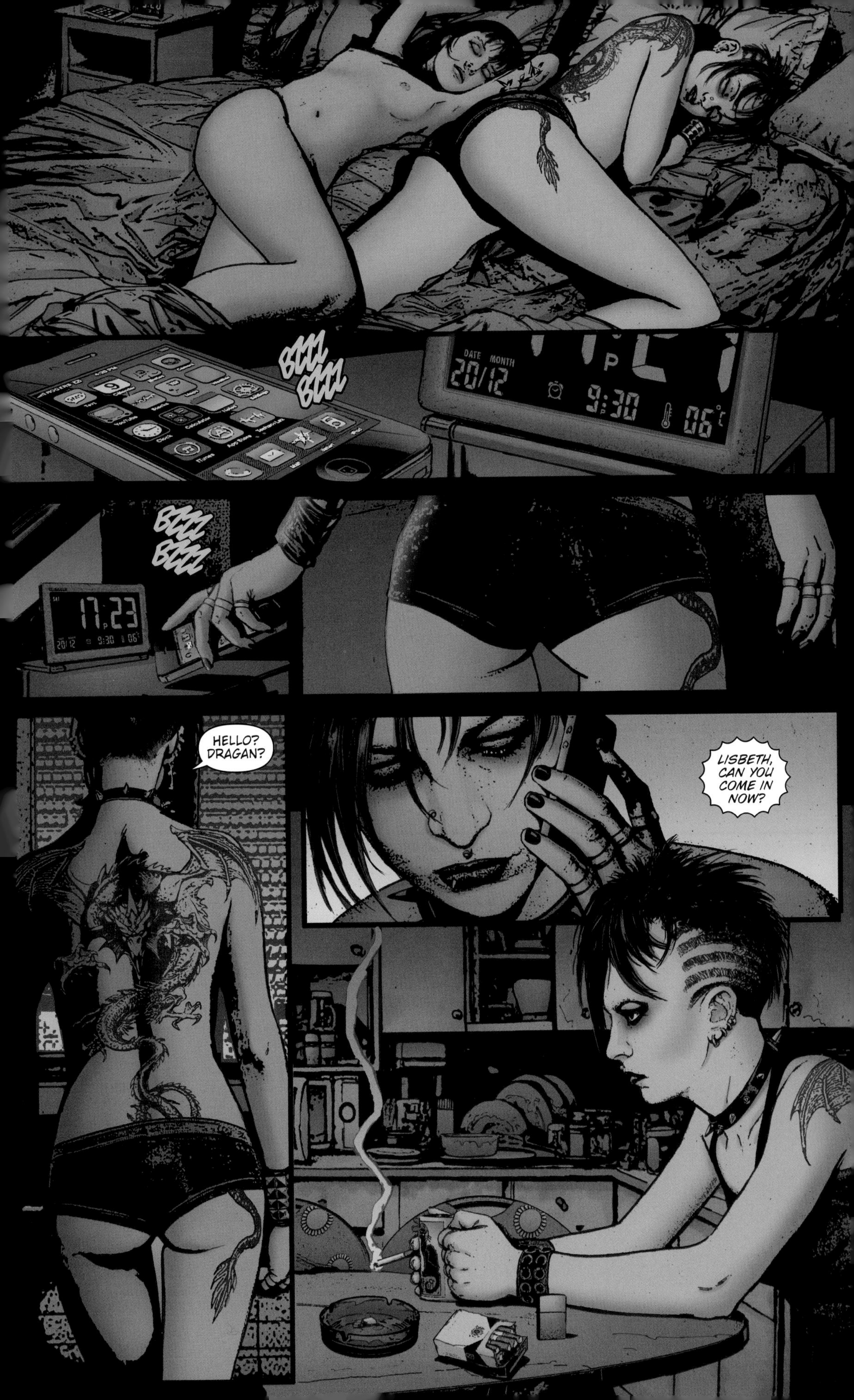

BZZZ
BZZZ
BZZZ
BZZZ
HELLO? DRAGAN?
LISBETH, CAN YOU COME IN NOW?

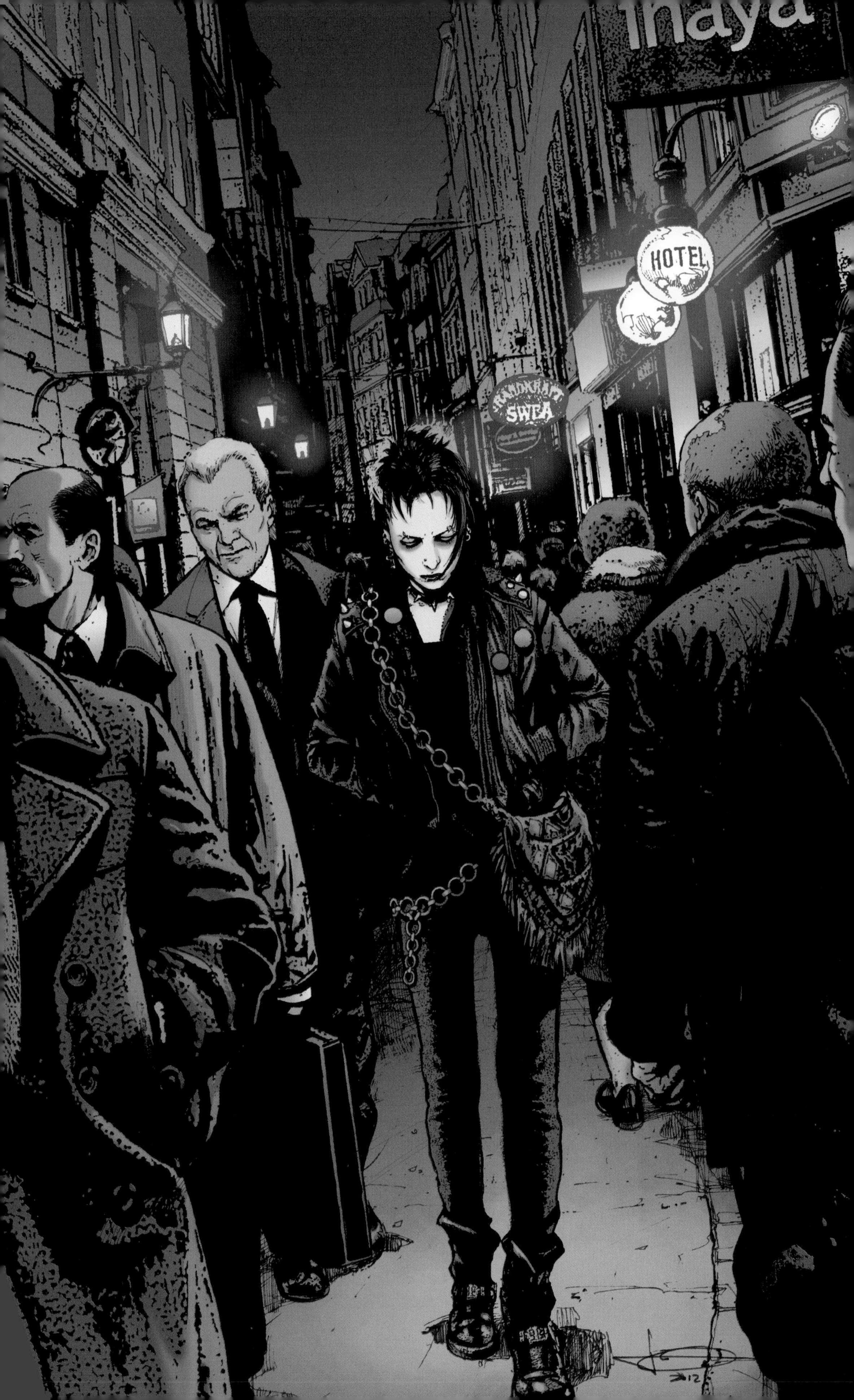
HOTEL
SWEA

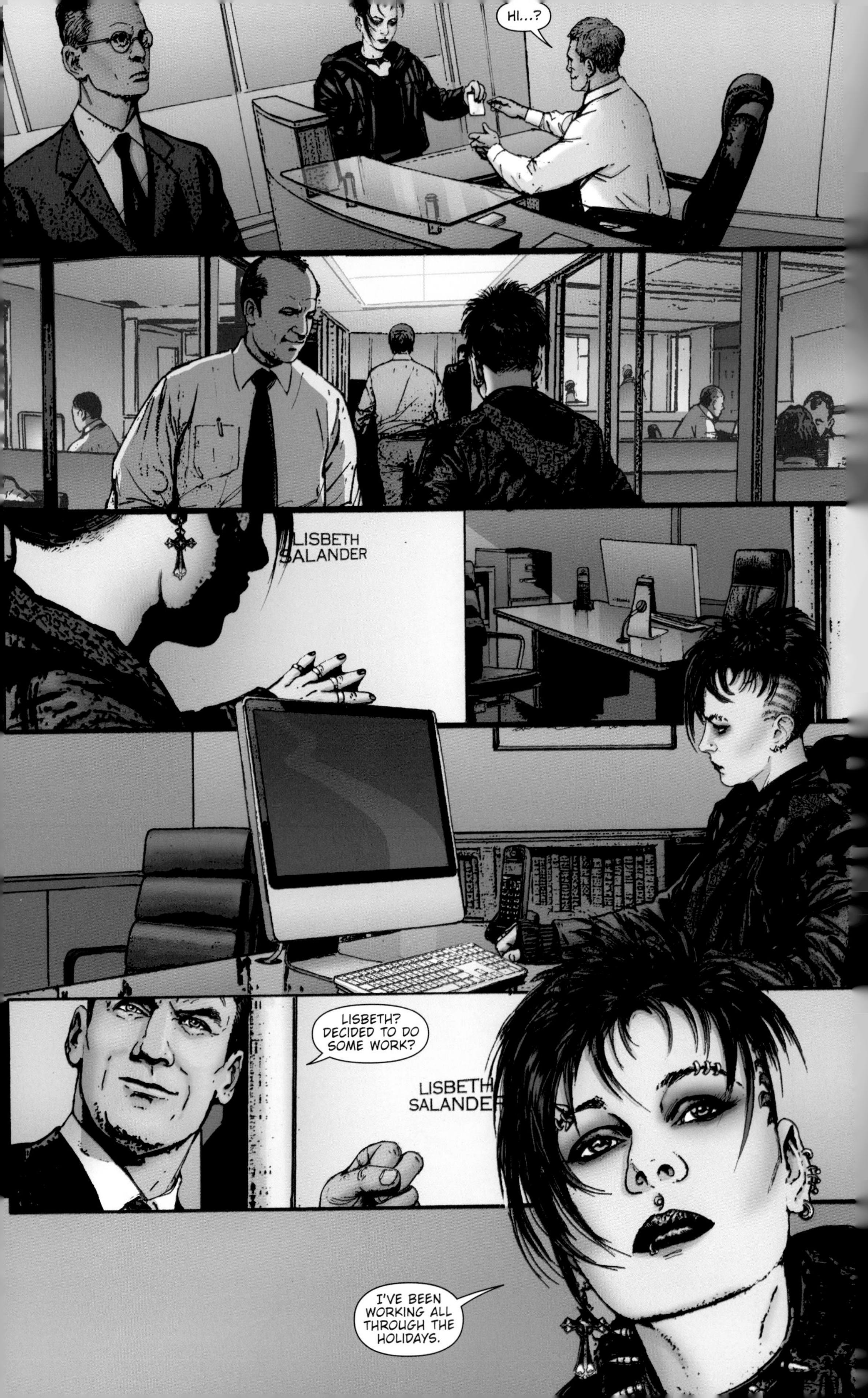
HI...?
LISBETH SALANDER
LISBETH?
DECIDED TO DO
SOME WORK?
LISBETH SALANDER
I'VE BEEN WORKING ALL THROUGH THE HOLIDAYS.

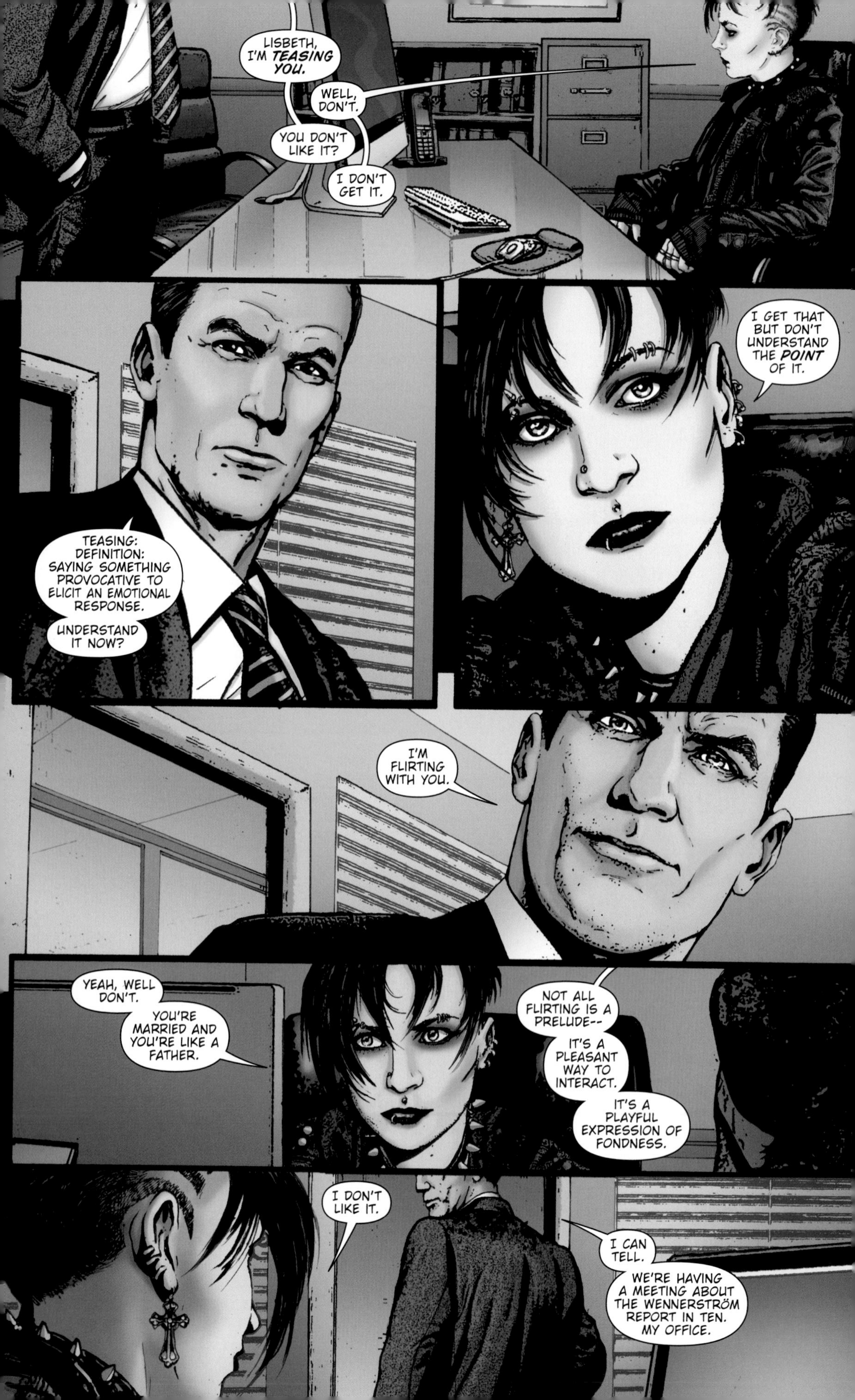
LISBETH, I'M *TEASING YOU.*
WELL, DON'T.
YOU DON'T LIKE IT?
I DON'T GET IT.
TEASING: DEFINITION: SAYING SOMETHING PROVOCATIVE TO ELICIT AN EMOTIONAL RESPONSE.
UNDERSTAND IT NOW?
I GET THAT BUT DON'T UNDERSTAND THE *POINT* OF IT.
I'M FLIRTING WITH YOU.
YEAH, WELL DON'T.
YOU'RE MARRIED AND YOU'RE LIKE A FATHER.
NOT ALL FLIRTING IS A PRELUDE--
IT'S A PLEASANT WAY TO INTERACT.
IT'S A PLAYFUL EXPRESSION OF FONDNESS.
I DON'T LIKE IT.
I CAN TELL.
WE'RE HAVING A MEETING ABOUT THE WENNERSTRÖM REPORT IN TEN. MY OFFICE.

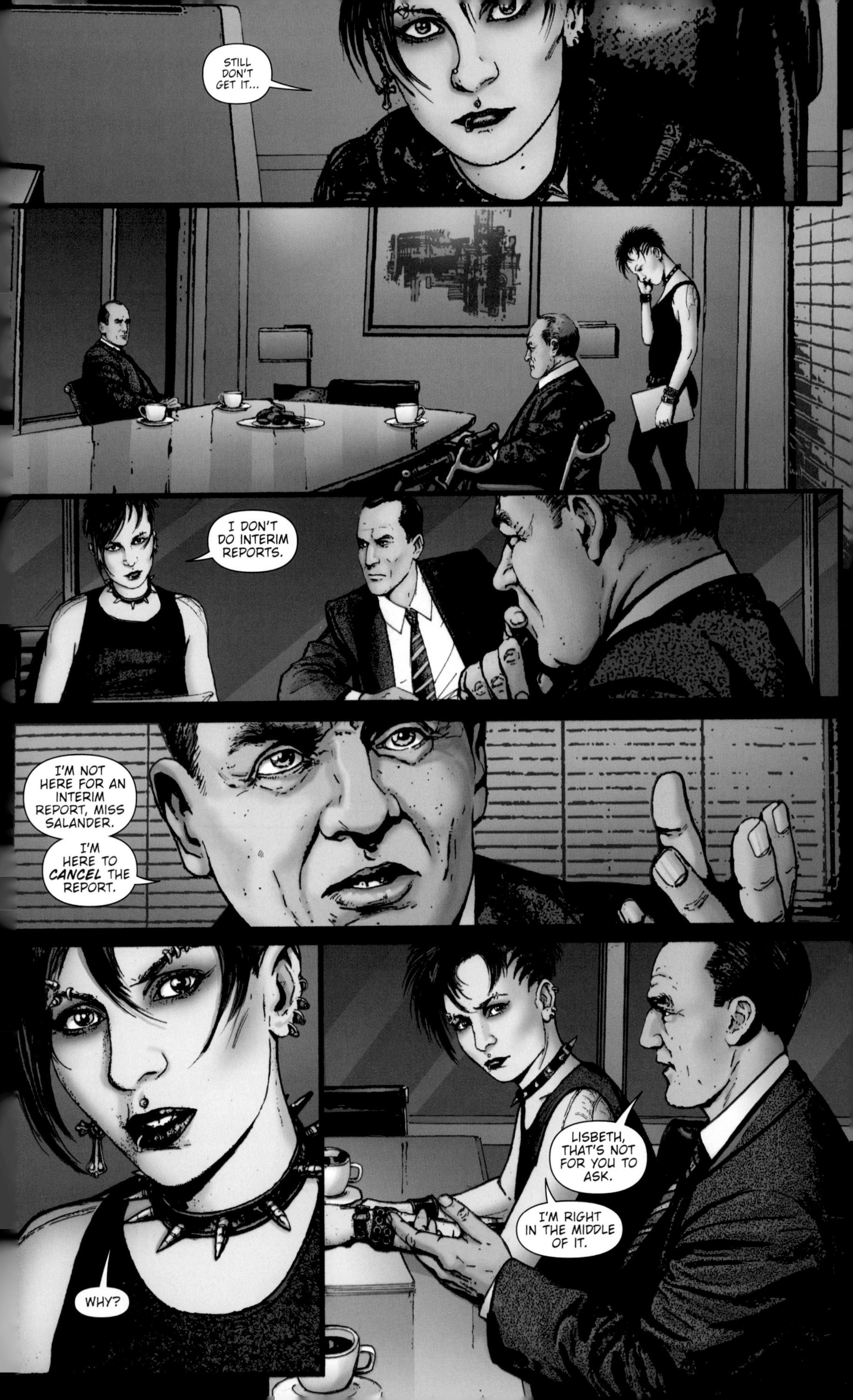
STILL DON'T GET IT...
I DON'T DO INTERIM REPORTS.
I'M NOT HERE FOR AN INTERIM REPORT, MISS SALANDER.
I'M HERE TO **CANCEL** THE REPORT.
WHY?
LISBETH, THAT'S NOT FOR YOU TO ASK.
I'M RIGHT IN THE MIDDLE OF IT.

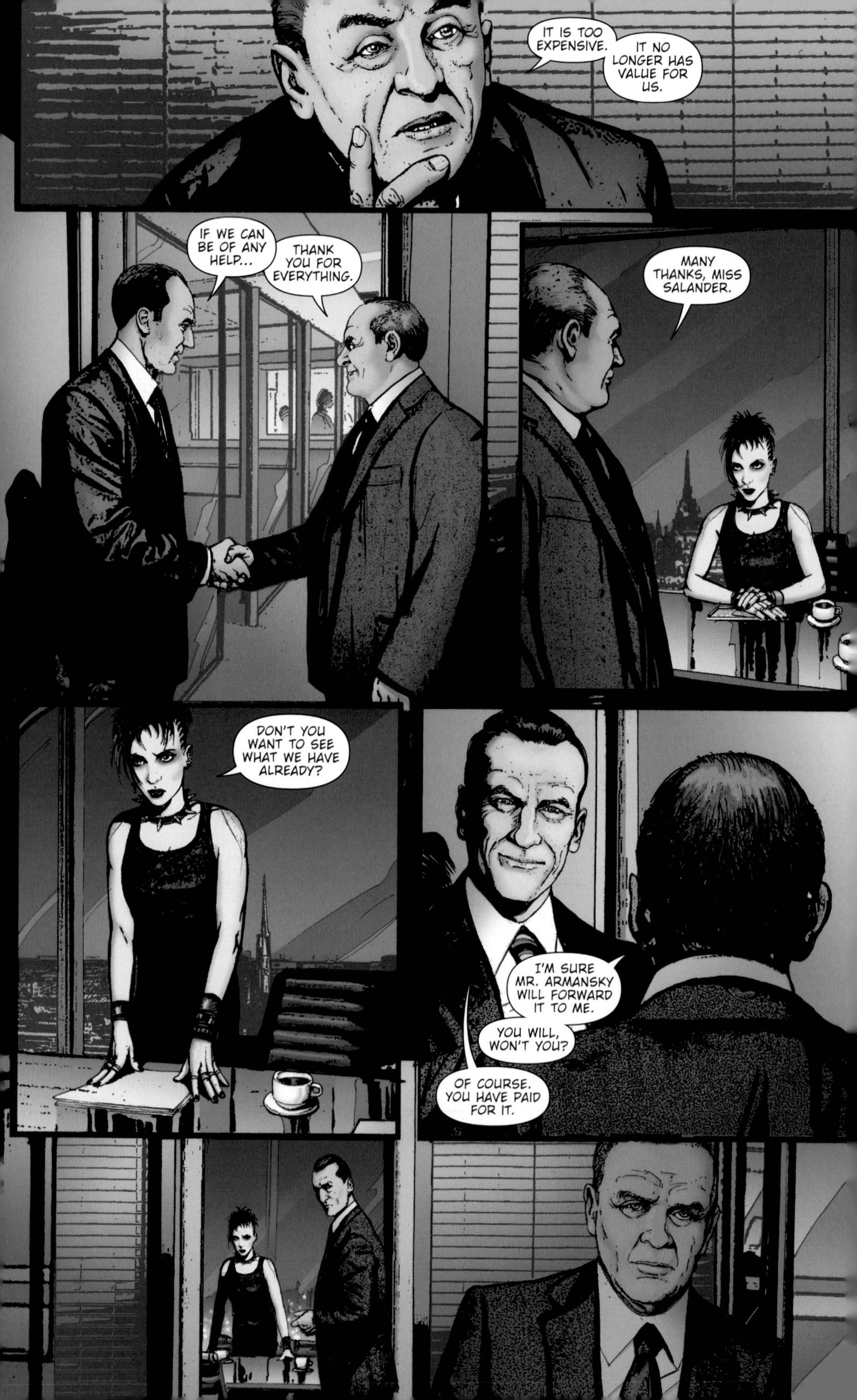
IT IS TOO EXPENSIVE.
IT NO LONGER HAS VALUE FOR US.
IF WE CAN BE OF ANY HELP...
THANK YOU FOR EVERYTHING.
MANY THANKS, MISS SALANDER.
DON'T YOU WANT TO SEE WHAT WE HAVE ALREADY?
I'M SURE MR. ARMANSKY WILL FORWARD IT TO ME.
YOU WILL, WON'T YOU?
OF COURSE. YOU HAVE PAID FOR IT.

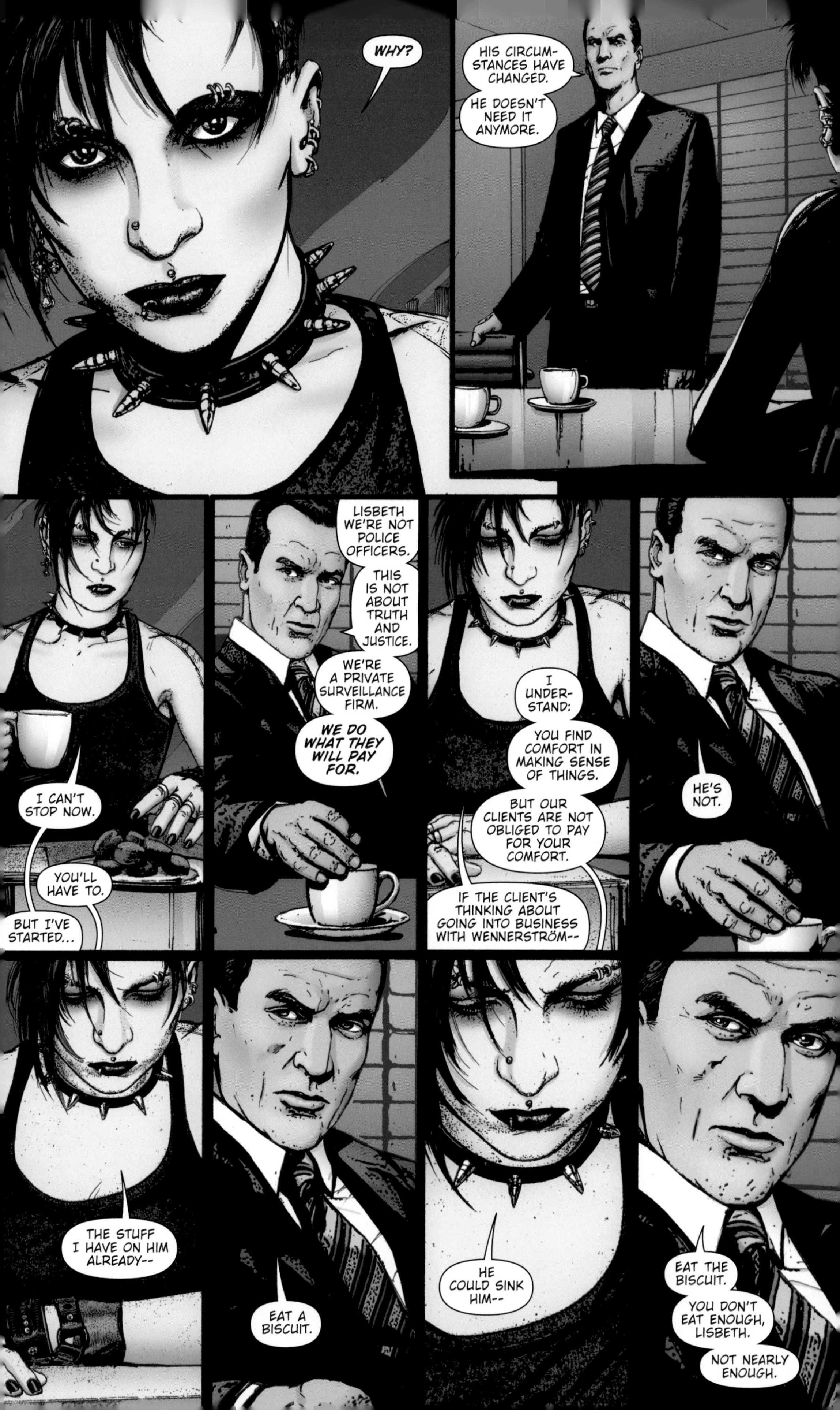
WHY?
HIS CIRCUM-STANCES HAVE CHANGED.
HE DOESN'T NEED IT ANYMORE.
I CAN'T STOP NOW.
YOU'LL HAVE TO.
BUT I'VE STARTED...
LISBETH WE'RE NOT POLICE OFFICERS.
THIS IS NOT ABOUT TRUTH AND JUSTICE.
WE'RE A PRIVATE SURVEILLANCE FIRM.
WE DO WHAT THEY WILL PAY FOR.
I UNDER-STAND:
YOU FIND COMFORT IN MAKING SENSE OF THINGS.
BUT OUR CLIENTS ARE NOT OBLIGED TO PAY FOR YOUR COMFORT.
IF THE CLIENT'S THINKING ABOUT GOING INTO BUSINESS WITH WENNERSTRÖM--
HE'S NOT.
THE STUFF I HAVE ON HIM ALREADY--
EAT A BISCUIT.
HE COULD SINK HIM--
EAT THE BISCUIT.
YOU DON'T EAT ENOUGH, LISBETH.
NOT NEARLY ENOUGH.

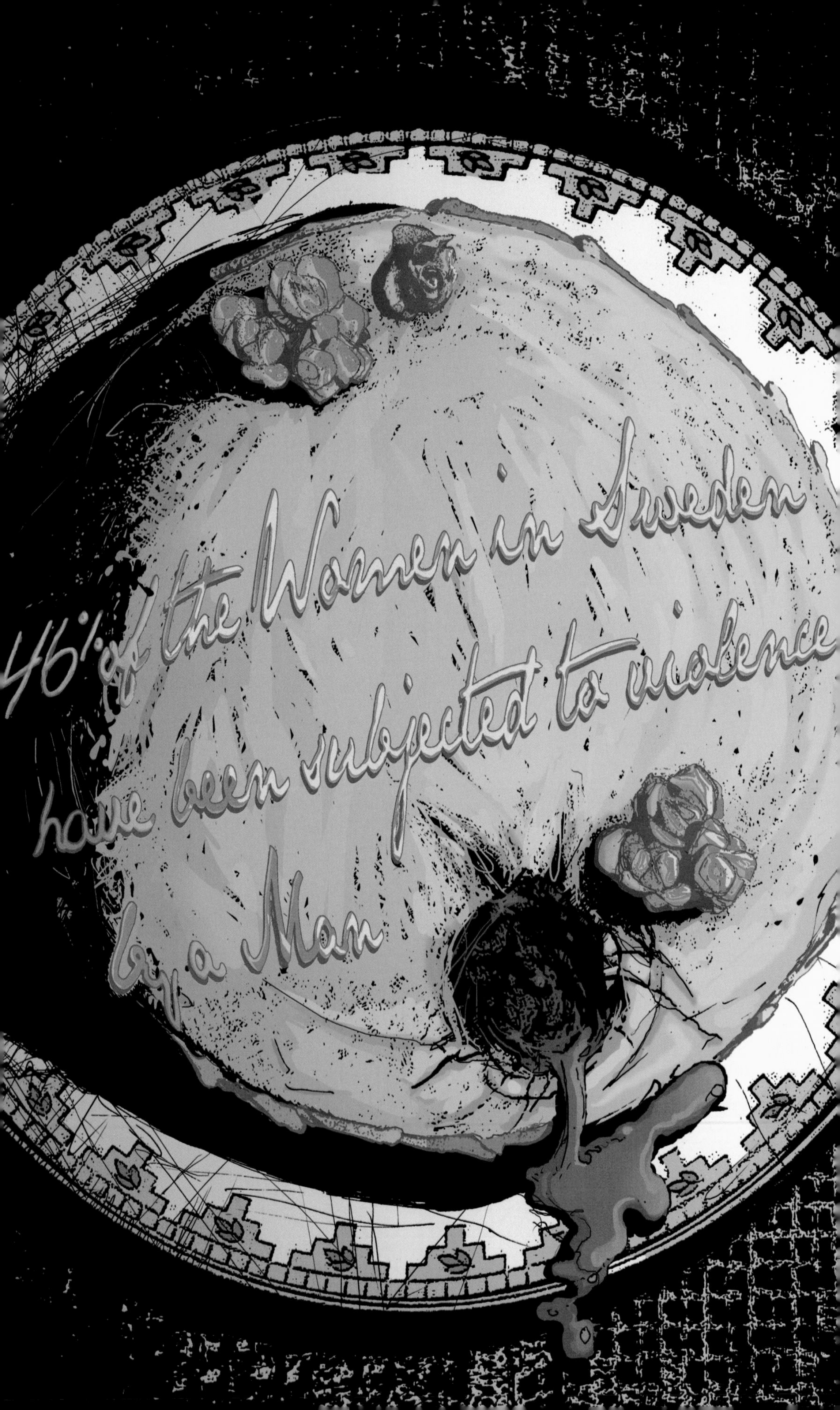
46% of the Women in Sweden
have been subjected to violence
by a Man

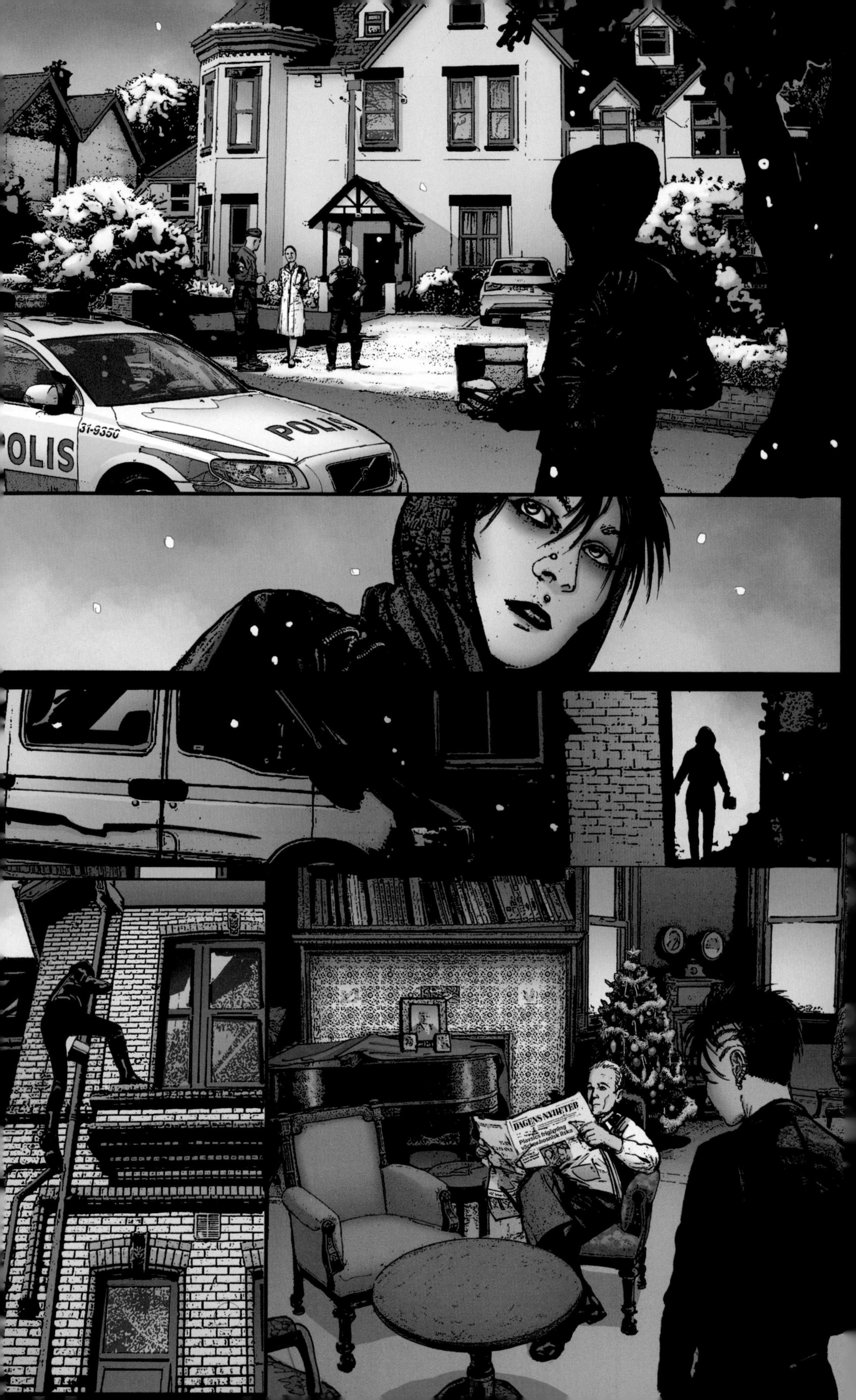
31-9350
POLIS
DAGENS NYHETER
Plavsics frigivning
bosnisk ilska

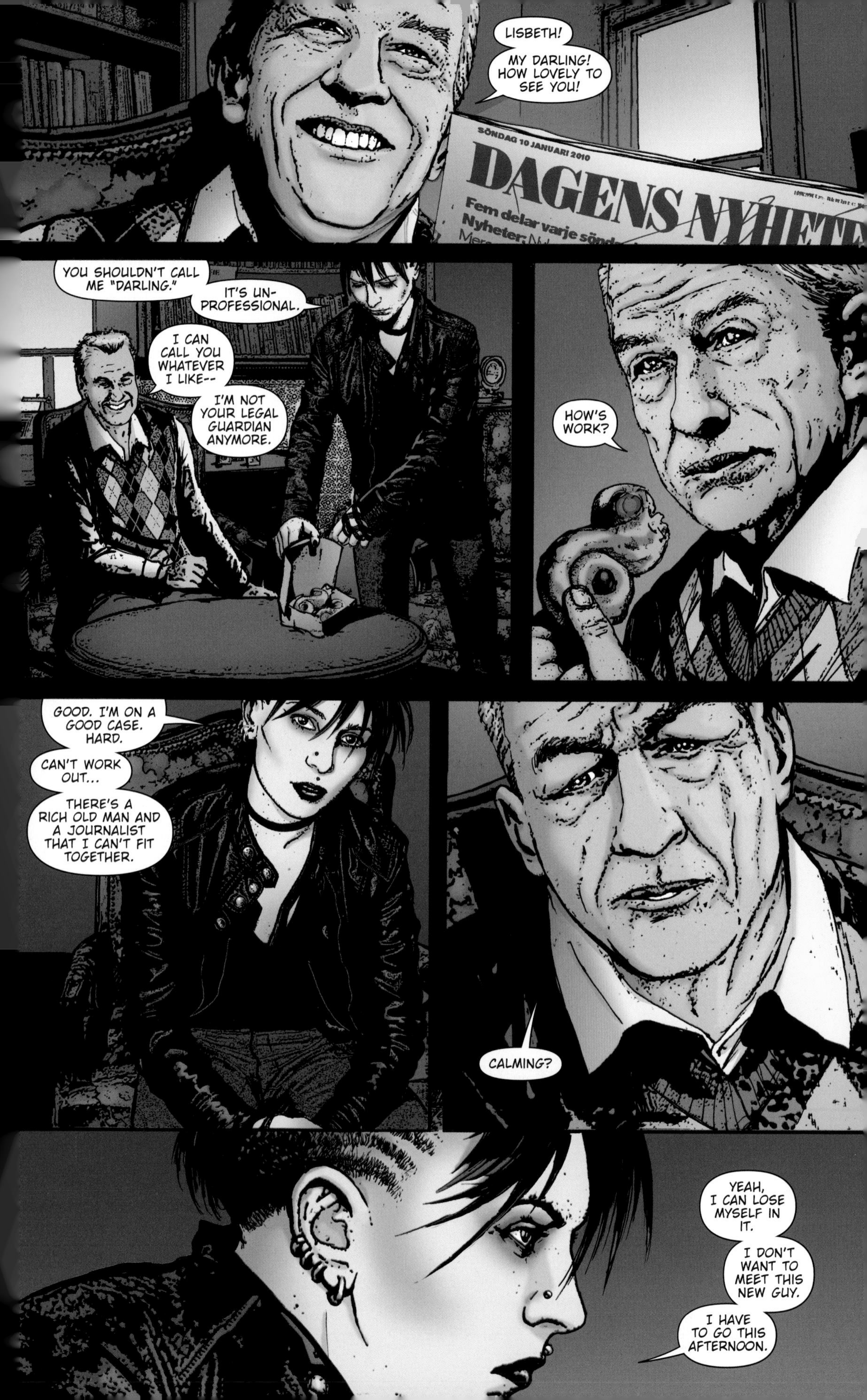
LISBETH!
MY DARLING! HOW LOVELY TO SEE YOU!
SÖNDAG 10 JANUARI 2010
DAGENS NYHETER
Fem delar varje sönd
YOU SHOULDN'T CALL ME "DARLING."
IT'S UN-PROFESSIONAL.
I CAN CALL YOU WHATEVER I LIKE--
I'M NOT YOUR LEGAL GUARDIAN ANYMORE.
HOW'S WORK?
GOOD. I'M ON A GOOD CASE. HARD.
CAN'T WORK OUT...
THERE'S A RICH OLD MAN AND A JOURNALIST THAT I CAN'T FIT TOGETHER.
CALMING?
YEAH, I CAN LOSE MYSELF IN IT.
I DON'T WANT TO MEET THIS NEW GUY.
I HAVE TO GO THIS AFTERNOON.

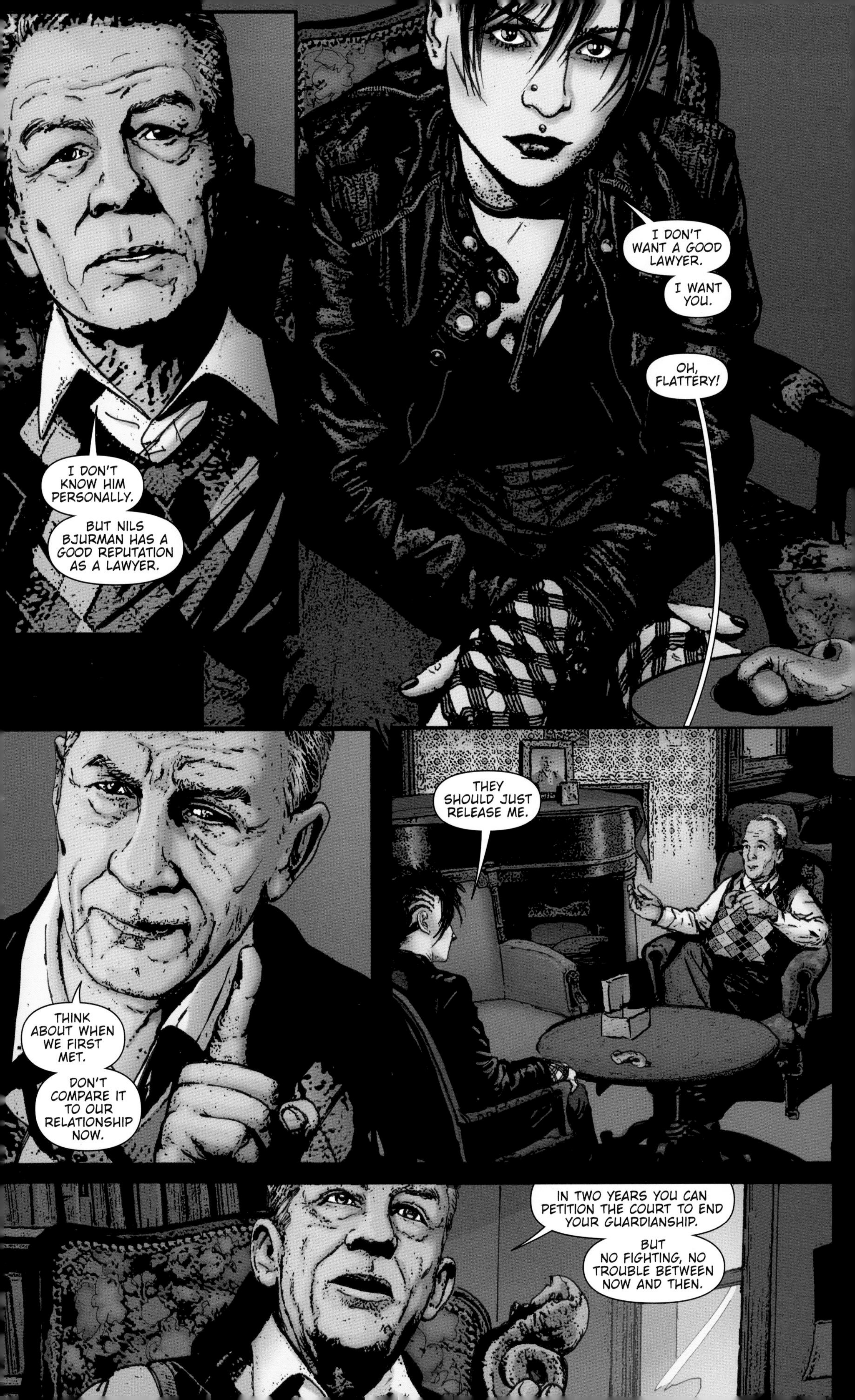
I DON'T KNOW HIM PERSONALLY.
BUT NILS BJURMAN HAS A GOOD REPUTATION AS A LAWYER.
I DON'T WANT A GOOD LAWYER.
I WANT YOU.
OH, FLATTERY!
THINK ABOUT WHEN WE FIRST MET.
DON'T COMPARE IT TO OUR RELATIONSHIP NOW.
THEY SHOULD JUST RELEASE ME.
IN TWO YEARS YOU CAN PETITION THE COURT TO END YOUR GUARDIANSHIP.
BUT NO FIGHTING, NO TROUBLE BETWEEN NOW AND THEN.

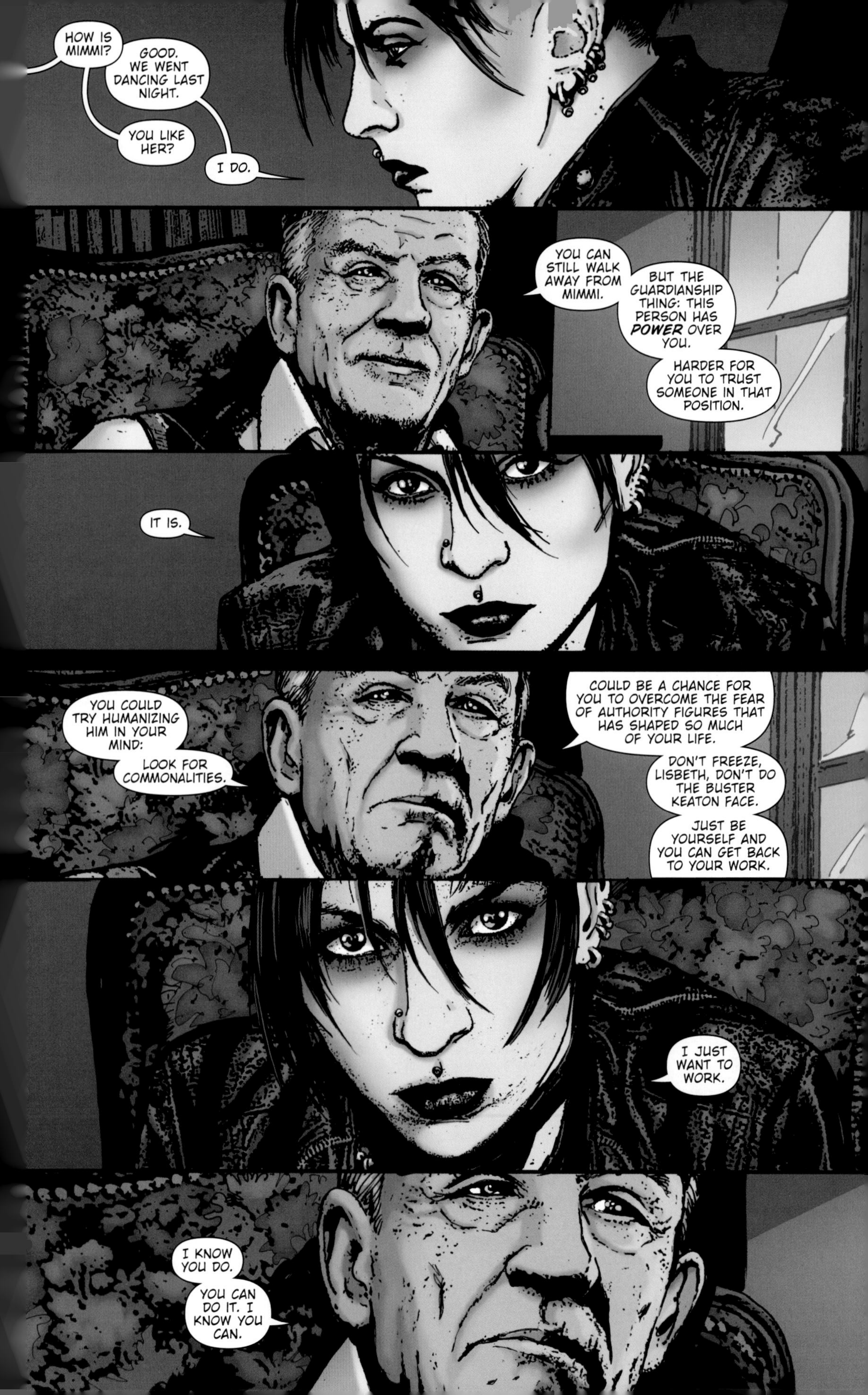
HOW IS MIMMI?
GOOD. WE WENT DANCING LAST NIGHT.
YOU LIKE HER?
I DO.
YOU CAN STILL WALK AWAY FROM MIMMI.
BUT THE GUARDIANSHIP THING: THIS PERSON HAS **POWER** OVER YOU.
HARDER FOR YOU TO TRUST SOMEONE IN THAT POSITION.
IT IS.
YOU COULD TRY HUMANIZING HIM IN YOUR MIND:
LOOK FOR COMMONALITIES.
COULD BE A CHANCE FOR YOU TO OVERCOME THE FEAR OF AUTHORITY FIGURES THAT HAS SHAPED SO MUCH OF YOUR LIFE.
DON'T FREEZE, LISBETH, DON'T DO THE BUSTER KEATON FACE.
JUST BE YOURSELF AND YOU CAN GET BACK TO YOUR WORK.
I JUST WANT TO WORK.
I KNOW YOU DO.
YOU CAN DO IT. I KNOW YOU CAN.

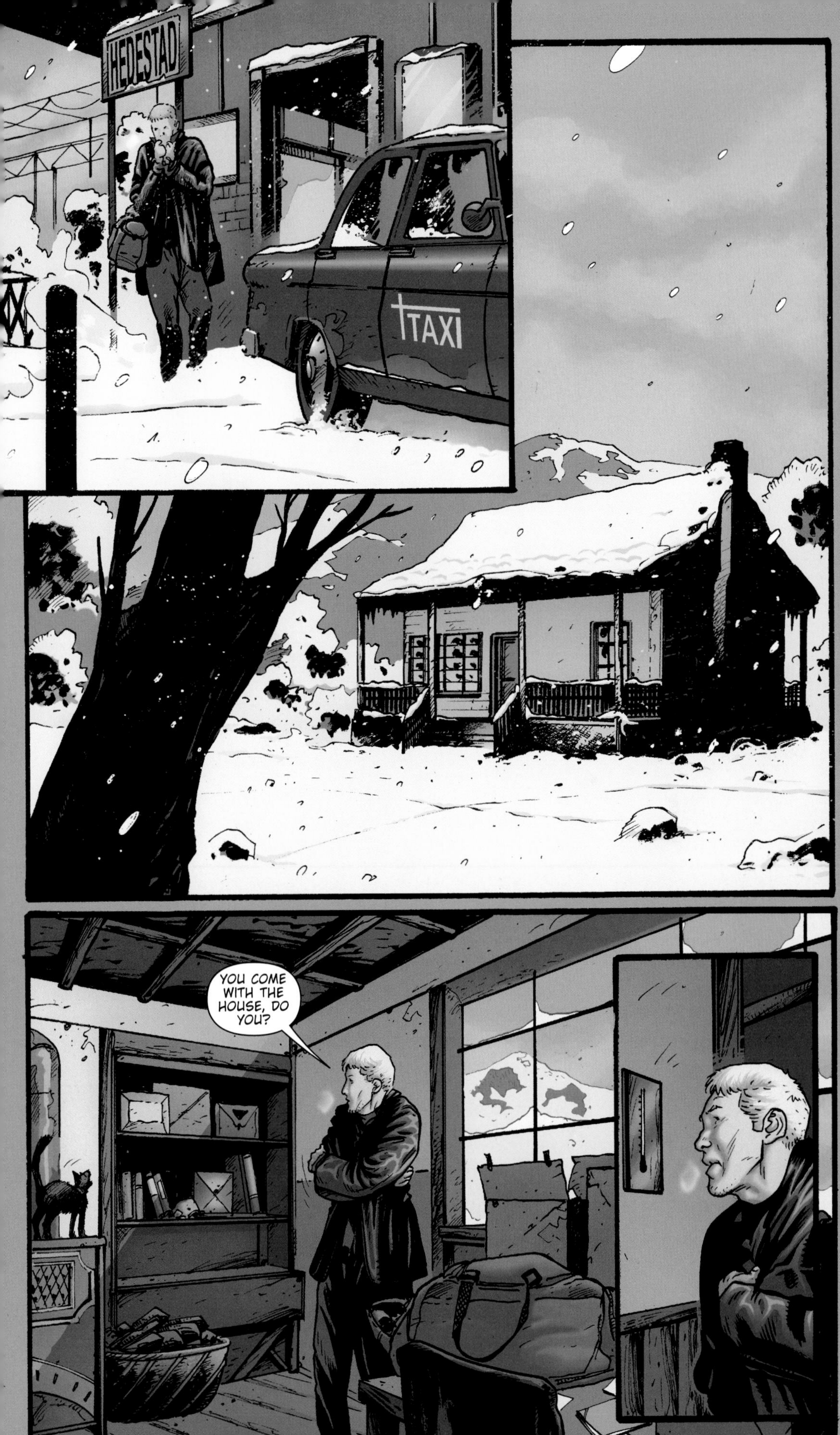
HEDESTAD
TAXI
YOU COME WITH THE HOUSE, DO YOU?

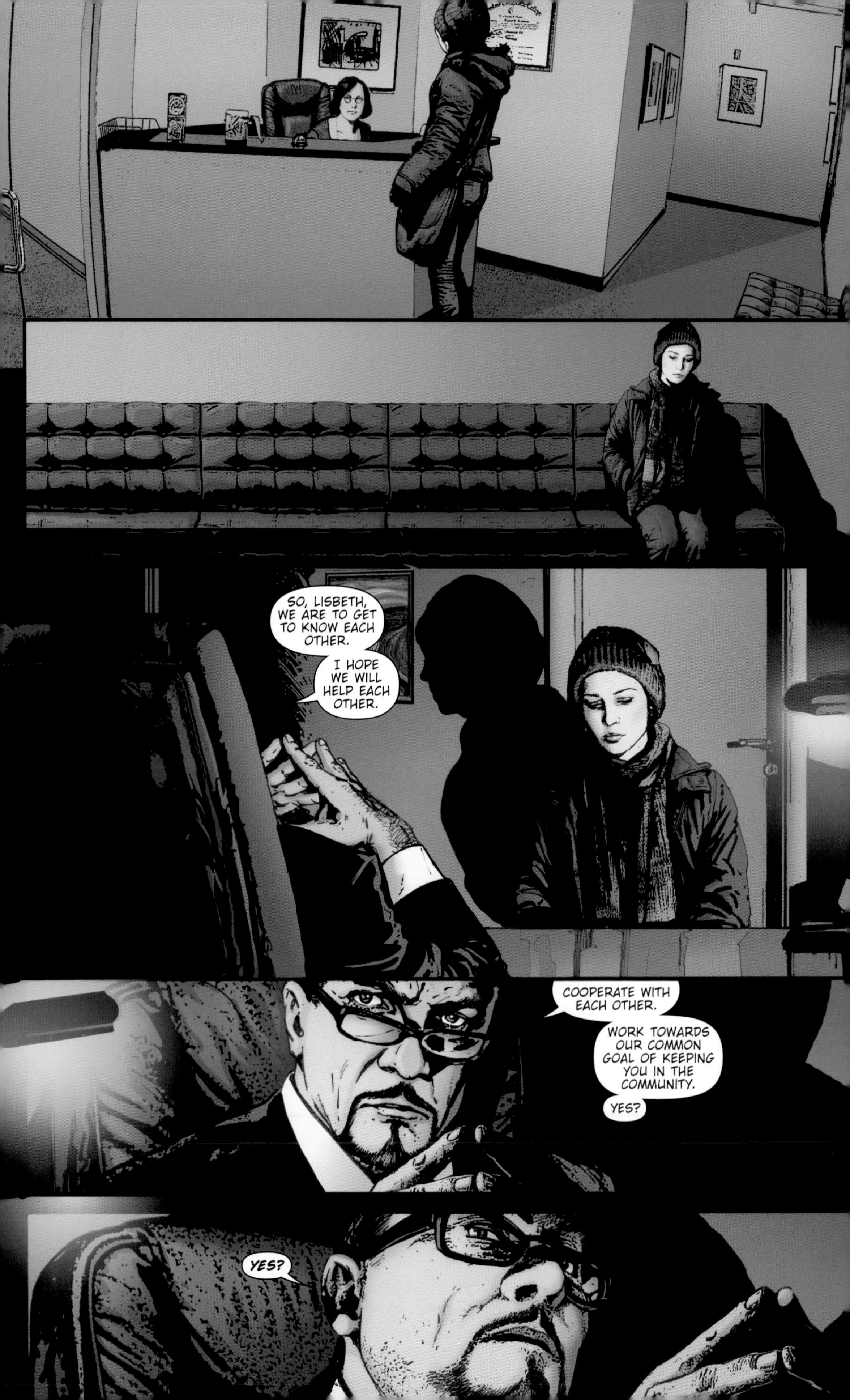
SO, LISBETH, WE ARE TO GET TO KNOW EACH OTHER.
I HOPE WE WILL HELP EACH OTHER.
COOPERATE WITH EACH OTHER.
WORK TOWARDS OUR COMMON GOAL OF KEEPING YOU IN THE COMMUNITY.
YES?
YES?

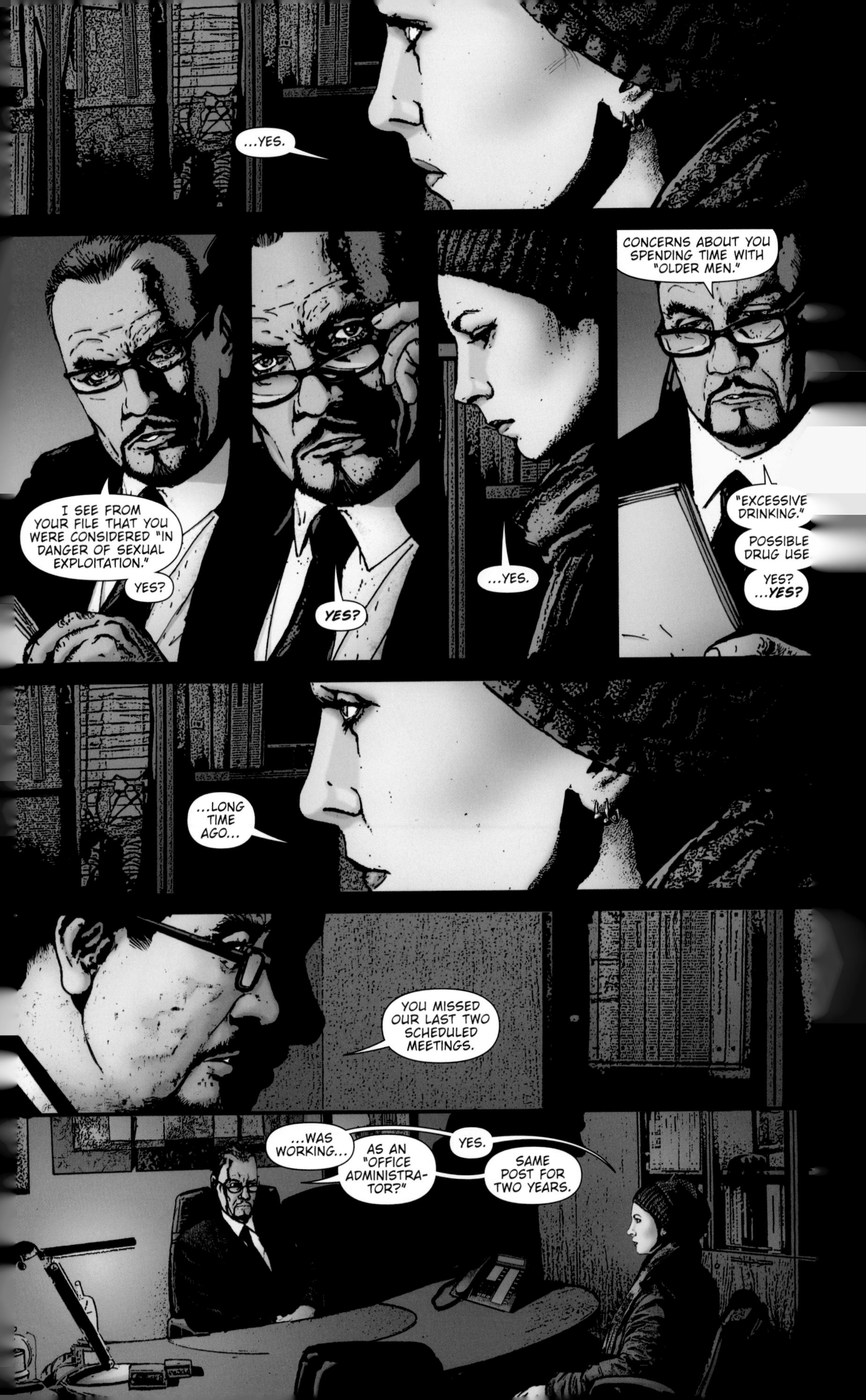
...YES.
I SEE FROM YOUR FILE THAT YOU WERE CONSIDERED "IN DANGER OF SEXUAL EXPLOITATION."
YES?
YES?
...YES.
CONCERNS ABOUT YOU SPENDING TIME WITH "OLDER MEN."
"EXCESSIVE DRINKING."
POSSIBLE DRUG USE
YES? ...YES?
...LONG TIME AGO...
YOU MISSED OUR LAST TWO SCHEDULED MEETINGS.
...WAS WORKING...
YES.
AS AN "OFFICE ADMINISTRA-TOR?"
SAME POST FOR TWO YEARS.

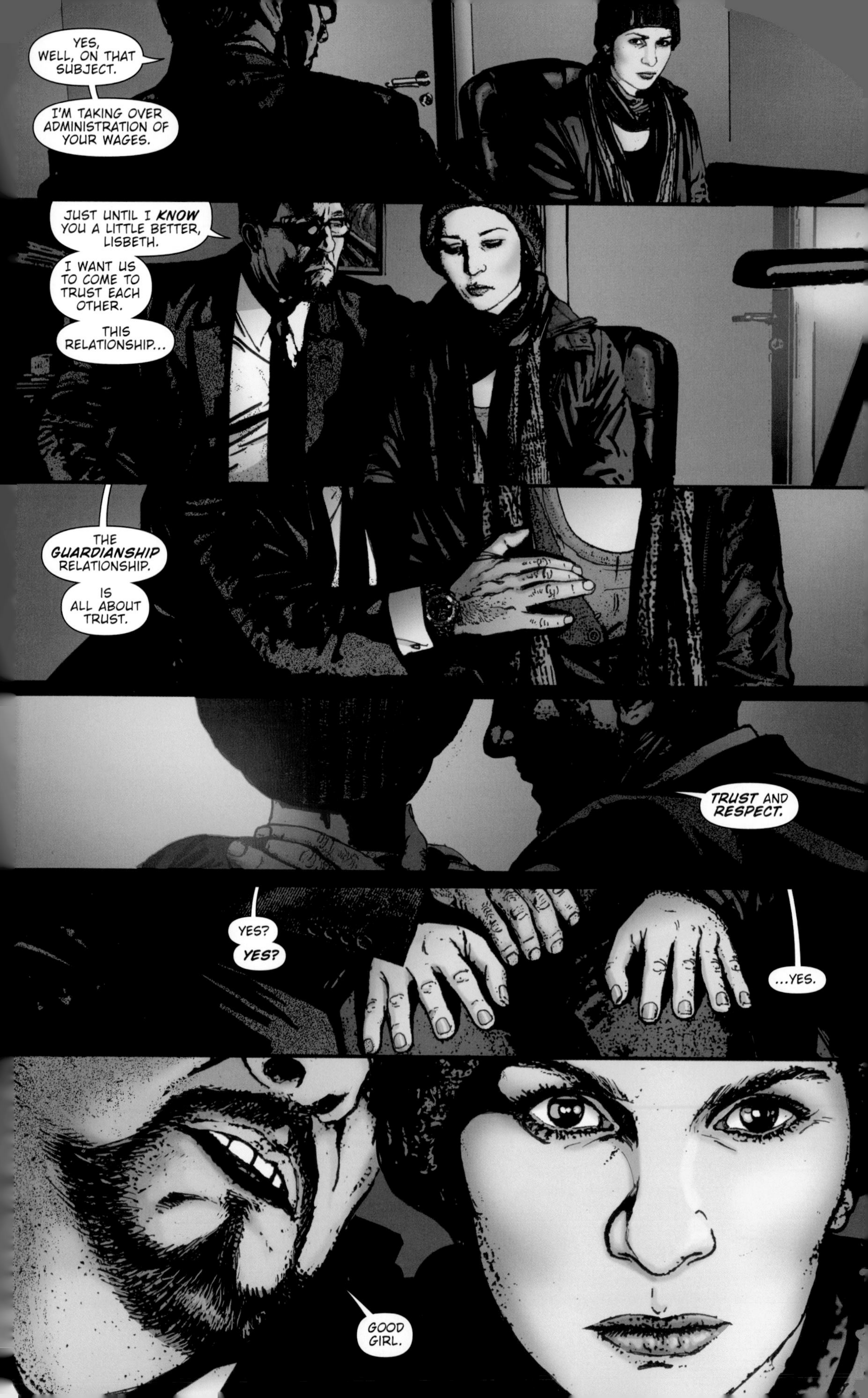
YES, WELL, ON THAT SUBJECT.
I'M TAKING OVER ADMINISTRATION OF YOUR WAGES.
JUST UNTIL I *KNOW* YOU A LITTLE BETTER, LISBETH.
I WANT US TO COME TO TRUST EACH OTHER.
THIS RELATIONSHIP...
THE *GUARDIANSHIP* RELATIONSHIP.
IS ALL ABOUT TRUST.
TRUST AND *RESPECT.*
YES?
YES?
...YES.
GOOD GIRL.

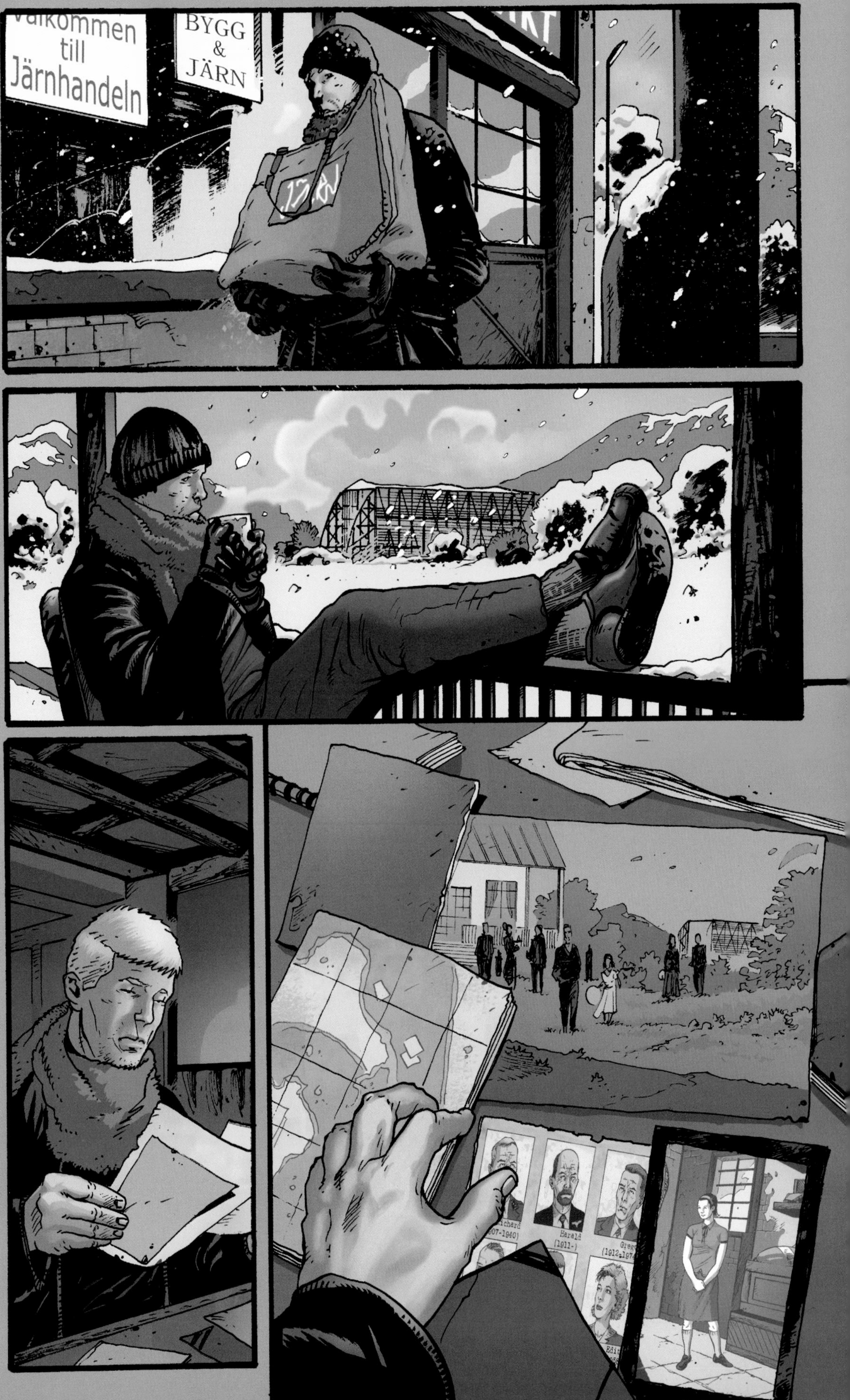
Välkommen
till
Järnhandeln
BYGG
&
JÄRN
Harald
(1911-)

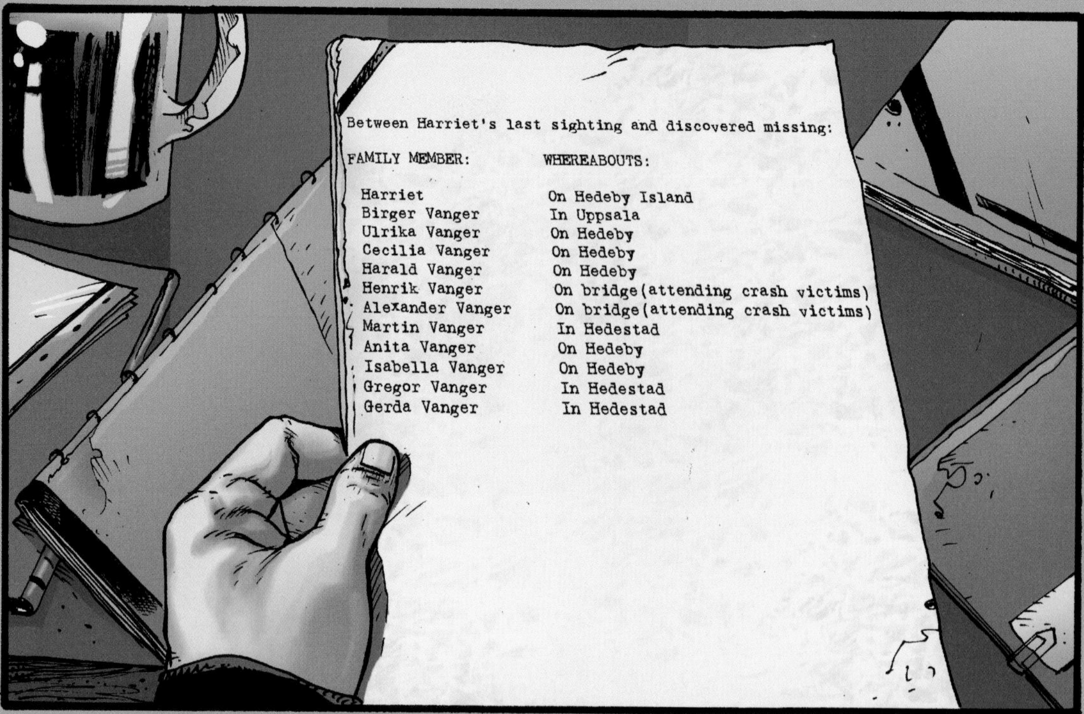
Between Harriet's last sighting and discovered missing:
FAMILY MEMBER: WHEREABOUTS:
Harriet On Hedeby Island
Birger Vanger In Uppsala
Ulrika Vanger On Hedeby
Cecilia Vanger On Hedeby
Harald Vanger On Hedeby
Henrik Vanger On bridge(attending crash victims)
Alexander Vanger On bridge(attending crash victims)
Martin Vanger In Hedestad
Anita Vanger On Hedeby
Isabella Vanger On Hedeby
Gregor Vanger In Hedestad
Gerda Vanger In Hedestad

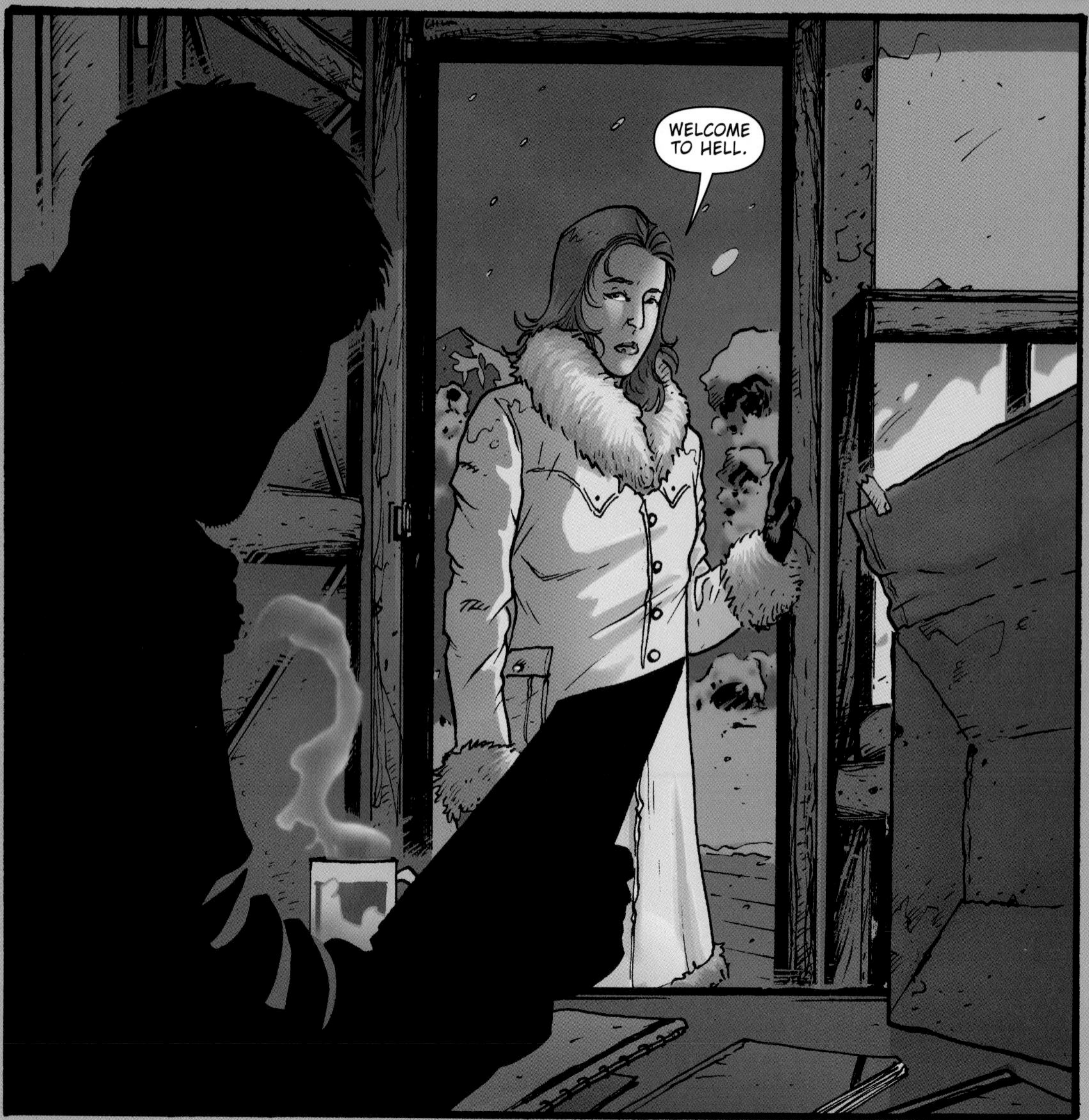
WELCOME TO HELL.

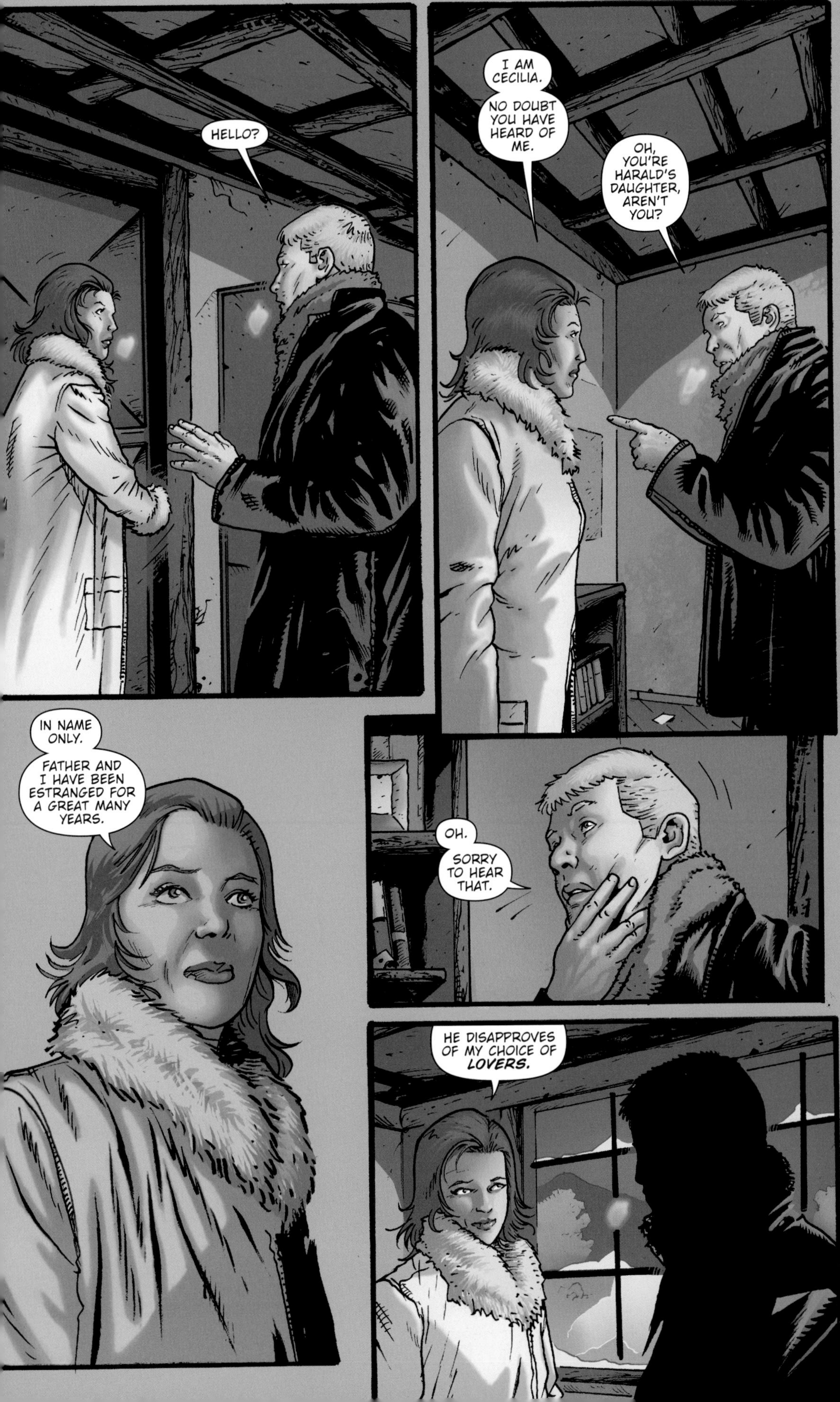
HELLO?
I AM CECILIA.
NO DOUBT YOU HAVE HEARD OF ME.
OH, YOU'RE HARALD'S DAUGHTER, AREN'T YOU?
IN NAME ONLY.
FATHER AND I HAVE BEEN ESTRANGED FOR A GREAT MANY YEARS.
OH.
SORRY TO HEAR THAT.
HE DISAPPROVES OF MY CHOICE OF ***LOVERS.***

PERHAPS YOU FIND ME SHOCKING?

UM, NO, NOT REALLY.

I DON'T CARE IF YOU DO. I JUST SAY WHAT I THINK.

OH, WELL.. GOOD FOR YOU...

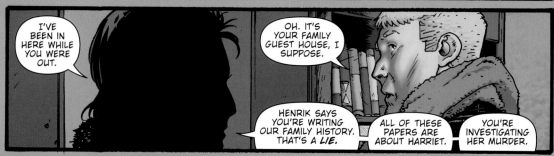

I'VE BEEN IN HERE WHILE YOU WERE OUT.

OH. IT'S YOUR FAMILY GUEST HOUSE, I SUPPOSE.

HENRIK SAYS YOU'RE WRITING OUR FAMILY HISTORY. THAT'S A *LIE.*

ALL OF THESE PAPERS ARE ABOUT HARRIET.

YOU'RE INVESTIGATING HER MURDER.

I'M *GLAD.* HENRIK WAS NEVER THE SAME, AFTERWARDS.

HE DESERVES TO FIND OUT THE TRUTH.

I HAVE INFORMATION FOR YOU.

COME TO MY HOUSE THIS EVENING...

...IF YOU WANT A *HOT* MEAL.

OKAY.

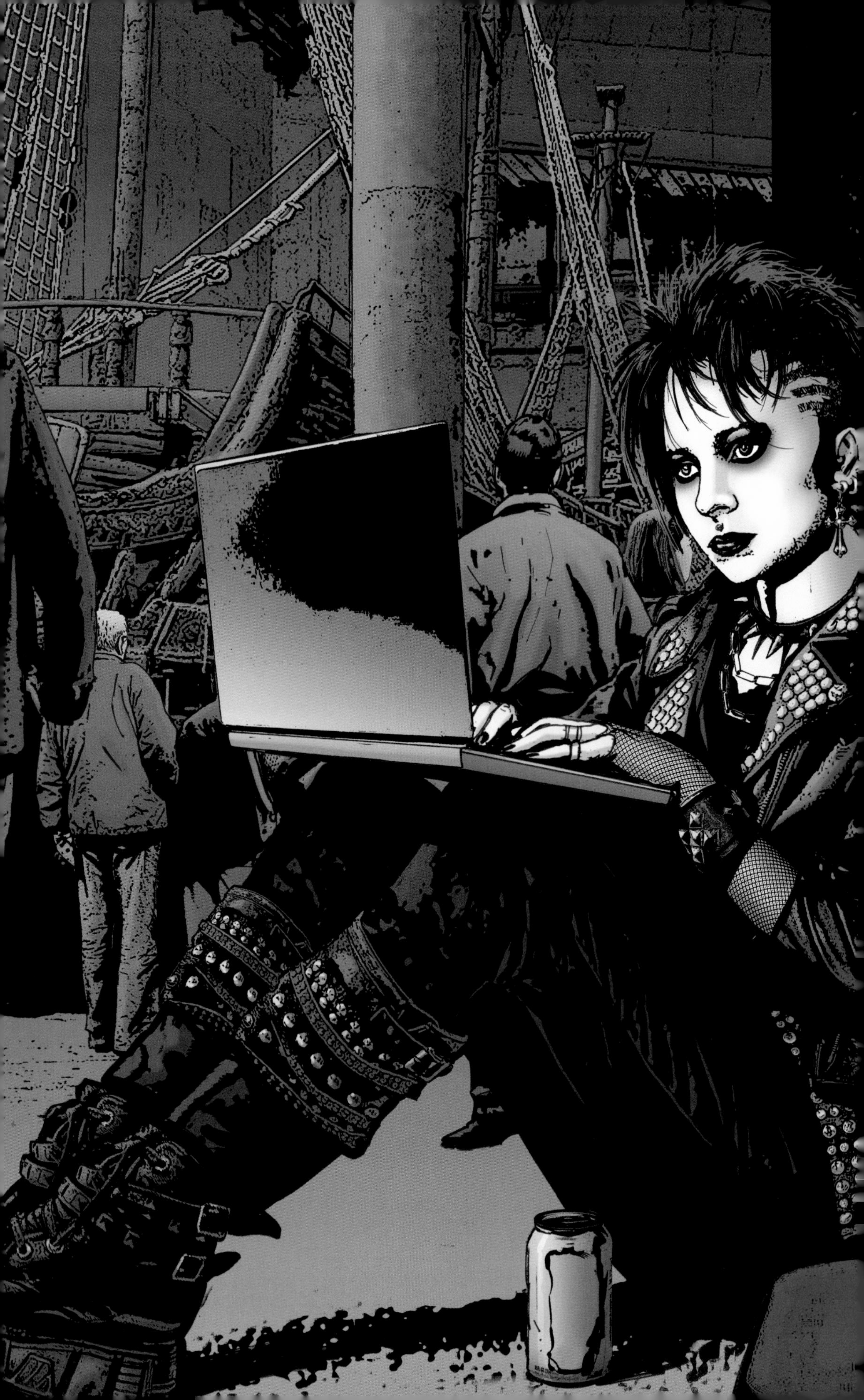

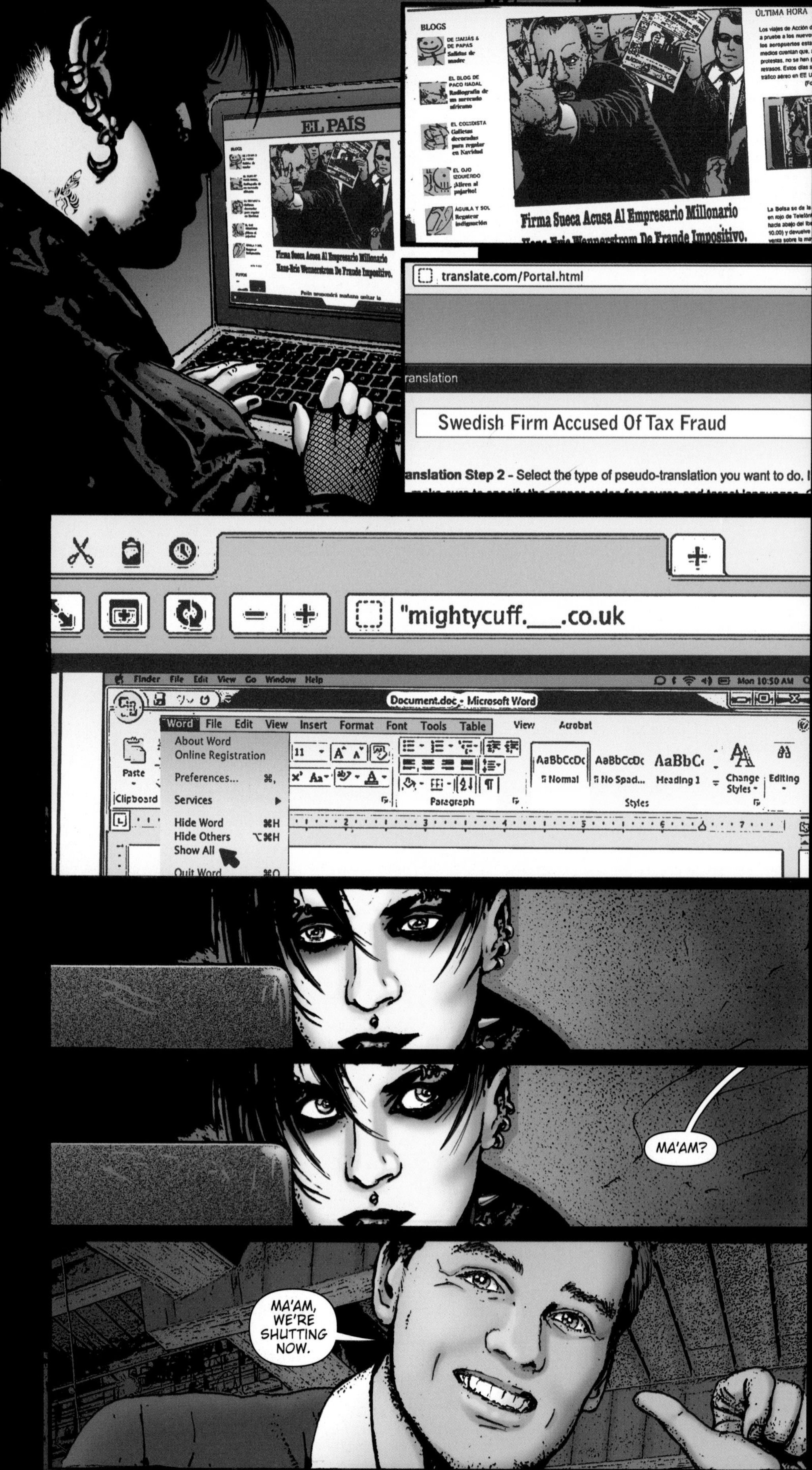

EL PAÍS
BLOGS
ÚLTIMA HORA
Firma Sueca Acusa Al Empresario Millonario
translate.com/Portal.html
Swedish Firm Accused Of Tax Fraud
"mightycuff.___.co.uk
Finder File Edit View Go Window Help
Mon 10:50 AM
Document.doc - Microsoft Word
Word File Edit View Insert Format Font Tools Table
About Word
Online Registration
Preferences...
Services
Hide Word
Hide Others
Show All
Paste
Clipboard
Paragraph
Styles
Normal
No Spaci...
Heading 1
Change Styles
Editing
MA'AM?
MA'AM, WE'RE SHUTTING NOW.

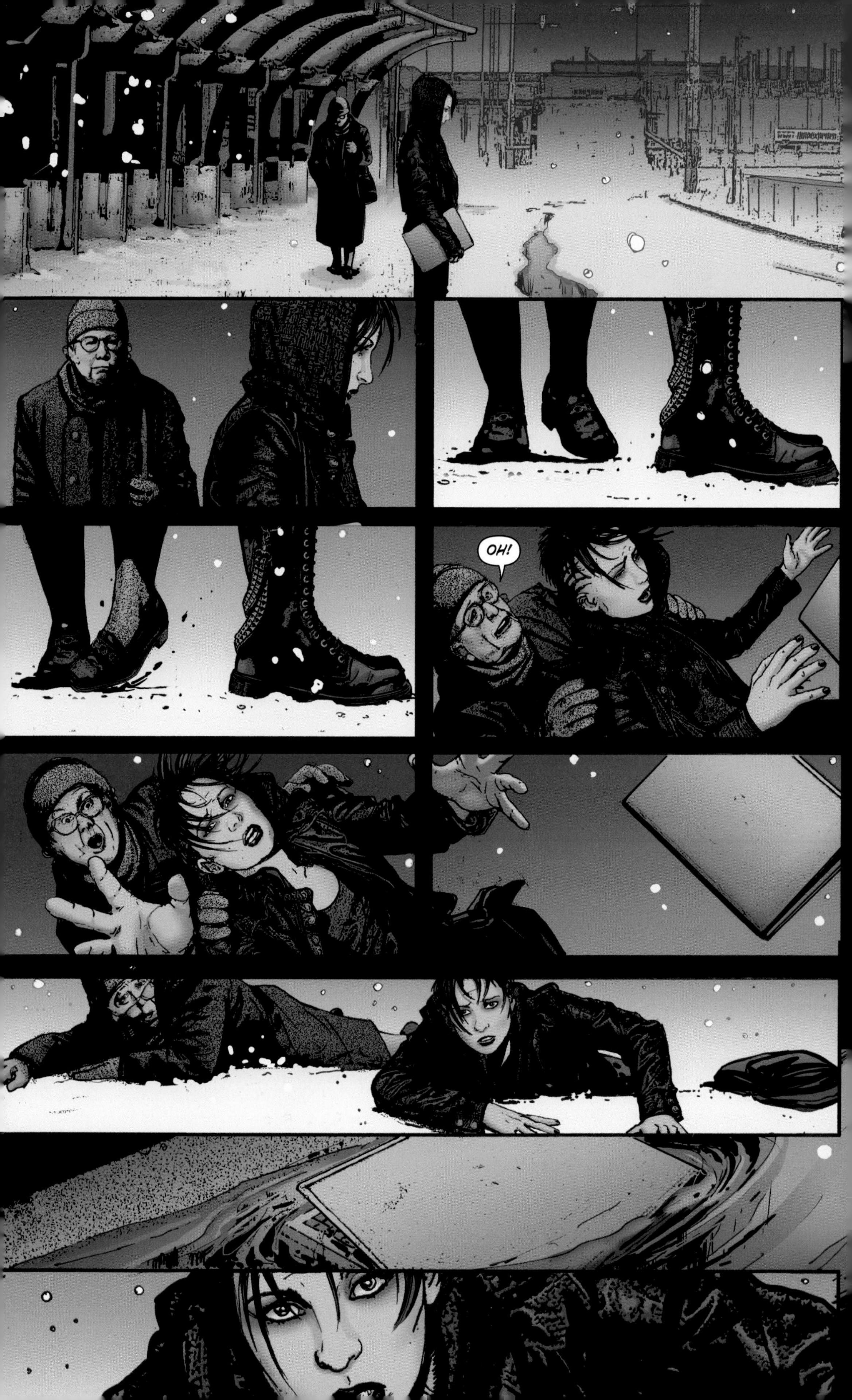
OH!

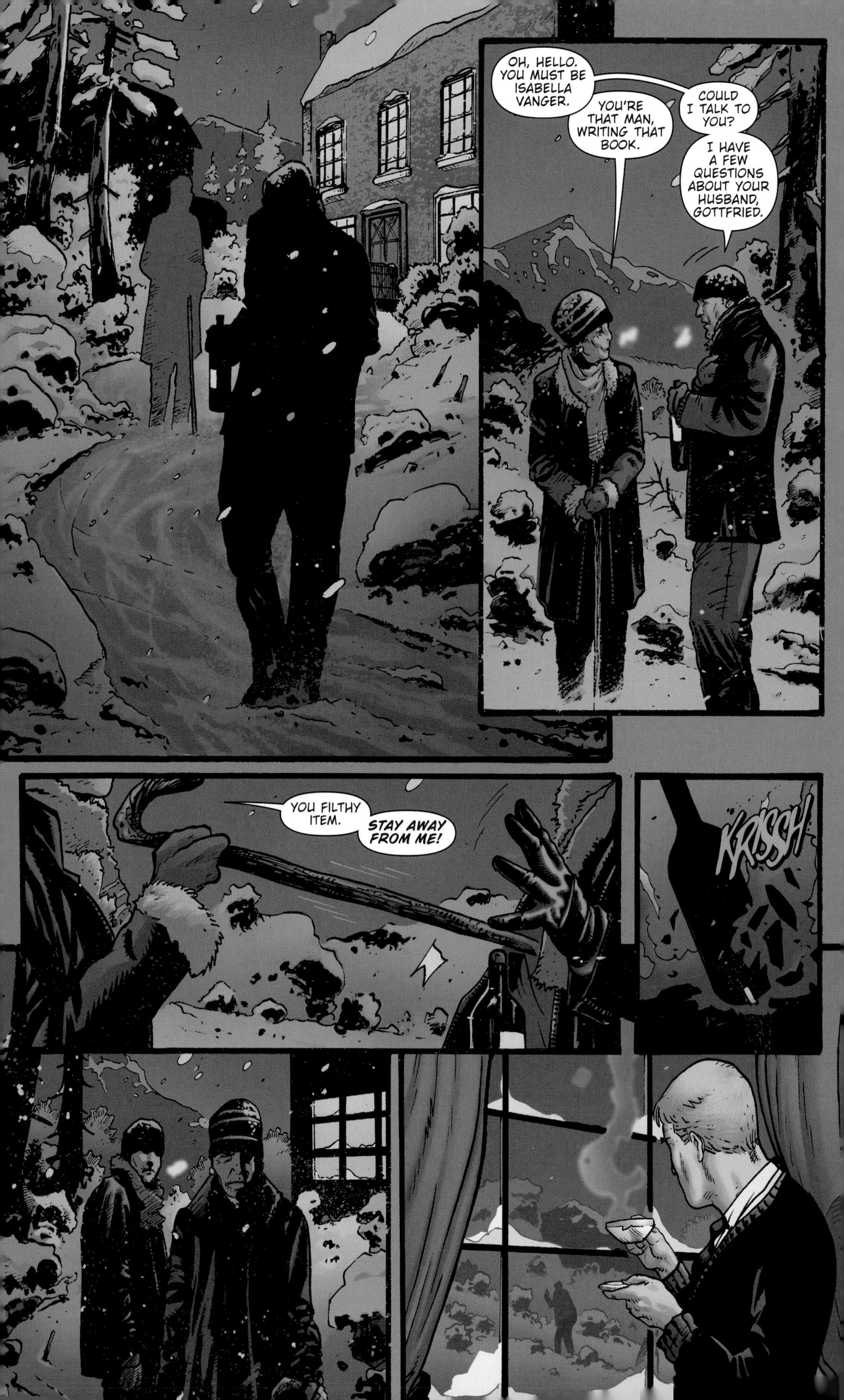
OH, HELLO. YOU MUST BE ISABELLA VANGER.
YOU'RE THAT MAN, WRITING THAT BOOK.
COULD I TALK TO YOU?
I HAVE A FEW QUESTIONS ABOUT YOUR HUSBAND, GOTTFRIED.
YOU FILTHY ITEM.
STAY AWAY FROM ME!
KRISSH

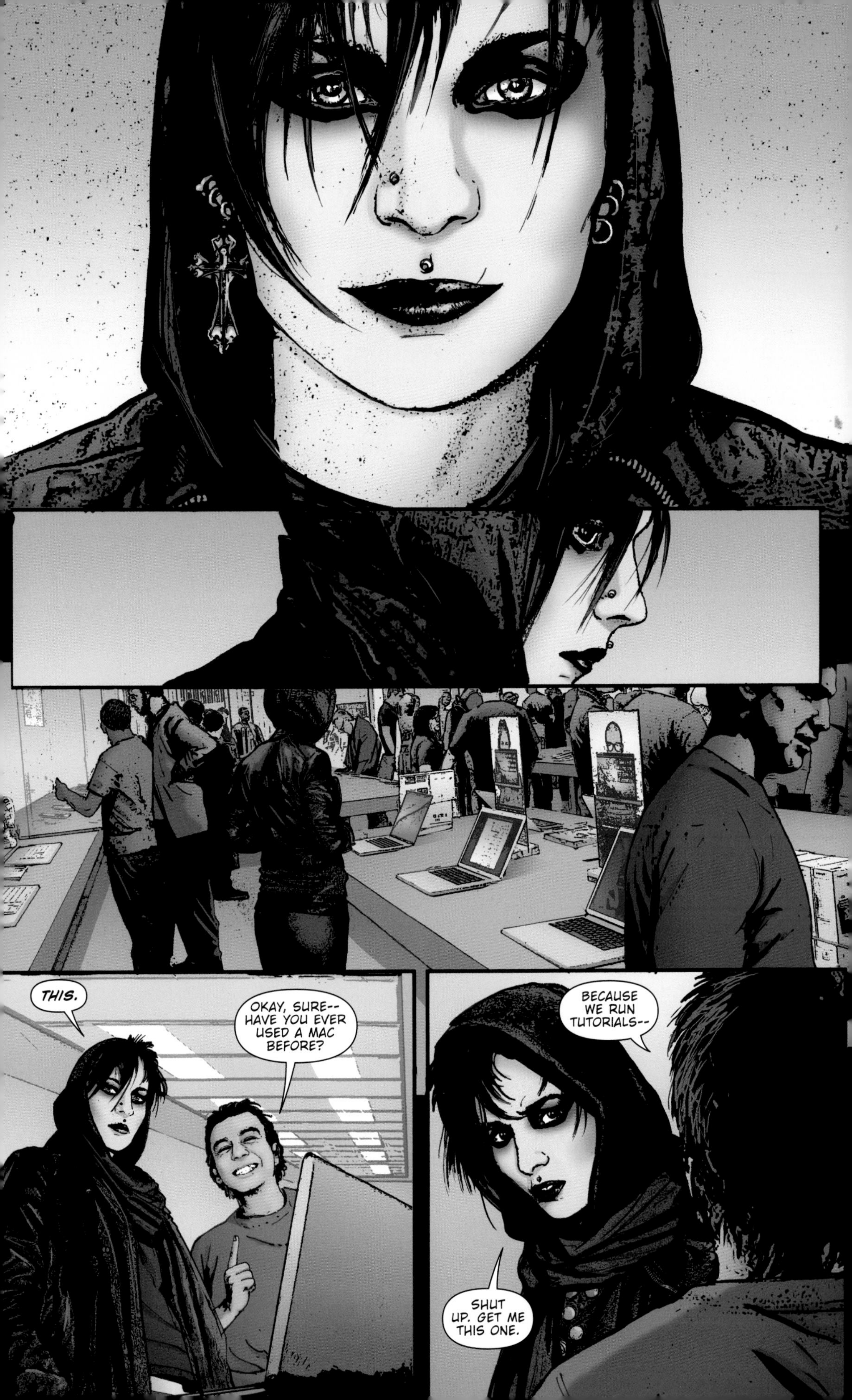
THIS.
OKAY, SURE-- HAVE YOU EVER USED A MAC BEFORE?
BECAUSE WE RUN TUTORIALS--
SHUT UP. GET ME THIS ONE.

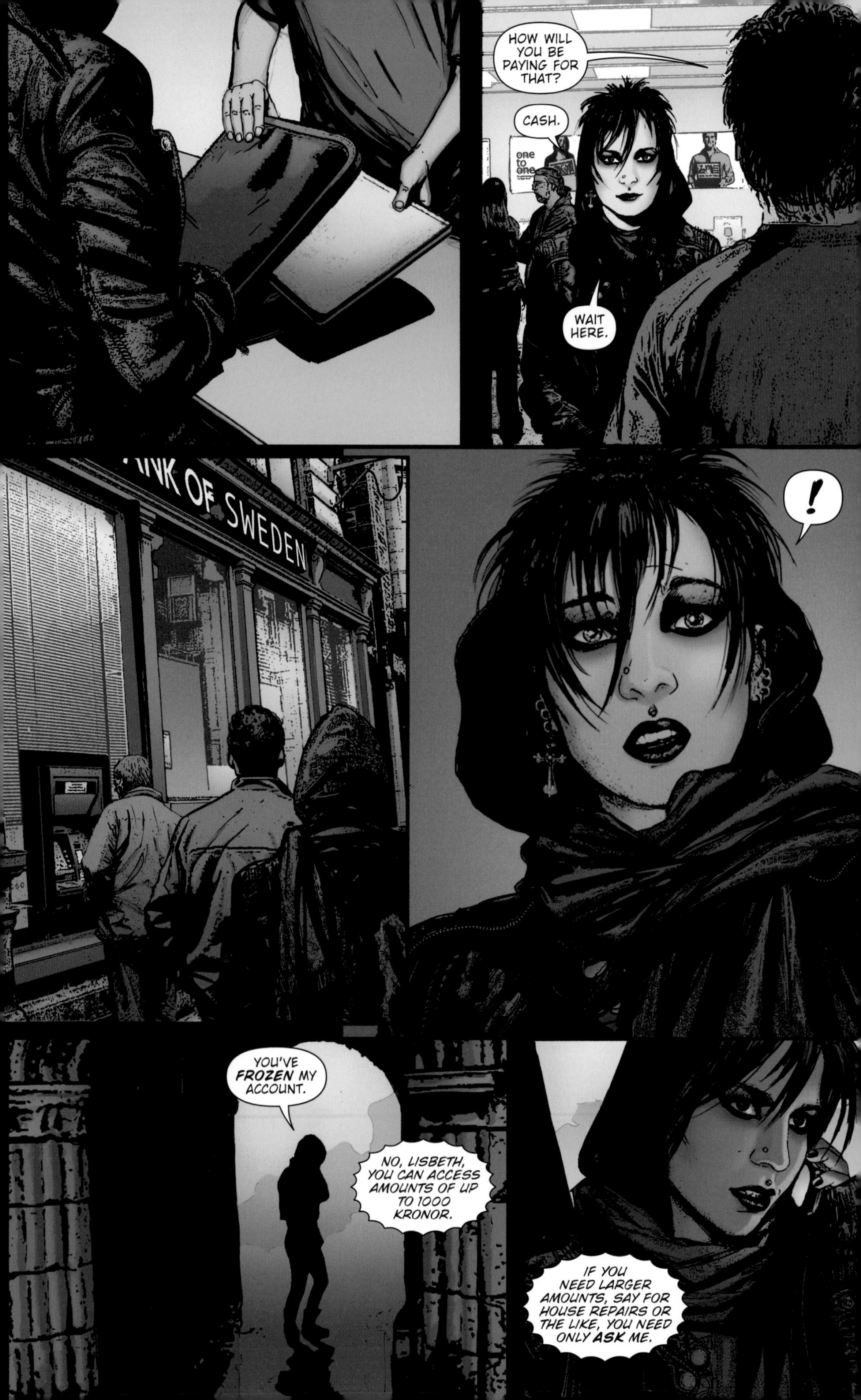
HOW WILL YOU BE PAYING FOR THAT?
CASH.
one to one
WAIT HERE.
ANK OF SWEDEN
!
YOU'VE FROZEN MY ACCOUNT.
NO, LISBETH, YOU CAN ACCESS AMOUNTS OF UP TO 1000 KRONOR.
IF YOU NEED LARGER AMOUNTS, SAY FOR HOUSE REPAIRS OR THE LIKE, YOU NEED ONLY ASK ME.

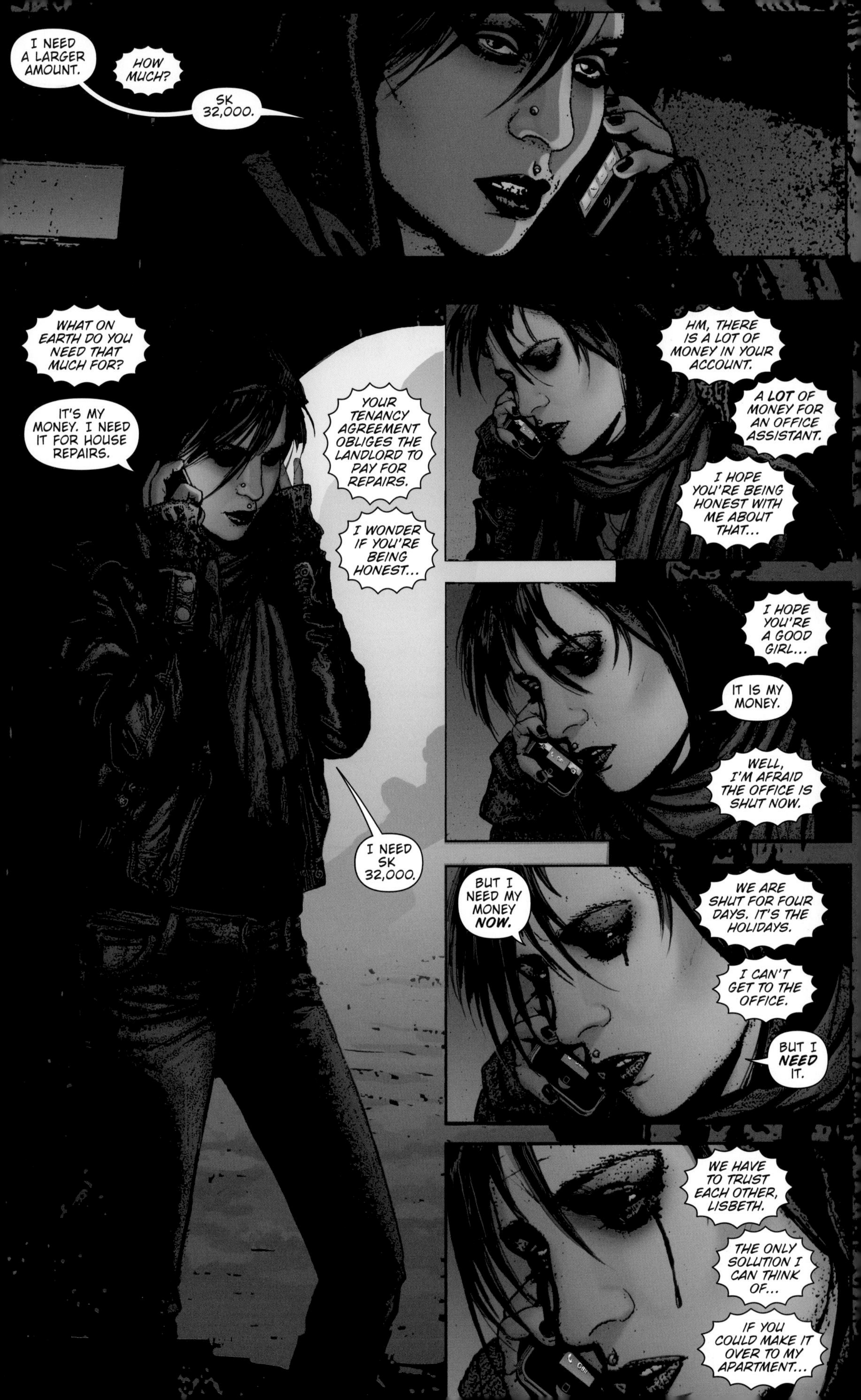
I NEED A LARGER AMOUNT.
HOW MUCH?
SK 32,000.
WHAT ON EARTH DO YOU NEED THAT MUCH FOR?
IT'S MY MONEY. I NEED IT FOR HOUSE REPAIRS.
YOUR TENANCY AGREEMENT OBLIGES THE LANDLORD TO PAY FOR REPAIRS.
I WONDER IF YOU'RE BEING HONEST...
I NEED SK 32,000.
HM, THERE IS A LOT OF MONEY IN YOUR ACCOUNT.
A LOT OF MONEY FOR AN OFFICE ASSISTANT.
I HOPE YOU'RE BEING HONEST WITH ME ABOUT THAT...
I HOPE YOU'RE A GOOD GIRL...
IT IS MY MONEY.
WELL, I'M AFRAID THE OFFICE IS SHUT NOW.
BUT I NEED MY MONEY NOW.
WE ARE SHUT FOR FOUR DAYS. IT'S THE HOLIDAYS.
I CAN'T GET TO THE OFFICE.
BUT I NEED IT.
WE HAVE TO TRUST EACH OTHER, LISBETH.
THE ONLY SOLUTION I CAN THINK OF...
IF YOU COULD MAKE IT OVER TO MY APARTMENT...

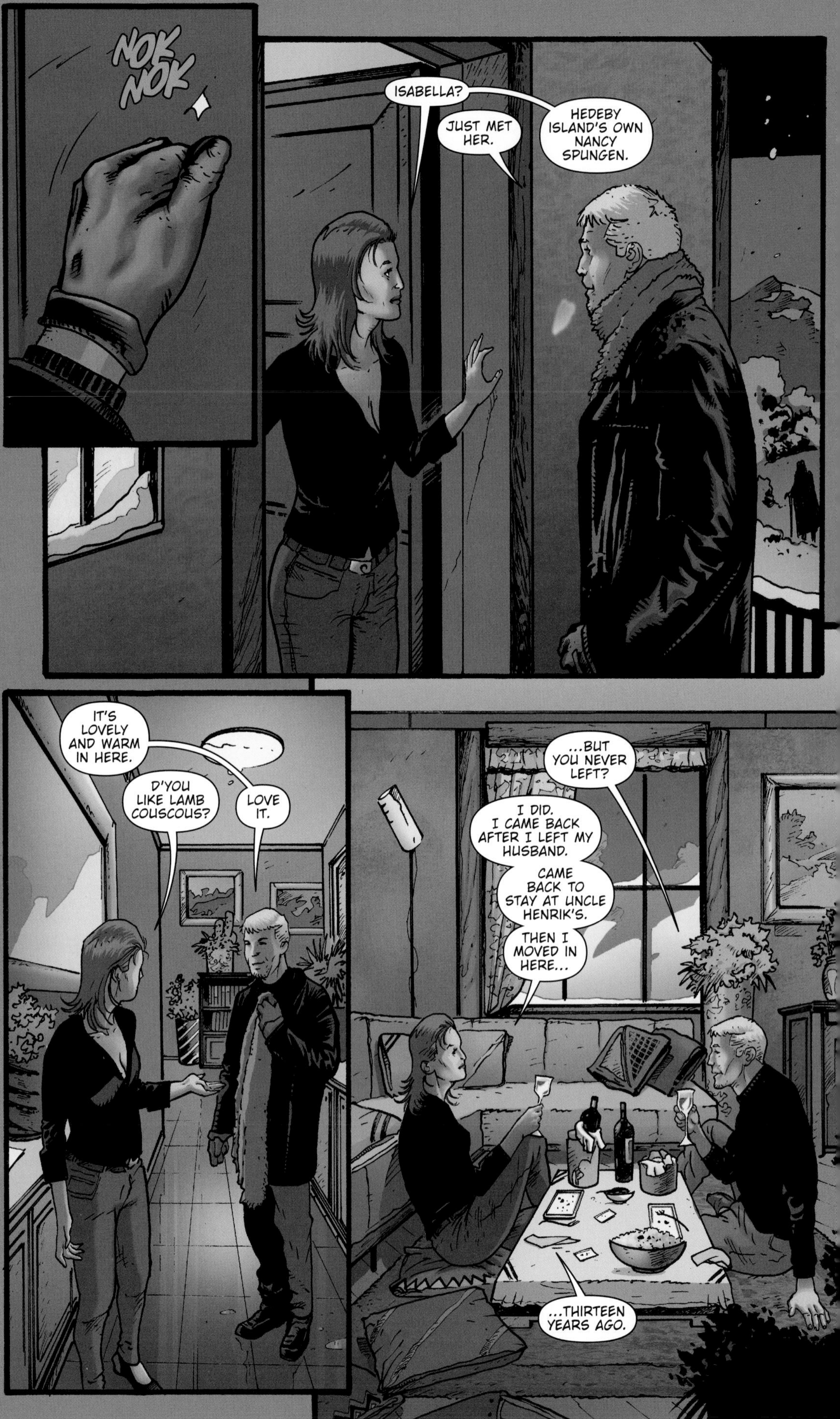
NOK NOK
ISABELLA?
JUST MET HER.
HEDEBY ISLAND'S OWN NANCY SPUNGEN.
IT'S LOVELY AND WARM IN HERE.
D'YOU LIKE LAMB COUSCOUS?
LOVE IT.
...BUT YOU NEVER LEFT?
I DID. I CAME BACK AFTER I LEFT MY HUSBAND.
CAME BACK TO STAY AT UNCLE HENRIK'S.
THEN I MOVED IN HERE...
...THIRTEEN YEARS AGO.

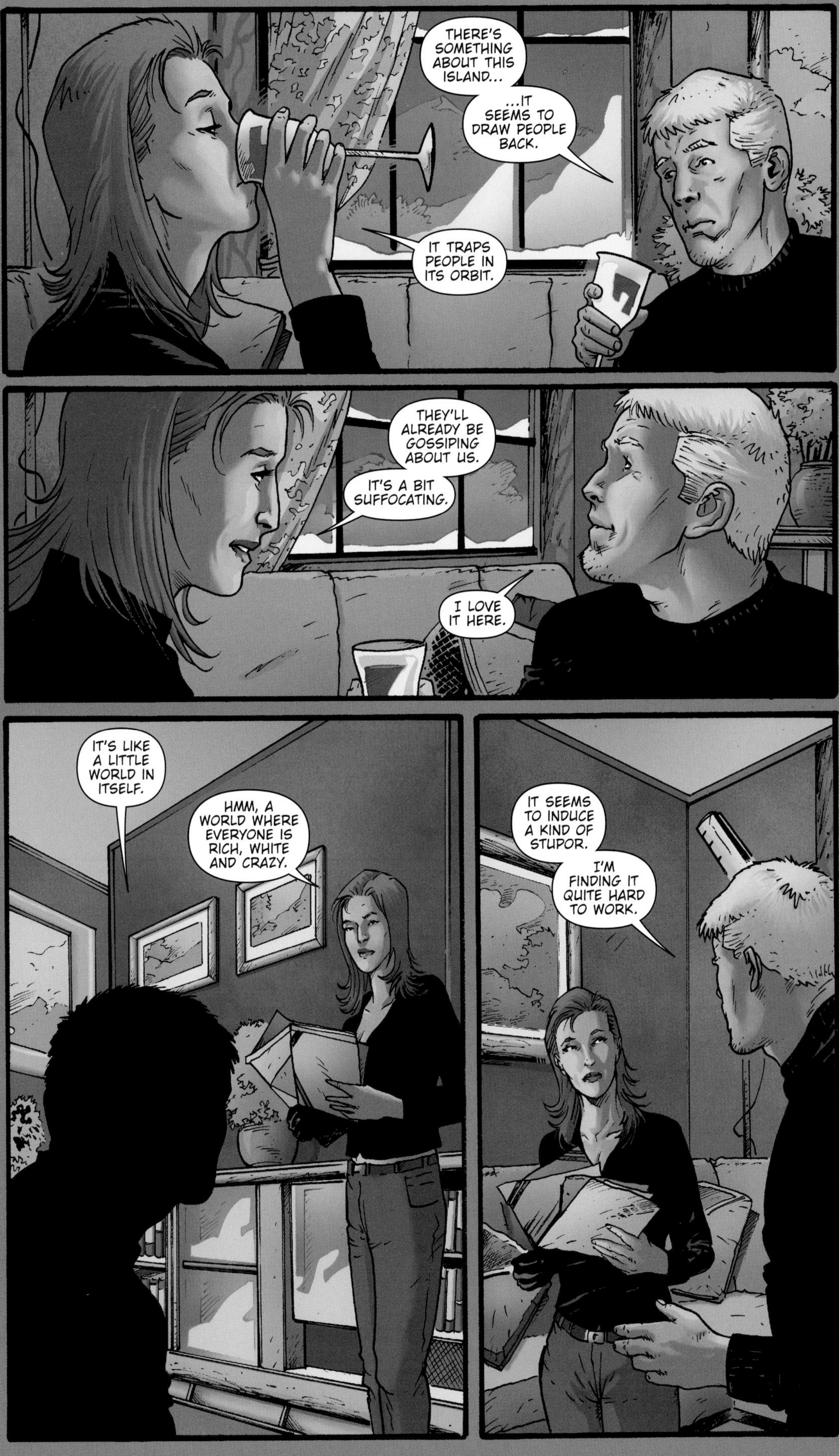
THERE'S SOMETHING ABOUT THIS ISLAND...
...IT SEEMS TO DRAW PEOPLE BACK.
IT TRAPS PEOPLE IN ITS ORBIT.
THEY'LL ALREADY BE GOSSIPING ABOUT US.
IT'S A BIT SUFFOCATING.
I LOVE IT HERE.
IT'S LIKE A LITTLE WORLD IN ITSELF.
HMM, A WORLD WHERE EVERYONE IS RICH, WHITE AND CRAZY.
IT SEEMS TO INDUCE A KIND OF STUPOR.
I'M FINDING IT QUITE HARD TO WORK.

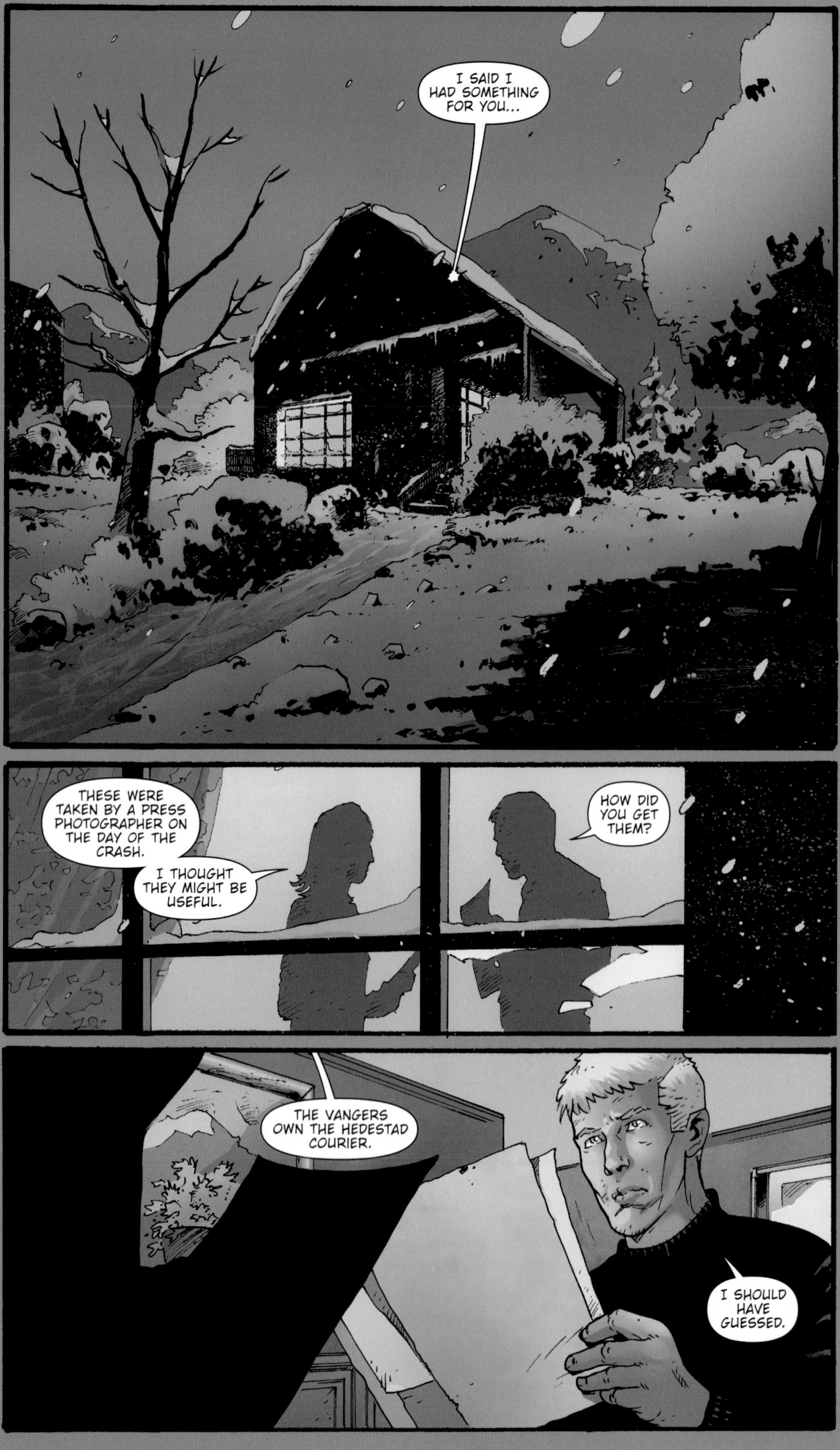
I SAID I HAD SOMETHING FOR YOU...
THESE WERE TAKEN BY A PRESS PHOTOGRAPHER ON THE DAY OF THE CRASH.
I THOUGHT THEY MIGHT BE USEFUL.
HOW DID YOU GET THEM?
THE VANGERS OWN THE HEDESTAD COURIER.
I SHOULD HAVE GUESSED.

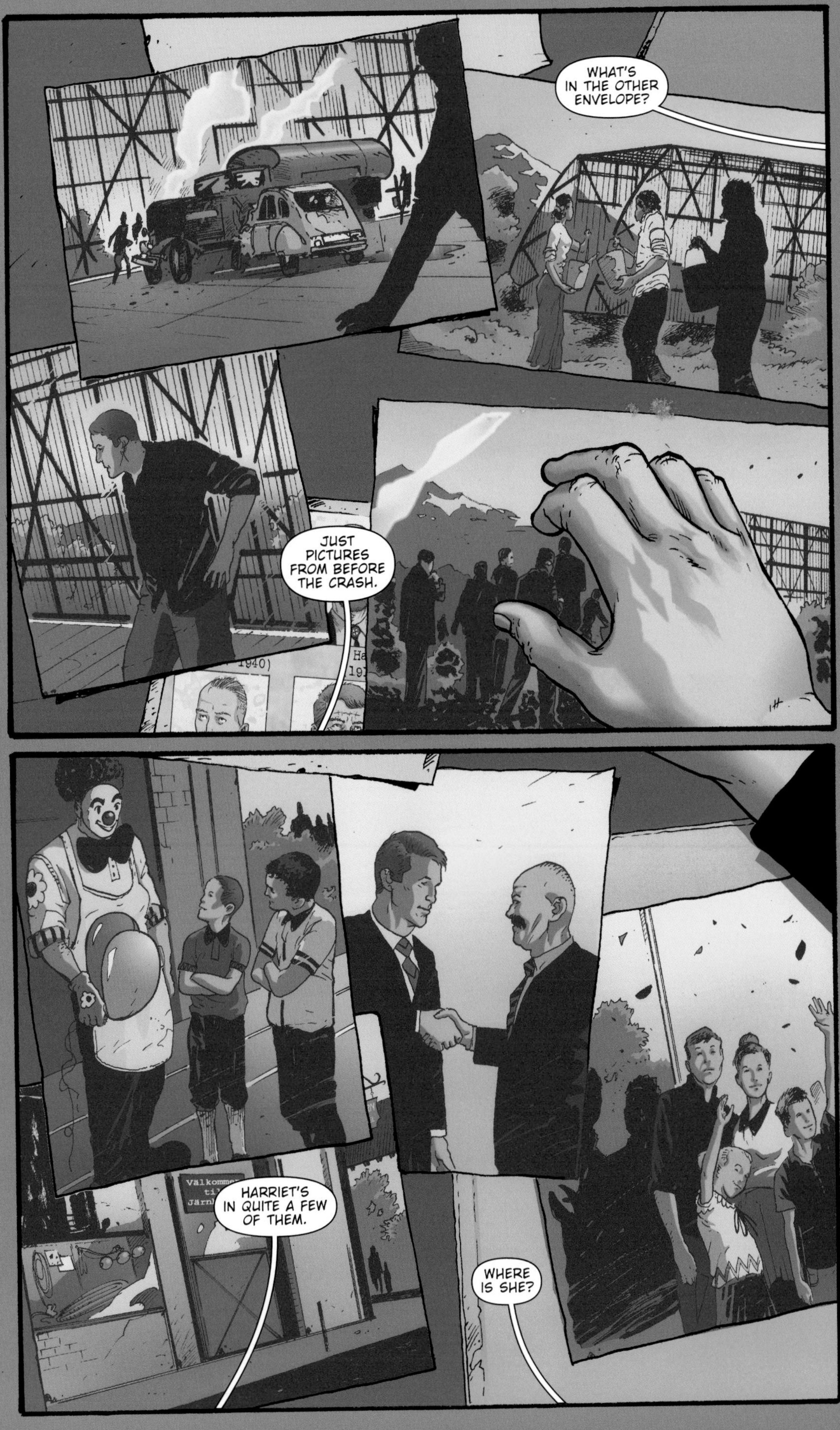
WHAT'S IN THE OTHER ENVELOPE?
JUST PICTURES FROM BEFORE THE CRASH.
HARRIET'S IN QUITE A FEW OF THEM.
WHERE IS SHE?

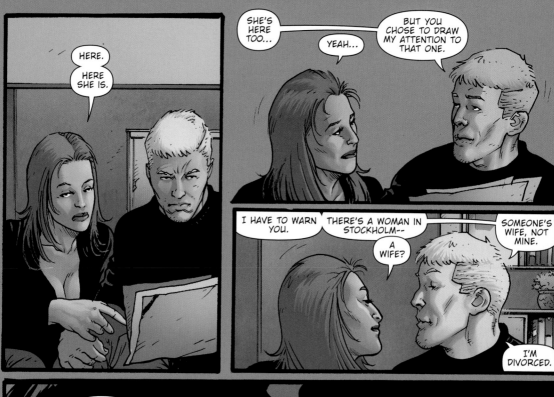

HERE. HERE SHE IS.

SHE'S HERE TOO...

YEAH...

BUT YOU CHOSE TO DRAW MY ATTENTION TO THAT ONE.

I HAVE TO WARN YOU.

THERE'S A WOMAN IN STOCKHOLM--

A WIFE?

SOMEONE'S WIFE, NOT MINE.

I'M DIVORCED.

YOU KNOW, I REALLY THINK I CAN HELP YOU.

I'D HATE FOR YOU TO MISS SOMETHING TERRIBLY IMPORTANT.

I'D *HATE* THAT.

WAKE UP!

YOU NEED TO LEAVE BEFORE MORNING.

IAMAWAKE

'MWIDEAWAKE

I DON'T WANT ANYONE TO KNOW ABOUT US.

OKAY OKAYOKAY.

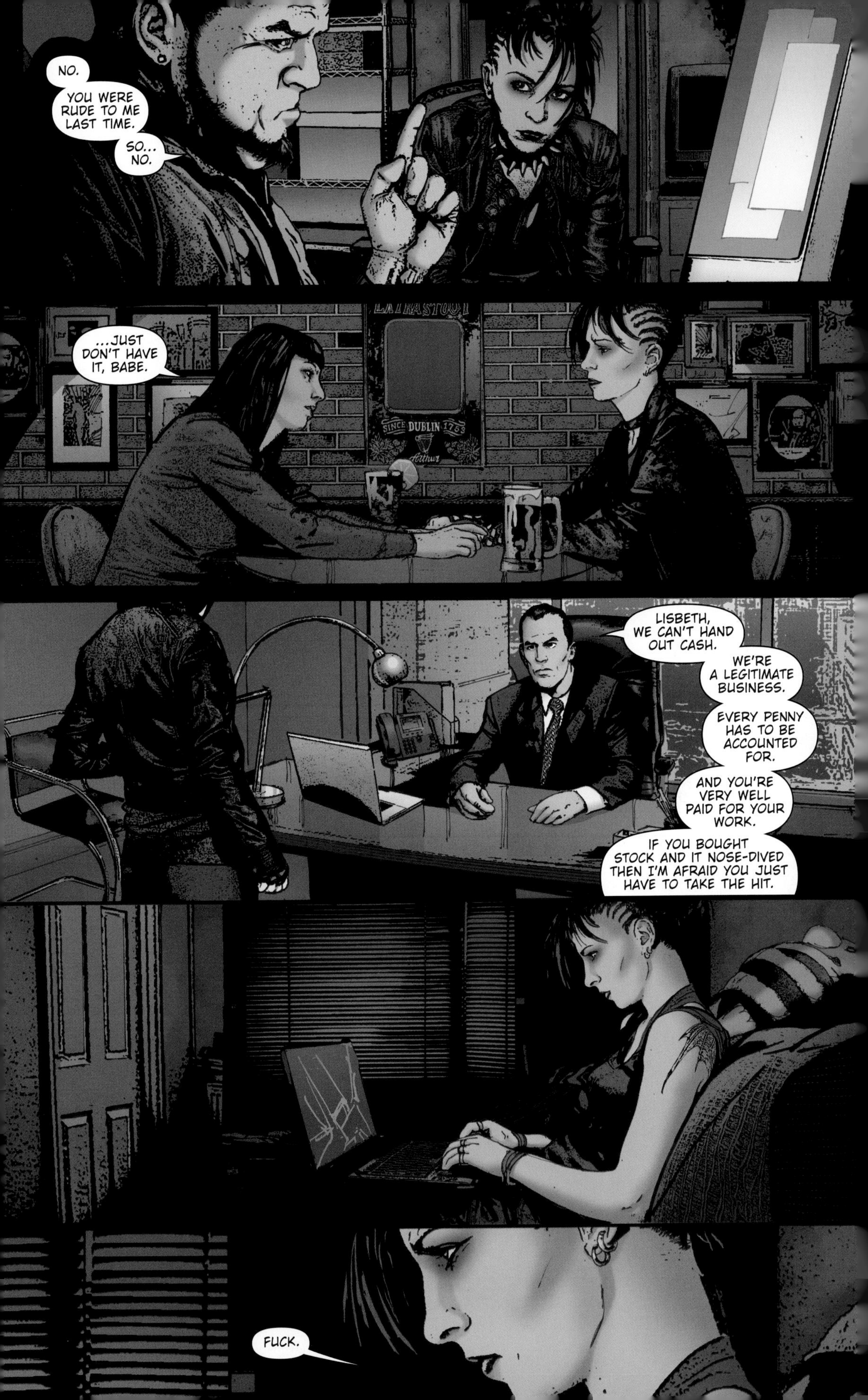
NO.
YOU WERE RUDE TO ME LAST TIME.
SO... NO.
...JUST DON'T HAVE IT, BABE.
SINCE DUBLIN 1759
LISBETH, WE CAN'T HAND OUT CASH.
WE'RE A LEGITIMATE BUSINESS.
EVERY PENNY HAS TO BE ACCOUNTED FOR.
AND YOU'RE VERY WELL PAID FOR YOUR WORK.
IF YOU BOUGHT STOCK AND IT NOSE-DIVED THEN I'M AFRAID YOU JUST HAVE TO TAKE THE HIT.
FUCK.

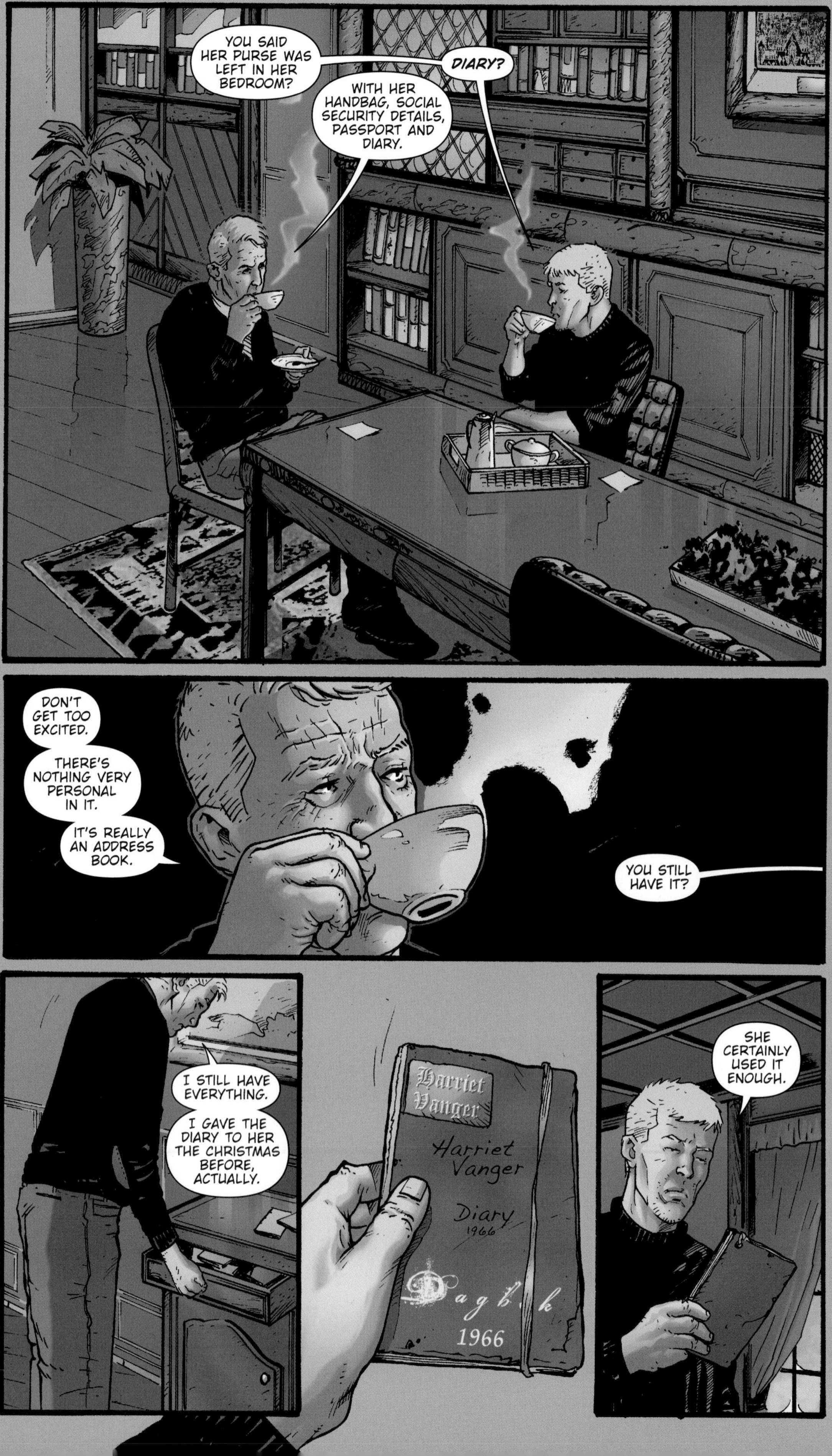
YOU SAID HER PURSE WAS LEFT IN HER BEDROOM?
WITH HER HANDBAG, SOCIAL SECURITY DETAILS, PASSPORT AND DIARY.
DIARY?
DON'T GET TOO EXCITED.
THERE'S NOTHING VERY PERSONAL IN IT.
IT'S REALLY AN ADDRESS BOOK.
YOU STILL HAVE IT?
I STILL HAVE EVERYTHING.
I GAVE THE DIARY TO HER THE CHRISTMAS BEFORE, ACTUALLY.
Harriet Vanger
Harriet Vanger
Diary 1966
1966
SHE CERTAINLY USED IT ENOUGH.

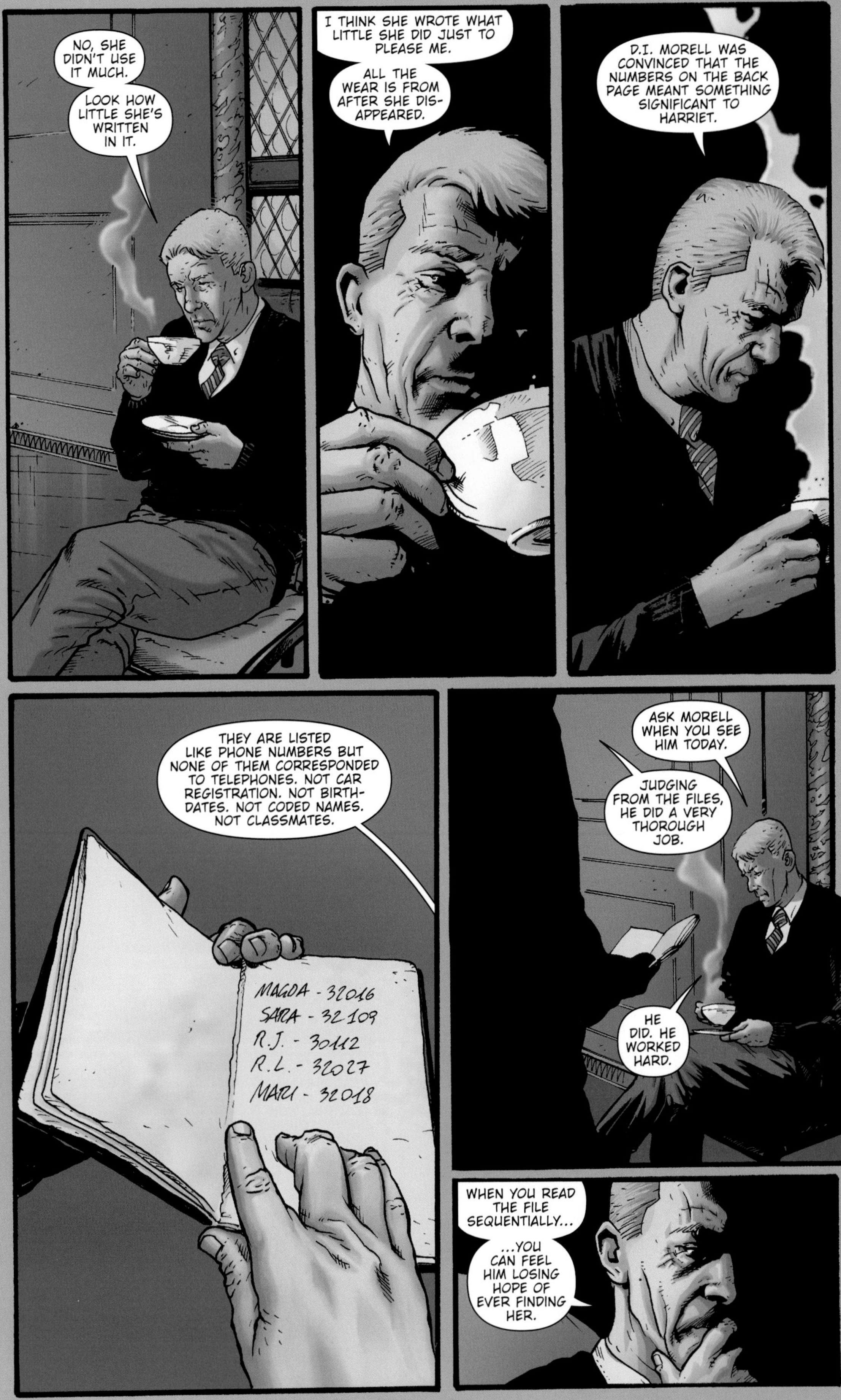
NO, SHE DIDN'T USE IT MUCH.
LOOK HOW LITTLE SHE'S WRITTEN IN IT.
I THINK SHE WROTE WHAT LITTLE SHE DID JUST TO PLEASE ME.
ALL THE WEAR IS FROM AFTER SHE DISAPPEARED.
D.I. MORELL WAS CONVINCED THAT THE NUMBERS ON THE BACK PAGE MEANT SOMETHING SIGNIFICANT TO HARRIET.
THEY ARE LISTED LIKE PHONE NUMBERS BUT NONE OF THEM CORRESPONDED TO TELEPHONES. NOT CAR REGISTRATION. NOT BIRTHDATES. NOT CODED NAMES. NOT CLASSMATES.
MAGDA - 32016
SARA - 32109
R.J. - 30112
R.L. - 32027
MARI - 32018
ASK MORELL WHEN YOU SEE HIM TODAY.
JUDGING FROM THE FILES, HE DID A VERY THOROUGH JOB.
HE DID. HE WORKED HARD.
WHEN YOU READ THE FILE SEQUENTIALLY...
...YOU CAN FEEL HIM LOSING HOPE OF EVER FINDING HER.

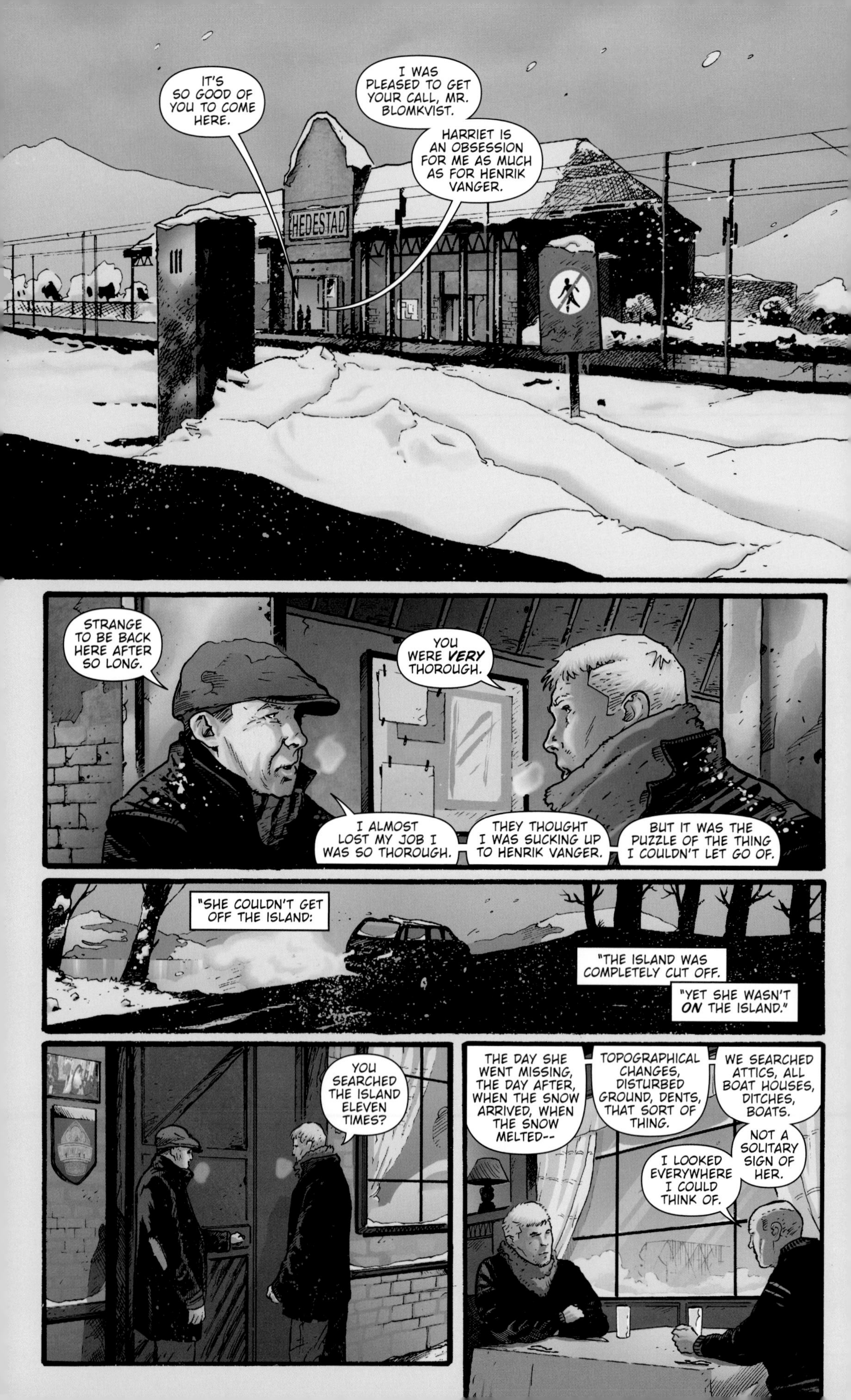
IT'S SO GOOD OF YOU TO COME HERE.
I WAS PLEASED TO GET YOUR CALL, MR. BLOMKVIST.
HARRIET IS AN OBSESSION FOR ME AS MUCH AS FOR HENRIK VANGER.
HEDESTAD
STRANGE TO BE BACK HERE AFTER SO LONG.
YOU WERE *VERY* THOROUGH.
I ALMOST LOST MY JOB I WAS SO THOROUGH.
THEY THOUGHT I WAS SUCKING UP TO HENRIK VANGER.
BUT IT WAS THE PUZZLE OF THE THING I COULDN'T LET GO OF.
"SHE COULDN'T GET OFF THE ISLAND:
"THE ISLAND WAS COMPLETELY CUT OFF.
"YET SHE WASN'T *ON* THE ISLAND."
YOU SEARCHED THE ISLAND ELEVEN TIMES?
THE DAY SHE WENT MISSING, THE DAY AFTER, WHEN THE SNOW ARRIVED, WHEN THE SNOW MELTED--
TOPOGRAPHICAL CHANGES, DISTURBED GROUND, DENTS, THAT SORT OF THING.
WE SEARCHED ATTICS, ALL BOAT HOUSES, DITCHES, BOATS.
NOT A SOLITARY SIGN OF HER.
I LOOKED EVERYWHERE I COULD THINK OF.

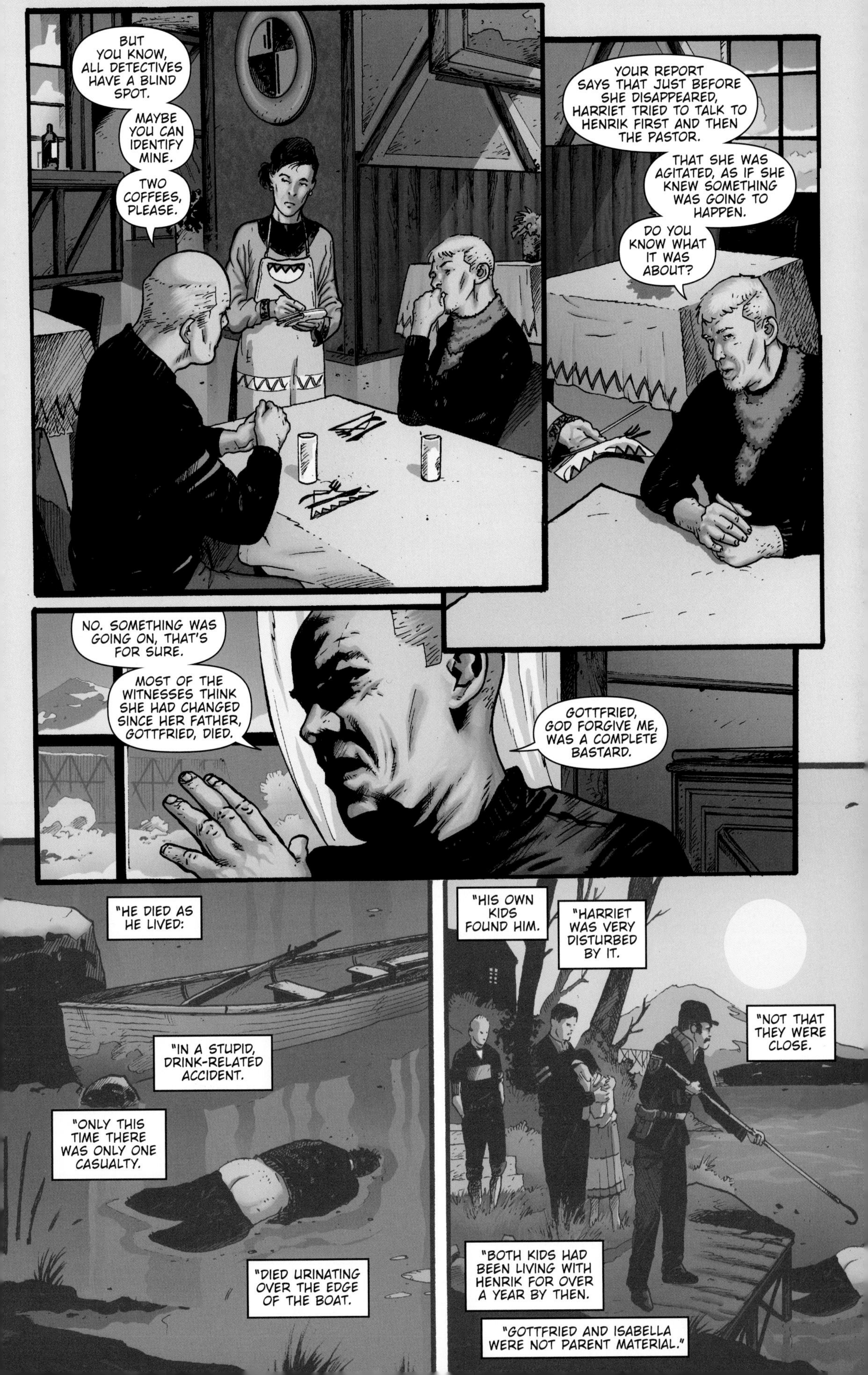

BUT YOU KNOW, ALL DETECTIVES HAVE A BLIND SPOT.
MAYBE YOU CAN IDENTIFY MINE.
TWO COFFEES, PLEASE.
YOUR REPORT SAYS THAT JUST BEFORE SHE DISAPPEARED, HARRIET TRIED TO TALK TO HENRIK FIRST AND THEN THE PASTOR.
THAT SHE WAS AGITATED, AS IF SHE KNEW SOMETHING WAS GOING TO HAPPEN.
DO YOU KNOW WHAT IT WAS ABOUT?
NO. SOMETHING WAS GOING ON, THAT'S FOR SURE.
MOST OF THE WITNESSES THINK SHE HAD CHANGED SINCE HER FATHER, GOTTFRIED, DIED.
GOTTFRIED, GOD FORGIVE ME, WAS A COMPLETE BASTARD.
"HE DIED AS HE LIVED:
"IN A STUPID, DRINK-RELATED ACCIDENT.
"ONLY THIS TIME THERE WAS ONLY ONE CASUALTY.
"DIED URINATING OVER THE EDGE OF THE BOAT.
"HIS OWN KIDS FOUND HIM.
"HARRIET WAS VERY DISTURBED BY IT.
"NOT THAT THEY WERE CLOSE.
"BOTH KIDS HAD BEEN LIVING WITH HENRIK FOR OVER A YEAR BY THEN.
"GOTTFRIED AND ISABELLA WERE NOT PARENT MATERIAL."

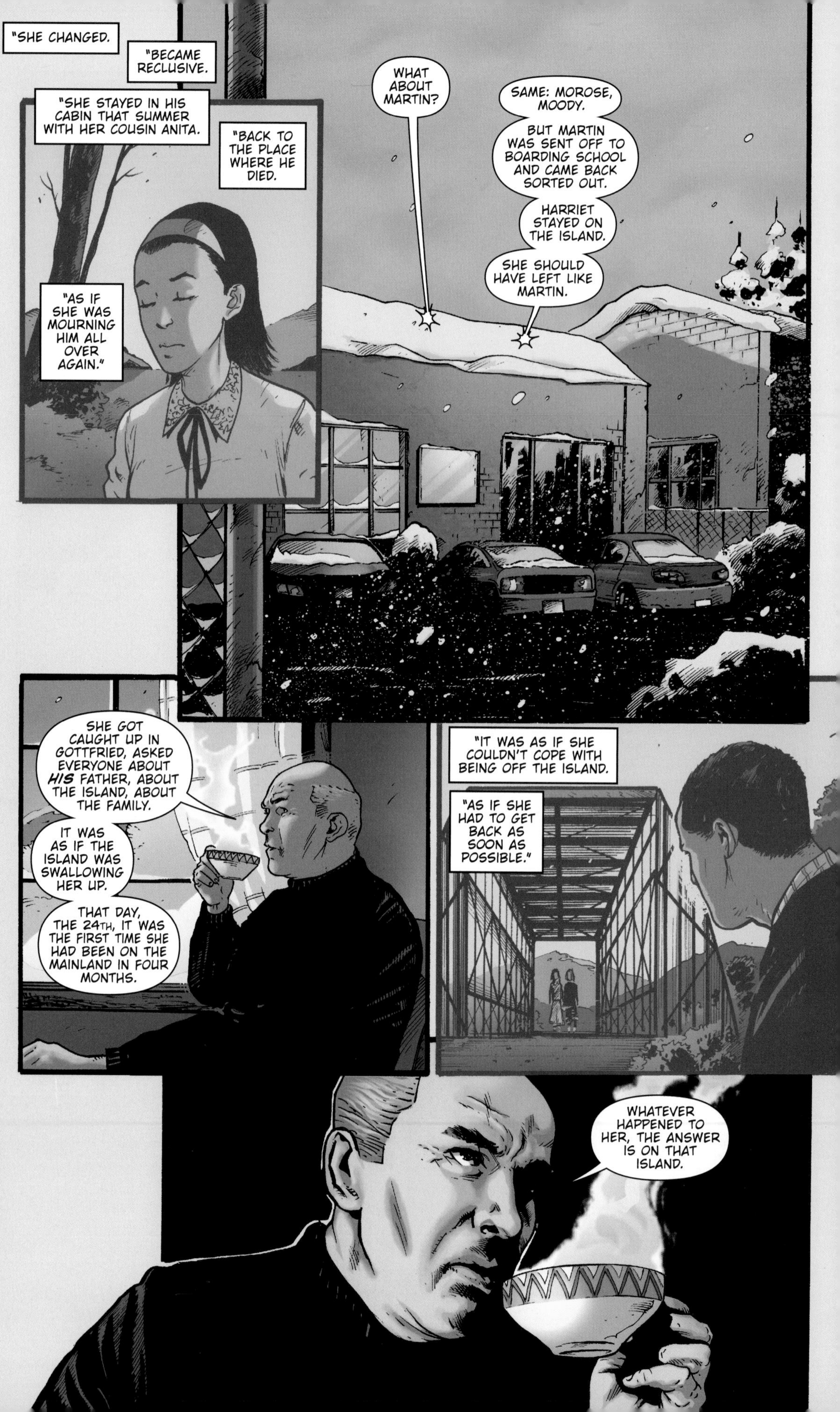
"SHE CHANGED.
"BECAME RECLUSIVE.
"SHE STAYED IN HIS CABIN THAT SUMMER WITH HER COUSIN ANITA.
"BACK TO THE PLACE WHERE HE DIED.
"AS IF SHE WAS MOURNING HIM ALL OVER AGAIN."
WHAT ABOUT MARTIN?
SAME: MOROSE, MOODY.
BUT MARTIN WAS SENT OFF TO BOARDING SCHOOL AND CAME BACK SORTED OUT.
HARRIET STAYED ON THE ISLAND.
SHE SHOULD HAVE LEFT LIKE MARTIN.
SHE GOT CAUGHT UP IN GOTTFRIED, ASKED EVERYONE ABOUT *HIS* FATHER, ABOUT THE ISLAND, ABOUT THE FAMILY.
IT WAS AS IF THE ISLAND WAS SWALLOWING HER UP.
THAT DAY, THE 24TH, IT WAS THE FIRST TIME SHE HAD BEEN ON THE MAINLAND IN FOUR MONTHS.
"IT WAS AS IF SHE COULDN'T COPE WITH BEING OFF THE ISLAND.
"AS IF SHE HAD TO GET BACK AS SOON AS POSSIBLE."
WHATEVER HAPPENED TO HER, THE ANSWER IS ON THAT ISLAND.

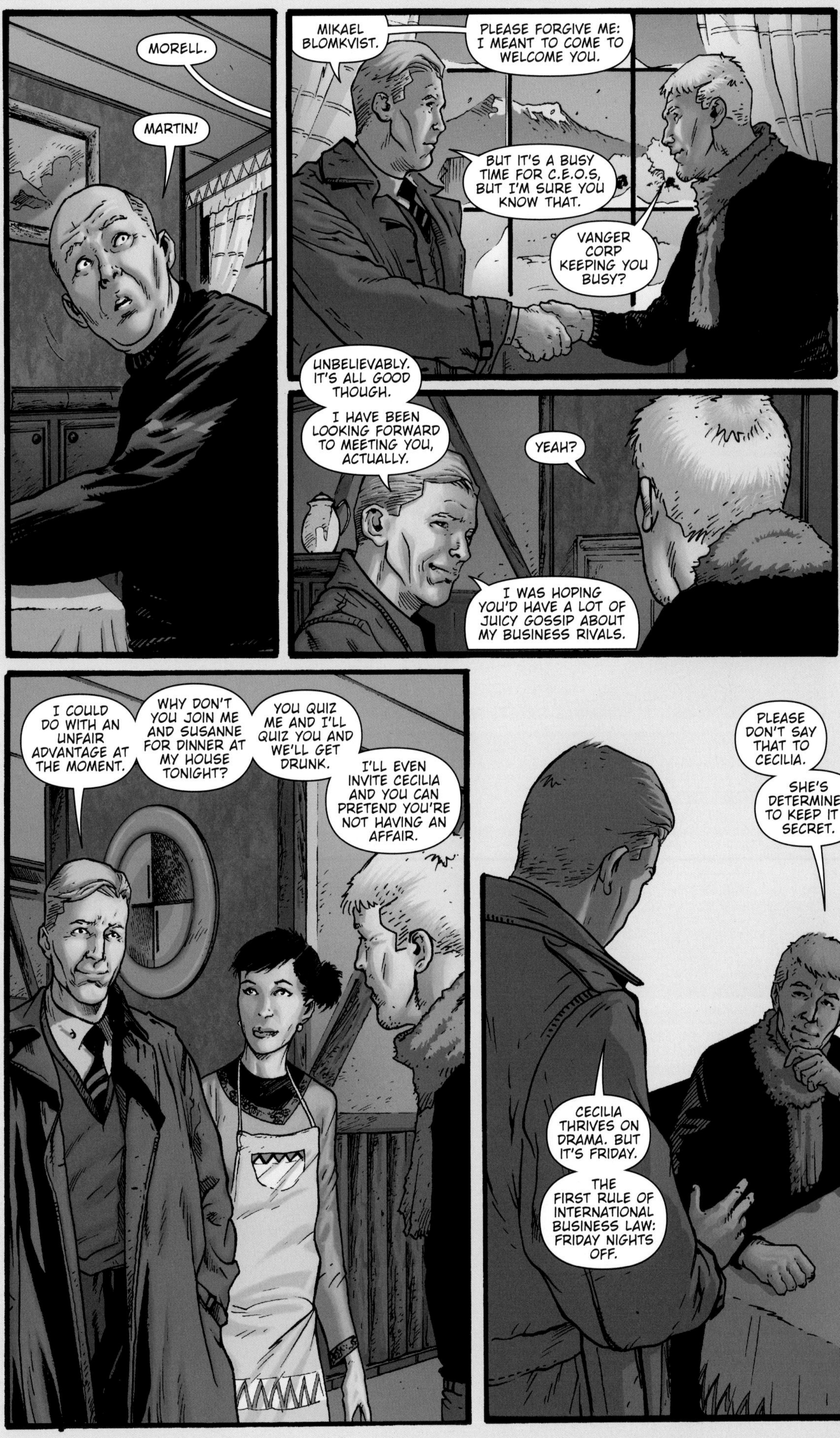
MORELL.
MARTIN!
MIKAEL BLOMKVIST.
PLEASE FORGIVE ME: I MEANT TO COME TO WELCOME YOU.
BUT IT'S A BUSY TIME FOR C.E.O.S, BUT I'M SURE YOU KNOW THAT.
VANGER CORP KEEPING YOU BUSY?
UNBELIEVABLY. IT'S ALL GOOD THOUGH.
I HAVE BEEN LOOKING FORWARD TO MEETING YOU, ACTUALLY.
YEAH?
I WAS HOPING YOU'D HAVE A LOT OF JUICY GOSSIP ABOUT MY BUSINESS RIVALS.
I COULD DO WITH AN UNFAIR ADVANTAGE AT THE MOMENT.
WHY DON'T YOU JOIN ME AND SUSANNE FOR DINNER AT MY HOUSE TONIGHT?
YOU QUIZ ME AND I'LL QUIZ YOU AND WE'LL GET DRUNK.
I'LL EVEN INVITE CECILIA AND YOU CAN PRETEND YOU'RE NOT HAVING AN AFFAIR.
PLEASE DON'T SAY THAT TO CECILIA.
SHE'S DETERMINED TO KEEP IT A SECRET.
CECILIA THRIVES ON DRAMA. BUT IT'S FRIDAY.
THE FIRST RULE OF INTERNATIONAL BUSINESS LAW: FRIDAY NIGHTS OFF.

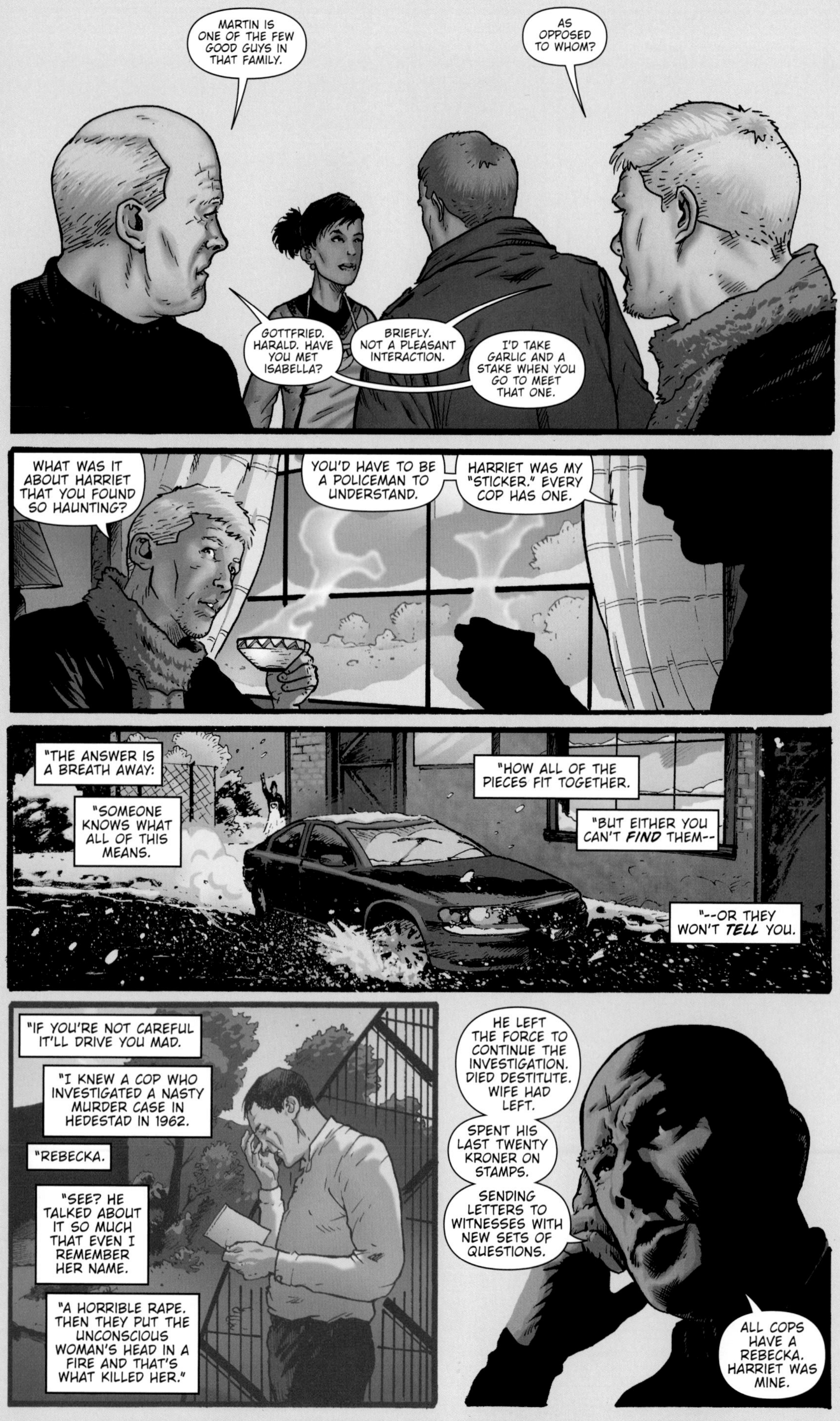
MARTIN IS ONE OF THE FEW GOOD GUYS IN THAT FAMILY.
AS OPPOSED TO WHOM?
GOTTFRIED. HARALD. HAVE YOU MET ISABELLA?
BRIEFLY. NOT A PLEASANT INTERACTION.
I'D TAKE GARLIC AND A STAKE WHEN YOU GO TO MEET THAT ONE.
WHAT WAS IT ABOUT HARRIET THAT YOU FOUND SO HAUNTING?
YOU'D HAVE TO BE A POLICEMAN TO UNDERSTAND.
HARRIET WAS MY "STICKER." EVERY COP HAS ONE.
"THE ANSWER IS A BREATH AWAY:
"SOMEONE KNOWS WHAT ALL OF THIS MEANS.
"HOW ALL OF THE PIECES FIT TOGETHER.
"BUT EITHER YOU CAN'T *FIND* THEM--
"--OR THEY WON'T *TELL* YOU.
"IF YOU'RE NOT CAREFUL IT'LL DRIVE YOU MAD.
"I KNEW A COP WHO INVESTIGATED A NASTY MURDER CASE IN HEDESTAD IN 1962.
"REBECKA.
"SEE? HE TALKED ABOUT IT SO MUCH THAT EVEN I REMEMBER HER NAME.
"A HORRIBLE RAPE. THEN THEY PUT THE UNCONSCIOUS WOMAN'S HEAD IN A FIRE AND THAT'S WHAT KILLED HER."
HE LEFT THE FORCE TO CONTINUE THE INVESTIGATION. DIED DESTITUTE. WIFE HAD LEFT.
SPENT HIS LAST TWENTY KRONER ON STAMPS.
SENDING LETTERS TO WITNESSES WITH NEW SETS OF QUESTIONS.
ALL COPS HAVE A REBECKA. HARRIET WAS MINE.

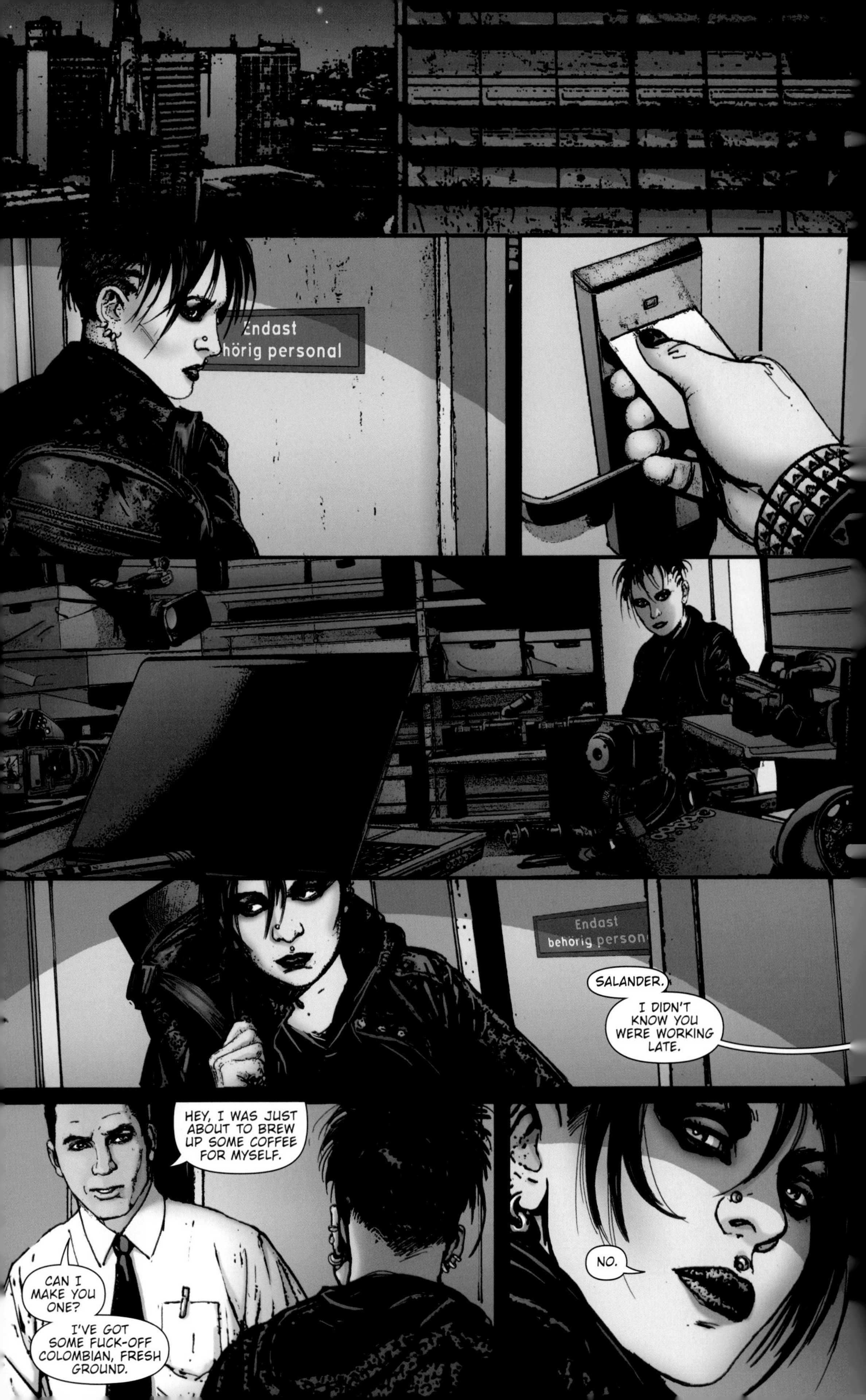
Endast
behörig personal
Endast
behörig persone
SALANDER.
I DIDN'T KNOW YOU WERE WORKING LATE.
HEY, I WAS JUST ABOUT TO BREW UP SOME COFFEE FOR MYSELF.
CAN I MAKE YOU ONE?
I'VE GOT SOME FUCK-OFF COLOMBIAN, FRESH GROUND.
NO.

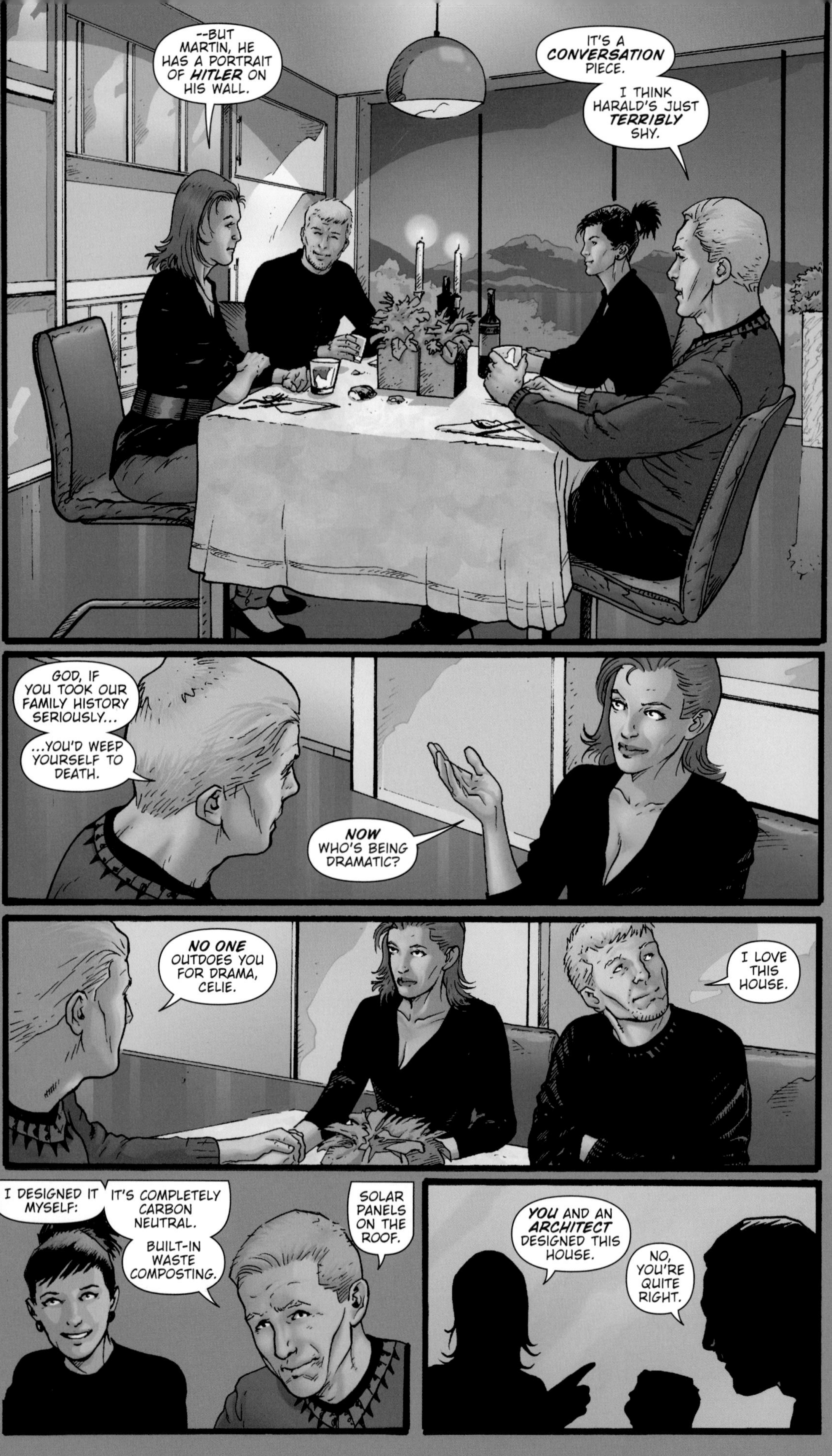

--BUT MARTIN, HE HAS A PORTRAIT OF HITLER ON HIS WALL.
IT'S A CONVERSATION PIECE.
I THINK HARALD'S JUST TERRIBLY SHY.
GOD, IF YOU TOOK OUR FAMILY HISTORY SERIOUSLY...
...YOU'D WEEP YOURSELF TO DEATH.
NOW WHO'S BEING DRAMATIC?
NO ONE OUTDOES YOU FOR DRAMA, CELIE.
I LOVE THIS HOUSE.
I DESIGNED IT MYSELF:
IT'S COMPLETELY CARBON NEUTRAL.
BUILT-IN WASTE COMPOSTING.
SOLAR PANELS ON THE ROOF.
YOU AND AN ARCHITECT DESIGNED THIS HOUSE.
NO, YOU'RE QUITE RIGHT.

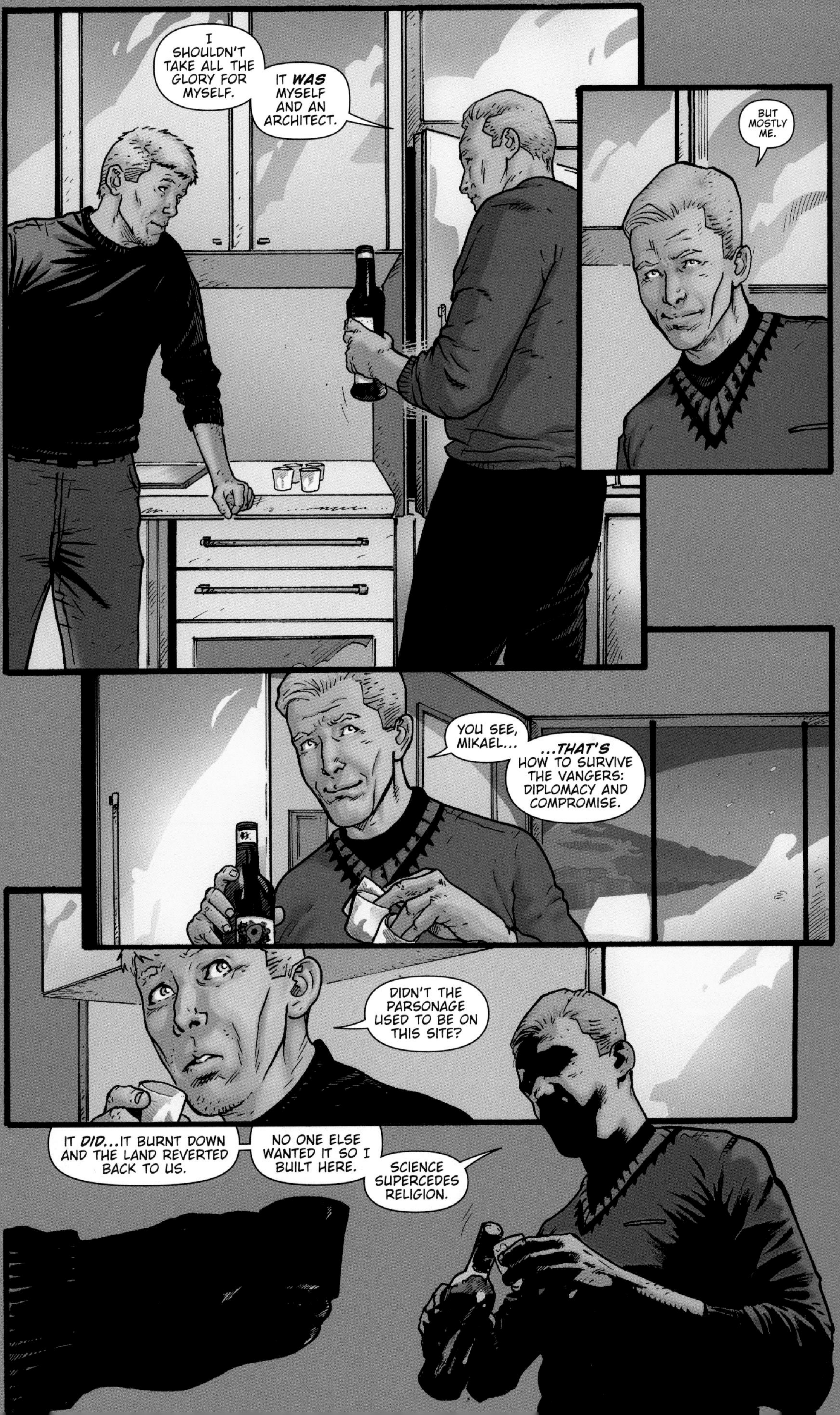

I SHOULDN'T TAKE ALL THE GLORY FOR MYSELF.
IT WAS MYSELF AND AN ARCHITECT.
BUT MOSTLY ME.
YOU SEE, MIKAEL...
...THAT'S HOW TO SURVIVE THE VANGERS: DIPLOMACY AND COMPROMISE.
DIDN'T THE PARSONAGE USED TO BE ON THIS SITE?
IT DID...IT BURNT DOWN AND THE LAND REVERTED BACK TO US.
NO ONE ELSE WANTED IT SO I BUILT HERE.
SCIENCE SUPERCEDES RELIGION.

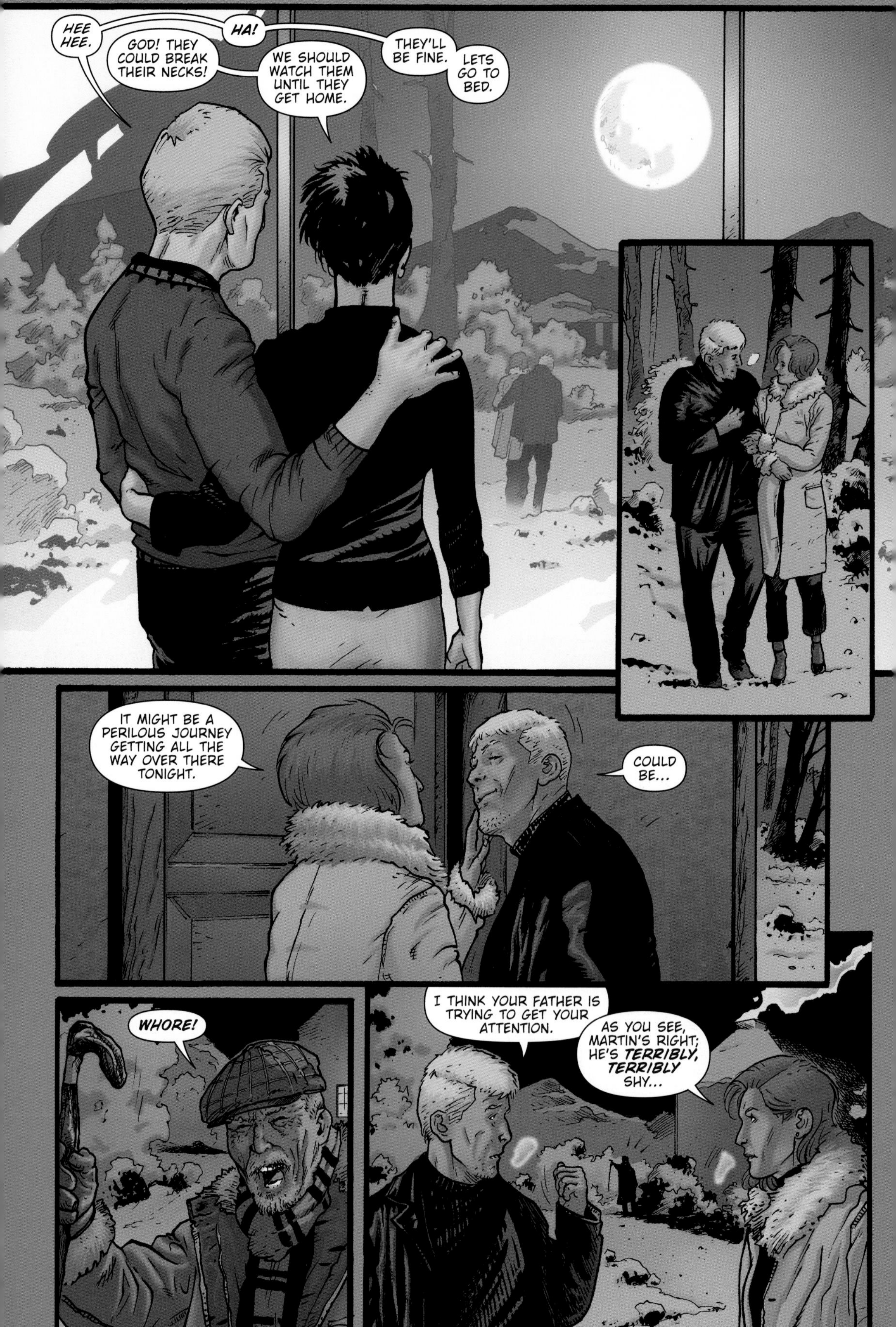
HEE HEE.
GOD! THEY COULD BREAK THEIR NECKS!
HA!
WE SHOULD WATCH THEM UNTIL THEY GET HOME.
THEY'LL BE FINE.
LETS GO TO BED.
IT MIGHT BE A PERILOUS JOURNEY GETTING ALL THE WAY OVER THERE TONIGHT.
COULD BE...
WHORE!
I THINK YOUR FATHER IS TRYING TO GET YOUR ATTENTION.
AS YOU SEE, MARTIN'S RIGHT; HE'S *TERRIBLY, TERRIBLY* SHY...

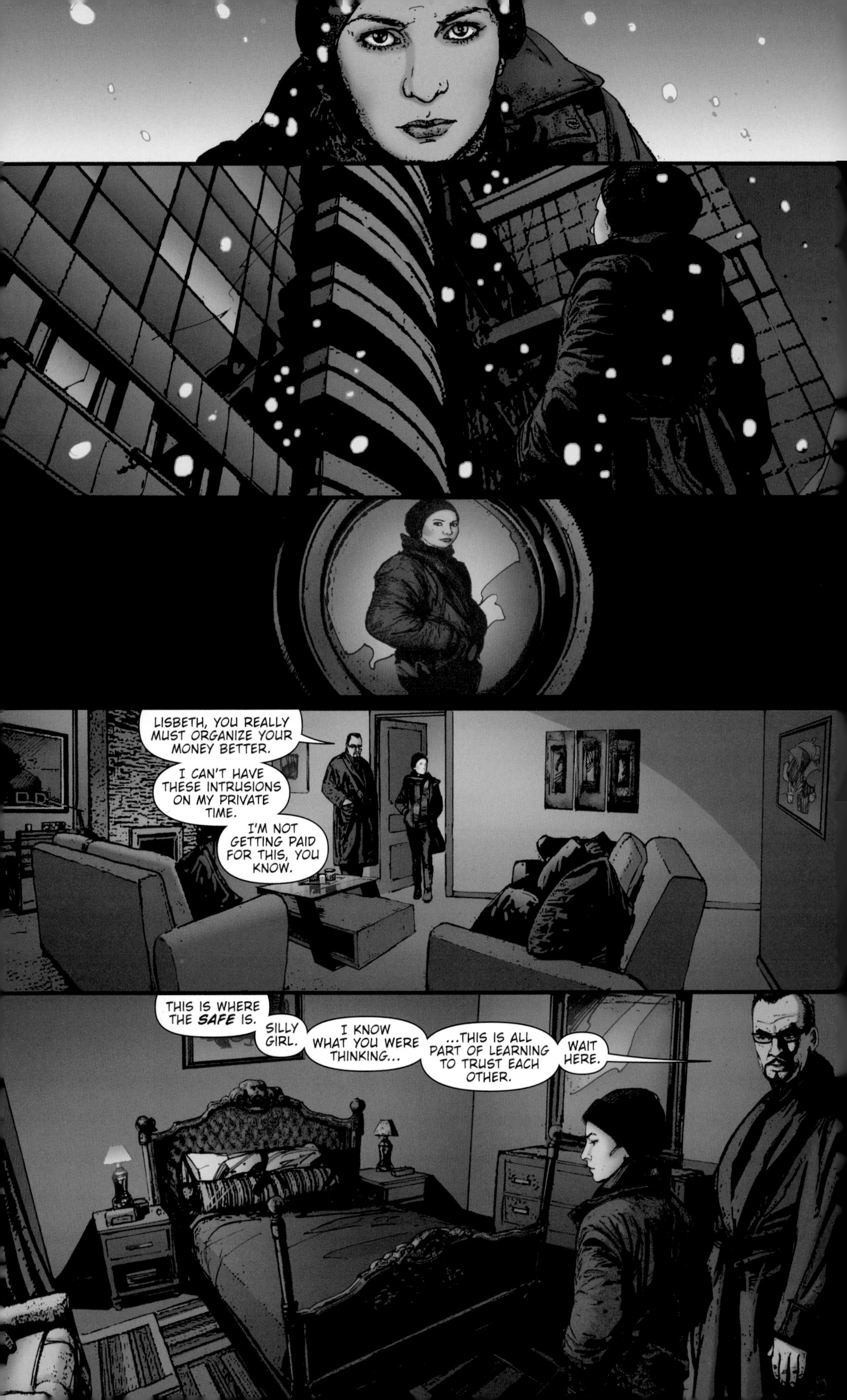
LISBETH, YOU REALLY MUST ORGANIZE YOUR MONEY BETTER.
I CAN'T HAVE THESE INTRUSIONS ON MY PRIVATE TIME.
I'M NOT GETTING PAID FOR THIS, YOU KNOW.
THIS IS WHERE THE *SAFE* IS.
SILLY GIRL.
I KNOW WHAT YOU WERE THINKING...
...THIS IS ALL PART OF LEARNING TO TRUST EACH OTHER.
WAIT HERE.

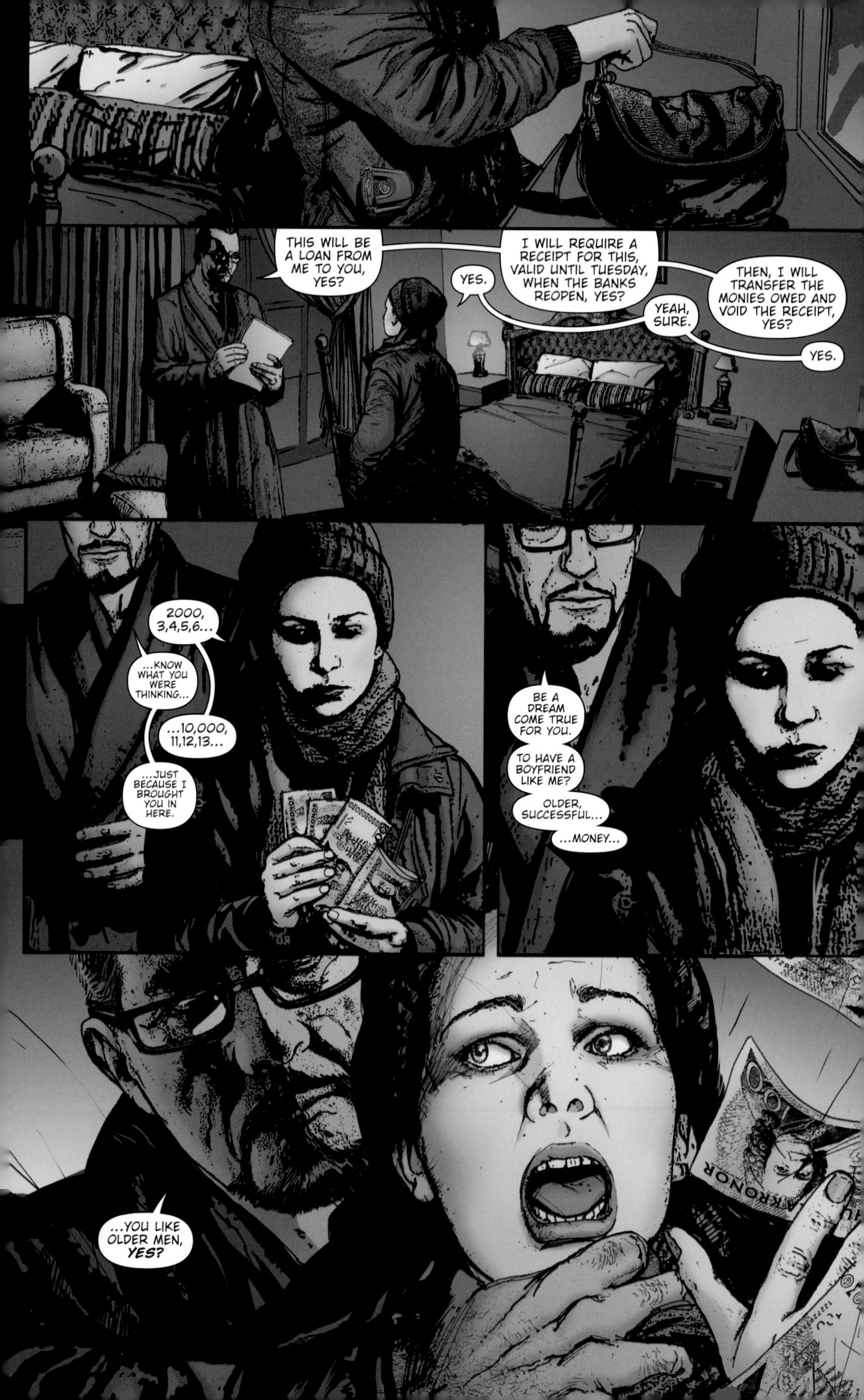
THIS WILL BE A LOAN FROM ME TO YOU, YES?
I WILL REQUIRE A RECEIPT FOR THIS, VALID UNTIL TUESDAY, WHEN THE BANKS REOPEN, YES?
YES.
THEN, I WILL TRANSFER THE MONIES OWED AND VOID THE RECEIPT, YES?
YEAH, SURE.
YES.
2000, 3,4,5,6...
...KNOW WHAT YOU WERE THINKING...
...10,000, 11,12,13...
...JUST BECAUSE I BROUGHT YOU IN HERE.
BE A DREAM COME TRUE FOR YOU.
TO HAVE A BOYFRIEND LIKE ME?
OLDER, SUCCESSFUL...
...MONEY...
...YOU LIKE OLDER MEN, *YES?*

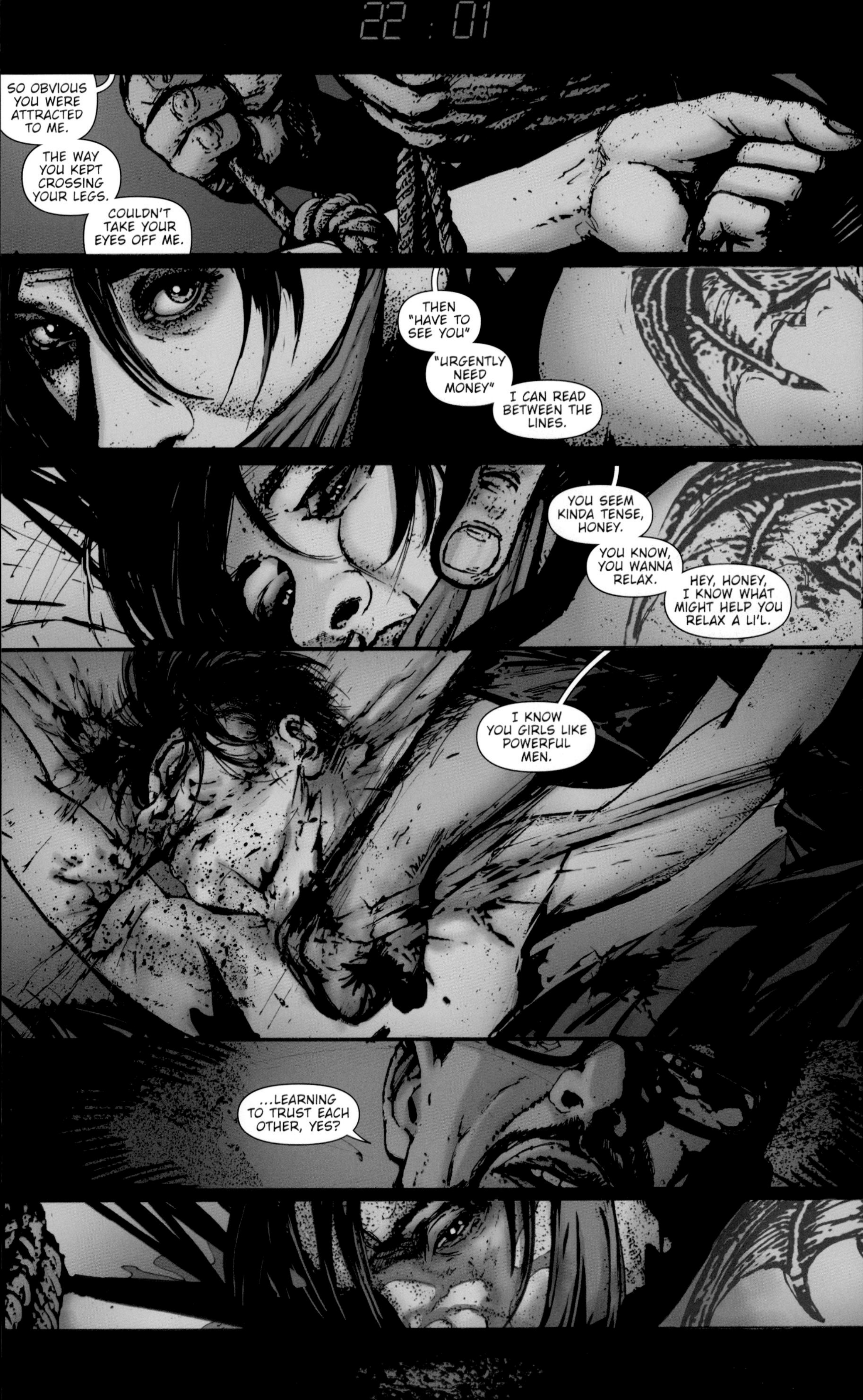
22:01
SO OBVIOUS YOU WERE ATTRACTED TO ME.
THE WAY YOU KEPT CROSSING YOUR LEGS.
COULDN'T TAKE YOUR EYES OFF ME.
THEN "HAVE TO SEE YOU"
"URGENTLY NEED MONEY"
I CAN READ BETWEEN THE LINES.
YOU SEEM KINDA TENSE, HONEY.
YOU KNOW, YOU WANNA RELAX.
HEY, HONEY, I KNOW WHAT MIGHT HELP YOU RELAX A LI'L.
I KNOW YOU GIRLS LIKE POWERFUL MEN.
...LEARNING TO TRUST EACH OTHER, YES?

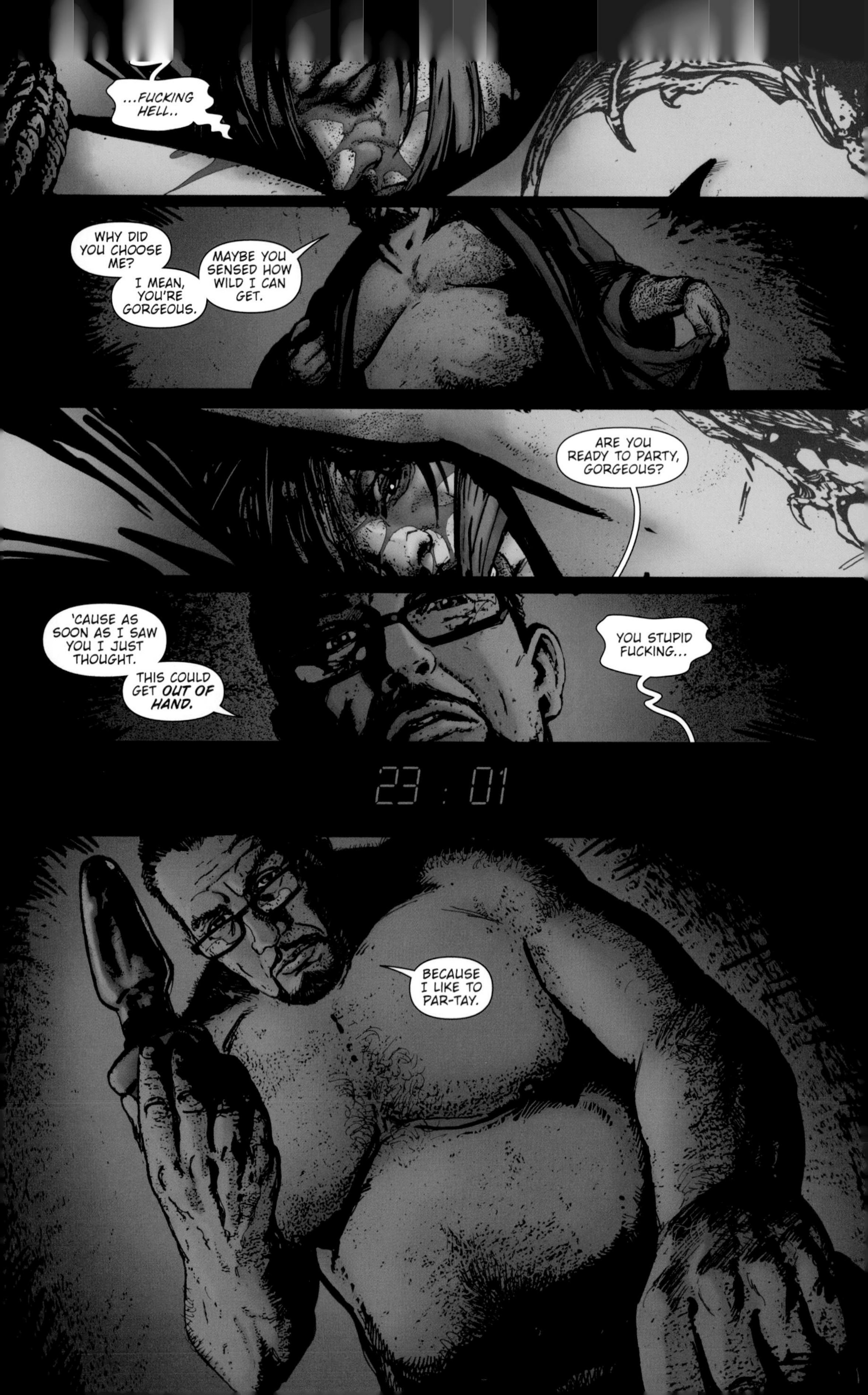
...FUCKING HELL..
WHY DID YOU CHOOSE ME?
I MEAN, YOU'RE GORGEOUS.
MAYBE YOU SENSED HOW WILD I CAN GET.
ARE YOU READY TO PARTY, GORGEOUS?
'CAUSE AS SOON AS I SAW YOU I JUST THOUGHT.
THIS COULD GET *OUT OF HAND.*
YOU STUPID FUCKING...
23 : 01
BECAUSE I LIKE TO PAR-TAY.

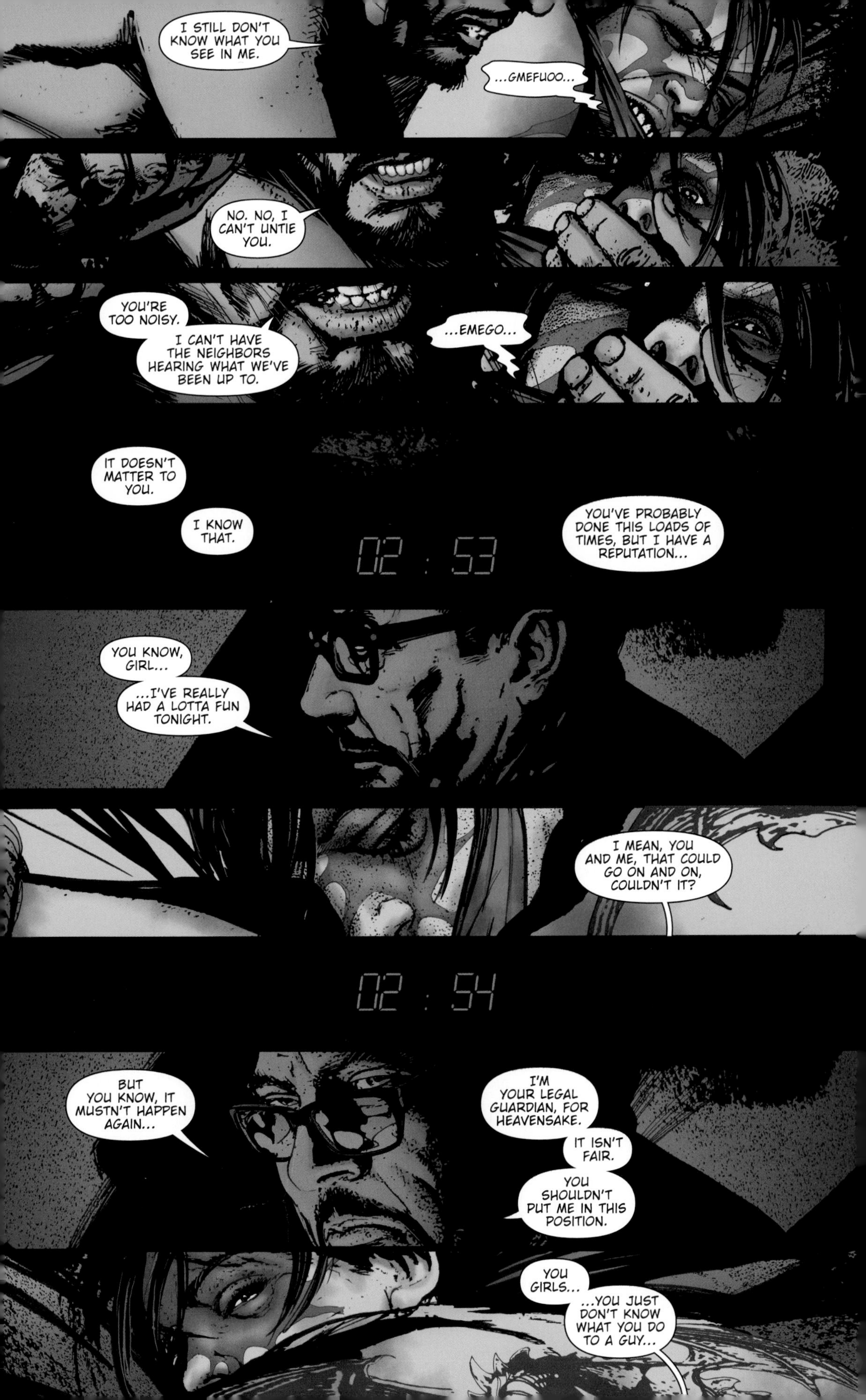
I STILL DON'T KNOW WHAT YOU SEE IN ME.
...GMEFUOO...
NO. NO, I CAN'T UNTIE YOU.
YOU'RE TOO NOISY.
I CAN'T HAVE THE NEIGHBORS HEARING WHAT WE'VE BEEN UP TO.
...EMEGO...
IT DOESN'T MATTER TO YOU.
I KNOW THAT.
02 : 53
YOU'VE PROBABLY DONE THIS LOADS OF TIMES, BUT I HAVE A REPUTATION...
YOU KNOW, GIRL...
...I'VE REALLY HAD A LOTTA FUN TONIGHT.
I MEAN, YOU AND ME, THAT COULD GO ON AND ON, COULDN'T IT?
02 : 54
BUT YOU KNOW, IT MUSTN'T HAPPEN AGAIN...
I'M YOUR LEGAL GUARDIAN, FOR HEAVENSAKE.
IT ISN'T FAIR.
YOU SHOULDN'T PUT ME IN THIS POSITION.
YOU GIRLS...
...YOU JUST DON'T KNOW WHAT YOU DO TO A GUY...

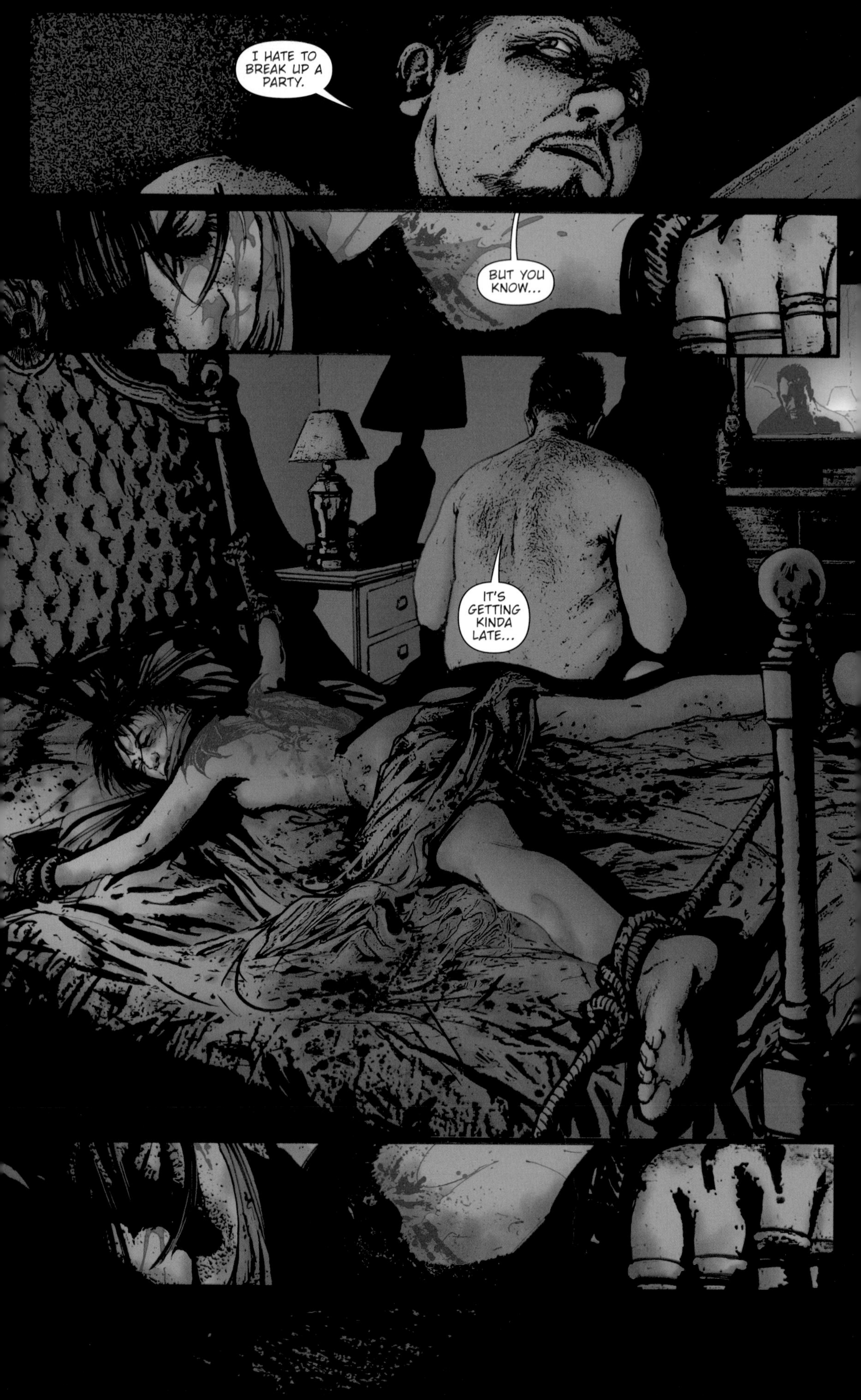
I HATE TO BREAK UP A PARTY.
BUT YOU KNOW...
IT'S GETTING KINDA LATE...

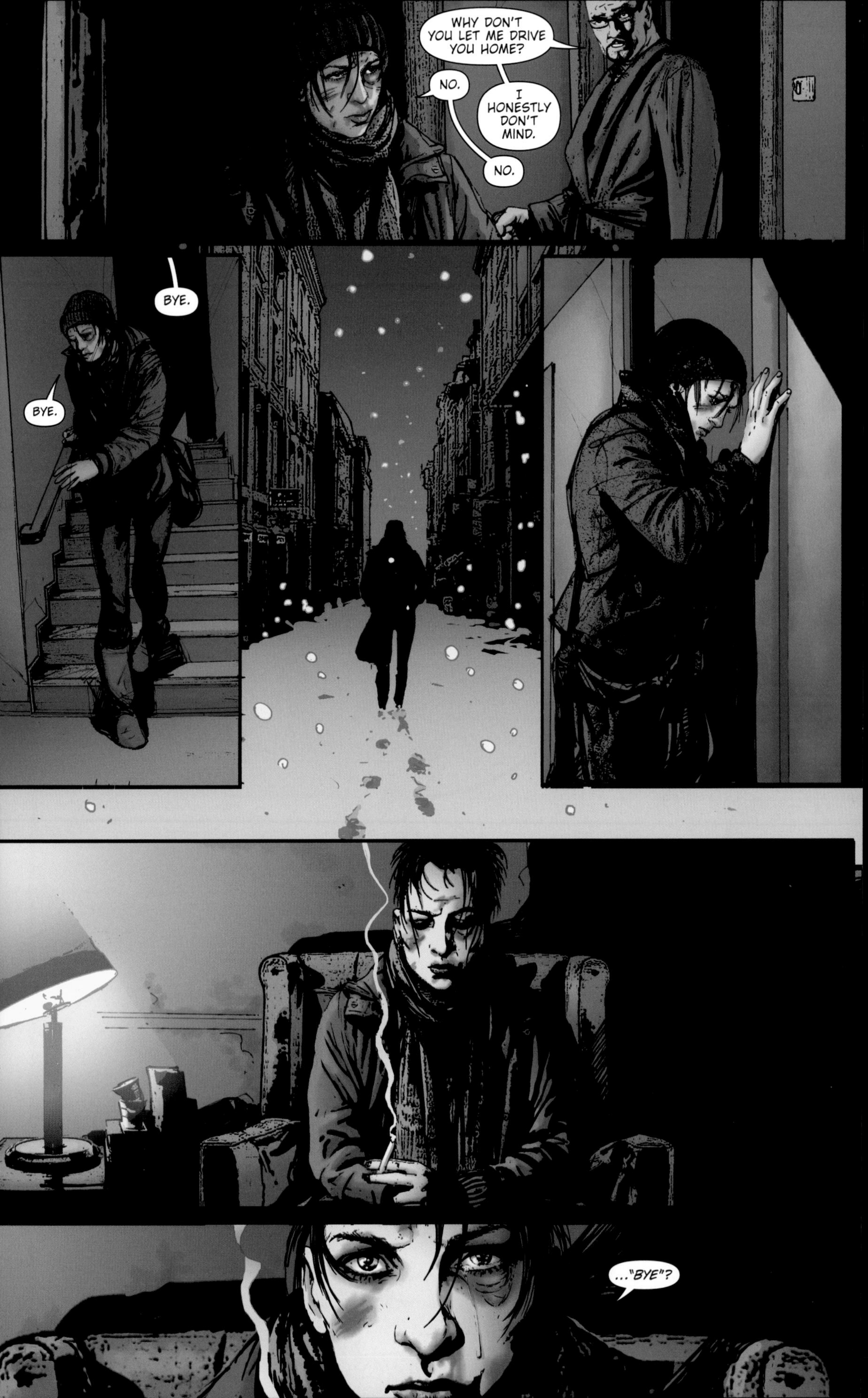
WHY DON'T YOU LET ME DRIVE YOU HOME?
NO.
I HONESTLY DON'T MIND.
NO.
BYE.
BYE.
..."BYE"?

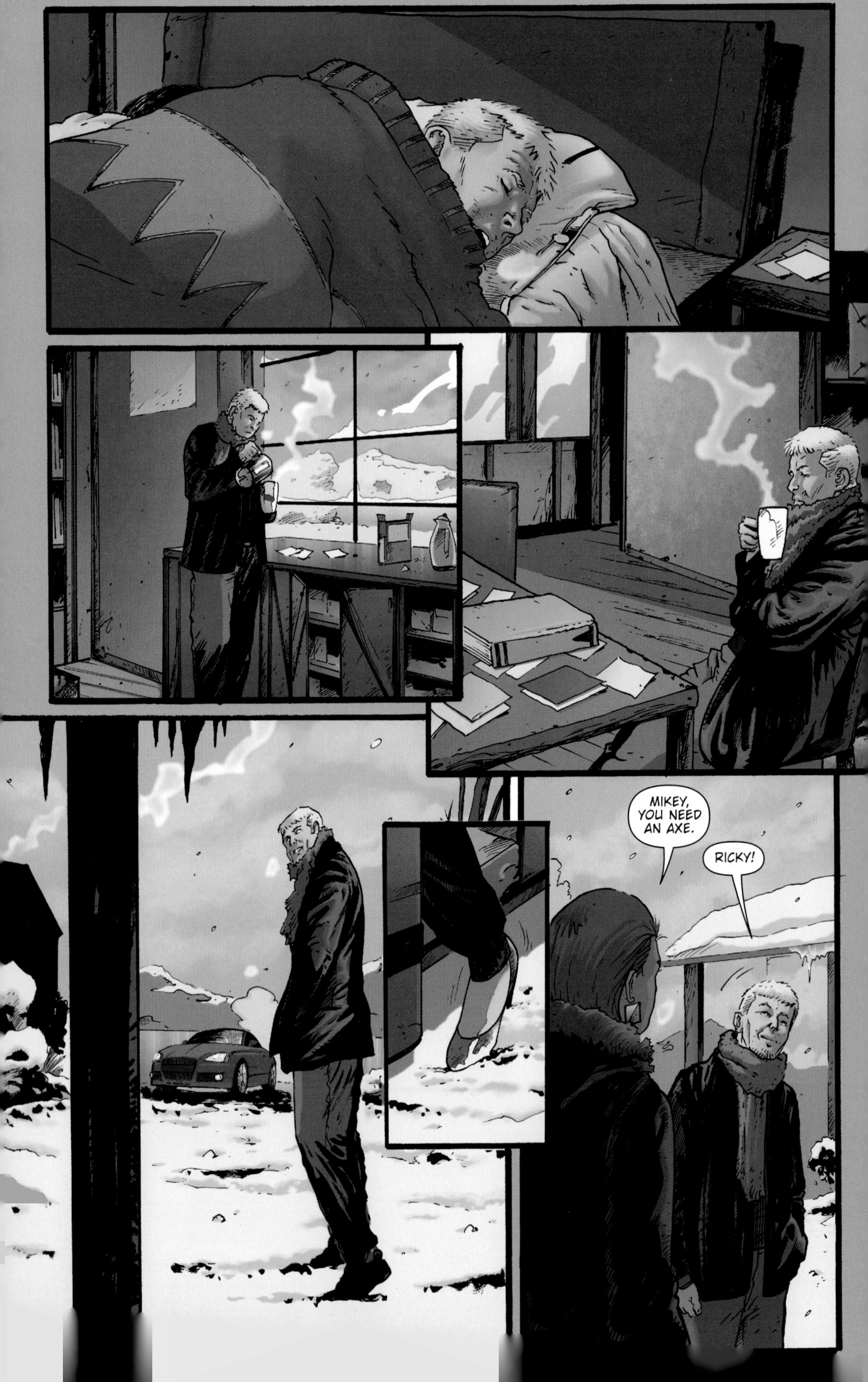
MIKEY, YOU NEED AN AXE.
RICKY!

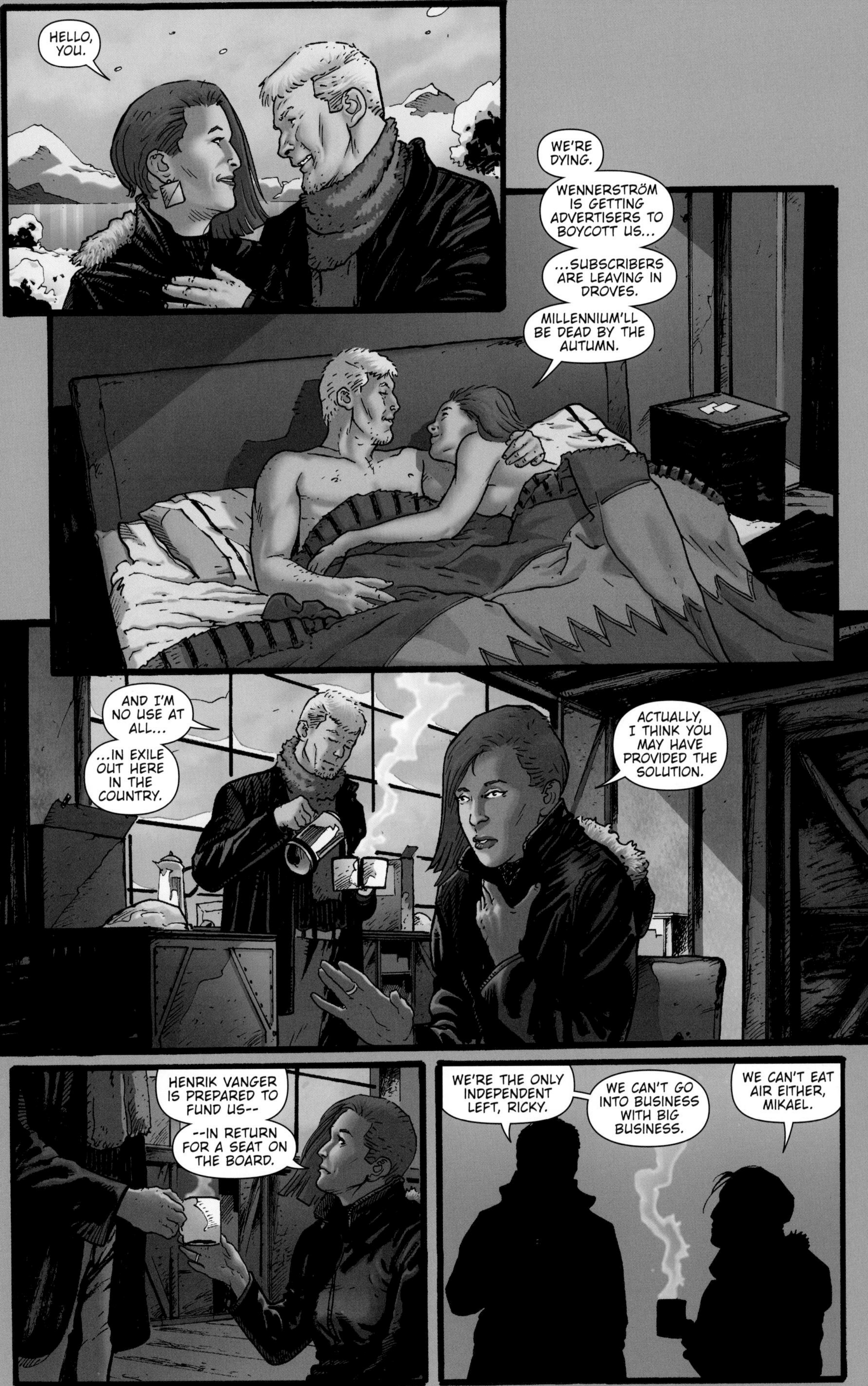
HELLO, YOU.
WE'RE DYING.
WENNERSTRÖM IS GETTING ADVERTISERS TO BOYCOTT US...
...SUBSCRIBERS ARE LEAVING IN DROVES.
MILLENNIUM'LL BE DEAD BY THE AUTUMN.
AND I'M NO USE AT ALL...
...IN EXILE OUT HERE IN THE COUNTRY.
ACTUALLY, I THINK YOU MAY HAVE PROVIDED THE SOLUTION.
HENRIK VANGER IS PREPARED TO FUND US--
--IN RETURN FOR A SEAT ON THE BOARD.
WE'RE THE ONLY INDEPENDENT LEFT, RICKY.
WE CAN'T GO INTO BUSINESS WITH BIG BUSINESS.
WE CAN'T EAT AIR EITHER, MIKAEL.

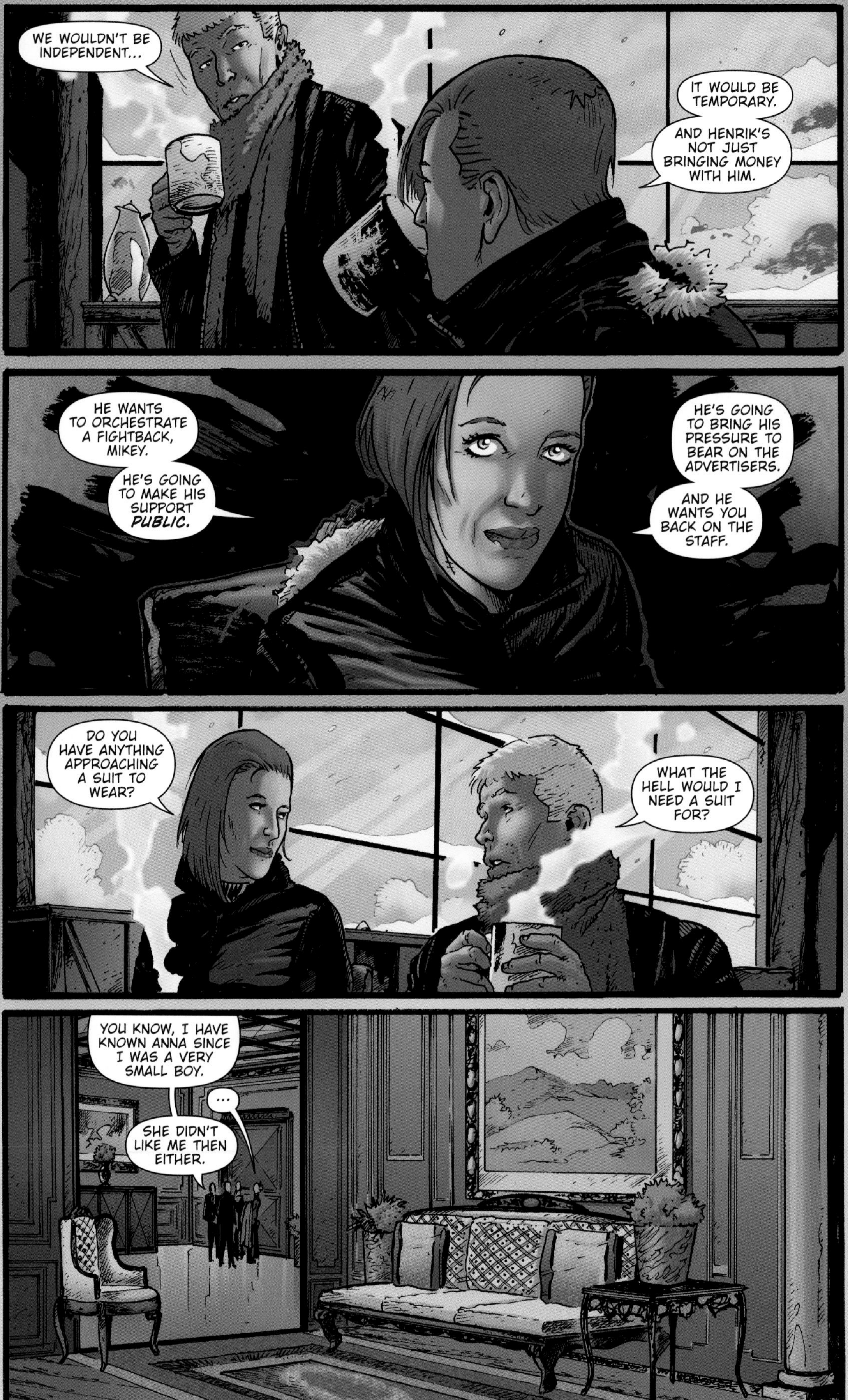
WE WOULDN'T BE INDEPENDENT...
IT WOULD BE TEMPORARY.
AND HENRIK'S NOT JUST BRINGING MONEY WITH HIM.
HE WANTS TO ORCHESTRATE A FIGHTBACK, MIKEY.
HE'S GOING TO MAKE HIS SUPPORT *PUBLIC.*
HE'S GOING TO BRING HIS PRESSURE TO BEAR ON THE ADVERTISERS.
AND HE WANTS YOU BACK ON THE STAFF.
DO YOU HAVE ANYTHING APPROACHING A SUIT TO WEAR?
WHAT THE HELL WOULD I NEED A SUIT FOR?
YOU KNOW, I HAVE KNOWN ANNA SINCE I WAS A VERY SMALL BOY.
...
SHE DIDN'T LIKE ME THEN EITHER.

--SAID, "I'M AFRAID HE'S IN A COMA." HE FELL TO HIS KNEES AND SAID "OH DEAR GOD! WHERE IS HE?" AND THE WIFE SAID, "OH, WELL, THE THING IS, IT'S AWKWARD BECAUSE HE DOESN'T WANT ANYONE TO KNOW HE'S IN A COMA."

MARVELOUS! MUST REMEMBER THAT ONE.

HA!

IN CASE YOU NEED IT, MARTIN?

WELL, YOU KNOW, THE WAY THINGS ARE GOING WITH THE VANGER CORPORATION...

EXACTLY!

GOOD TO HAVE A FEW MOVES UP YOUR SLEEVE?

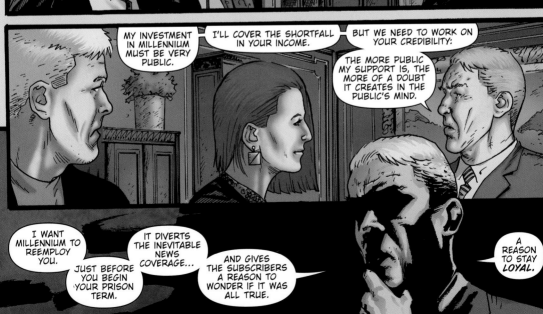

MY INVESTMENT IN MILLENNIUM MUST BE VERY PUBLIC.

I'LL COVER THE SHORTFALL IN YOUR INCOME.

BUT WE NEED TO WORK ON YOUR CREDIBILITY:

THE MORE PUBLIC MY SUPPORT IS, THE MORE OF A DOUBT IT CREATES IN THE PUBLIC'S MIND.

I WANT MILLENNIUM TO REEMPLOY YOU.

JUST BEFORE YOU BEGIN YOUR PRISON TERM.

IT DIVERTS THE INEVITABLE NEWS COVERAGE...

AND GIVES THE SUBSCRIBERS A REASON TO WONDER IF IT WAS ALL TRUE.

A REASON TO STAY *LOYAL*.

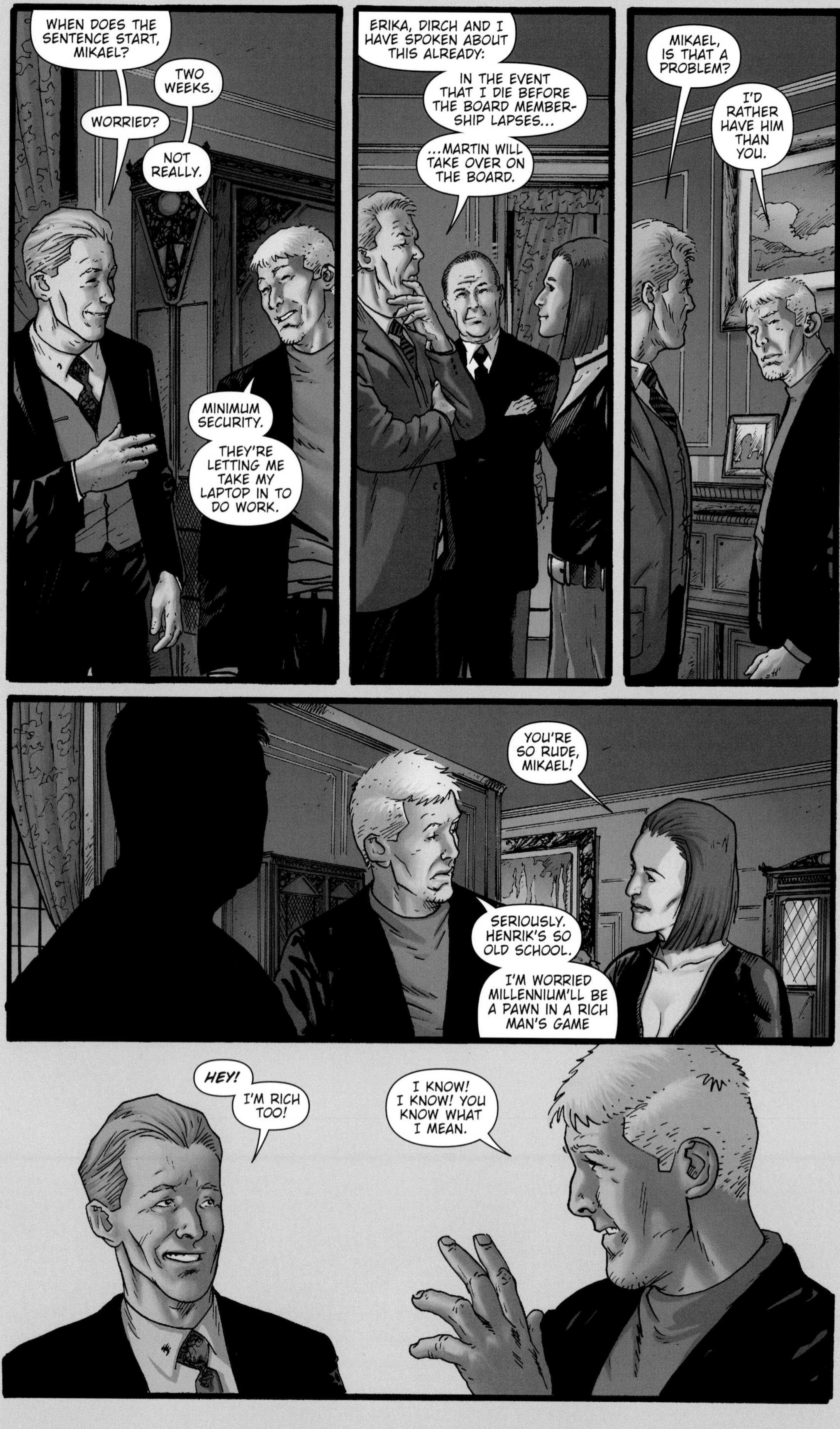
WHEN DOES THE SENTENCE START, MIKAEL?
TWO WEEKS.
WORRIED?
NOT REALLY.
MINIMUM SECURITY.
THEY'RE LETTING ME TAKE MY LAPTOP IN TO DO WORK.
ERIKA, DIRCH AND I HAVE SPOKEN ABOUT THIS ALREADY:
IN THE EVENT THAT I DIE BEFORE THE BOARD MEMBERSHIP LAPSES...
...MARTIN WILL TAKE OVER ON THE BOARD.
MIKAEL, IS THAT A PROBLEM?
I'D RATHER HAVE HIM THAN YOU.
YOU'RE SO RUDE, MIKAEL!
SERIOUSLY. HENRIK'S SO OLD SCHOOL.
I'M WORRIED MILLENNIUM'LL BE A PAWN IN A RICH MAN'S GAME
HEY!
I'M RICH TOO!
I KNOW! I KNOW! YOU KNOW WHAT I MEAN.

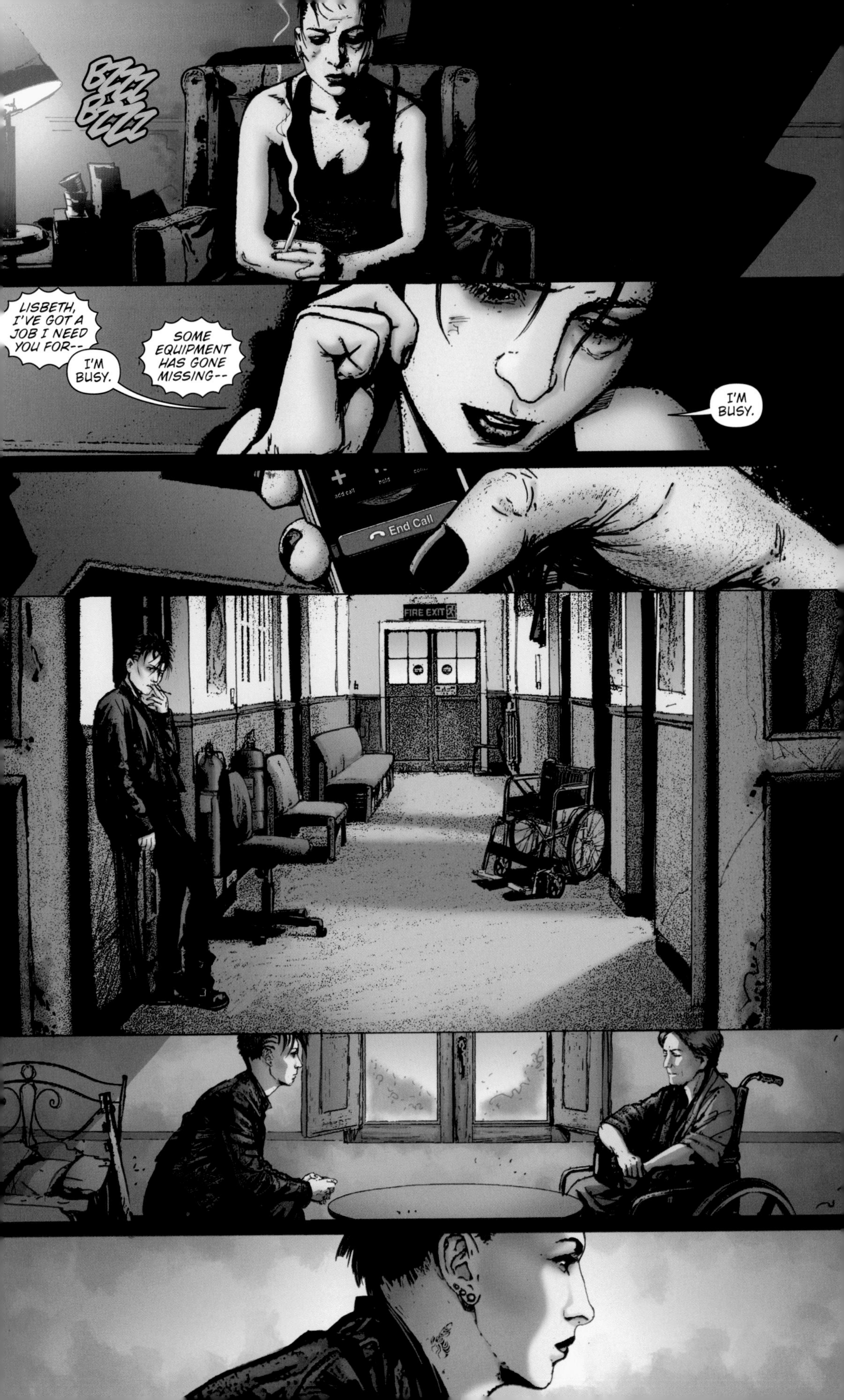
BZZZ BZZZ
LISBETH, I'VE GOT A JOB I NEED YOU FOR--
I'M BUSY.
SOME EQUIPMENT HAS GONE MISSING--
I'M BUSY.
End Call
FIRE EXIT

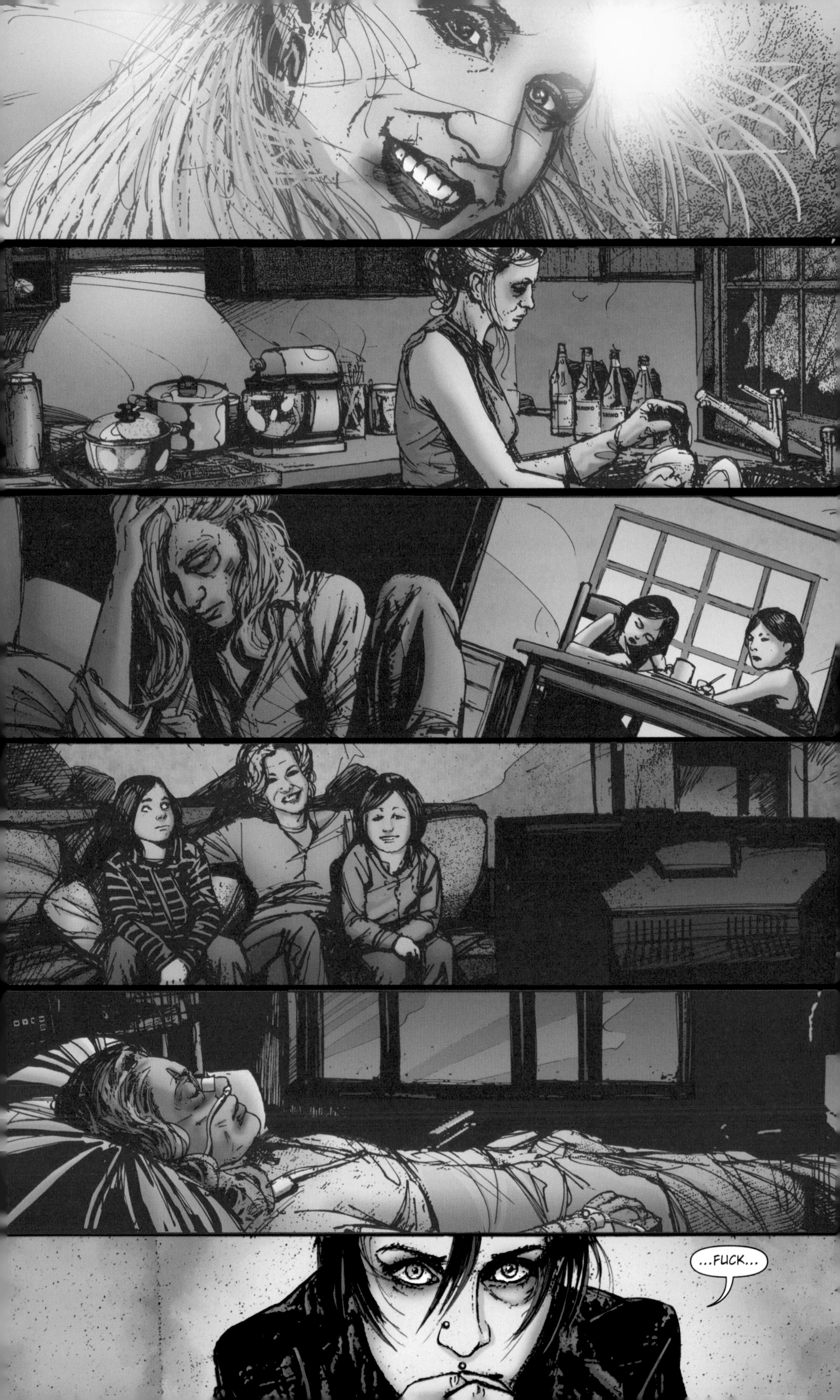
...FUCK...

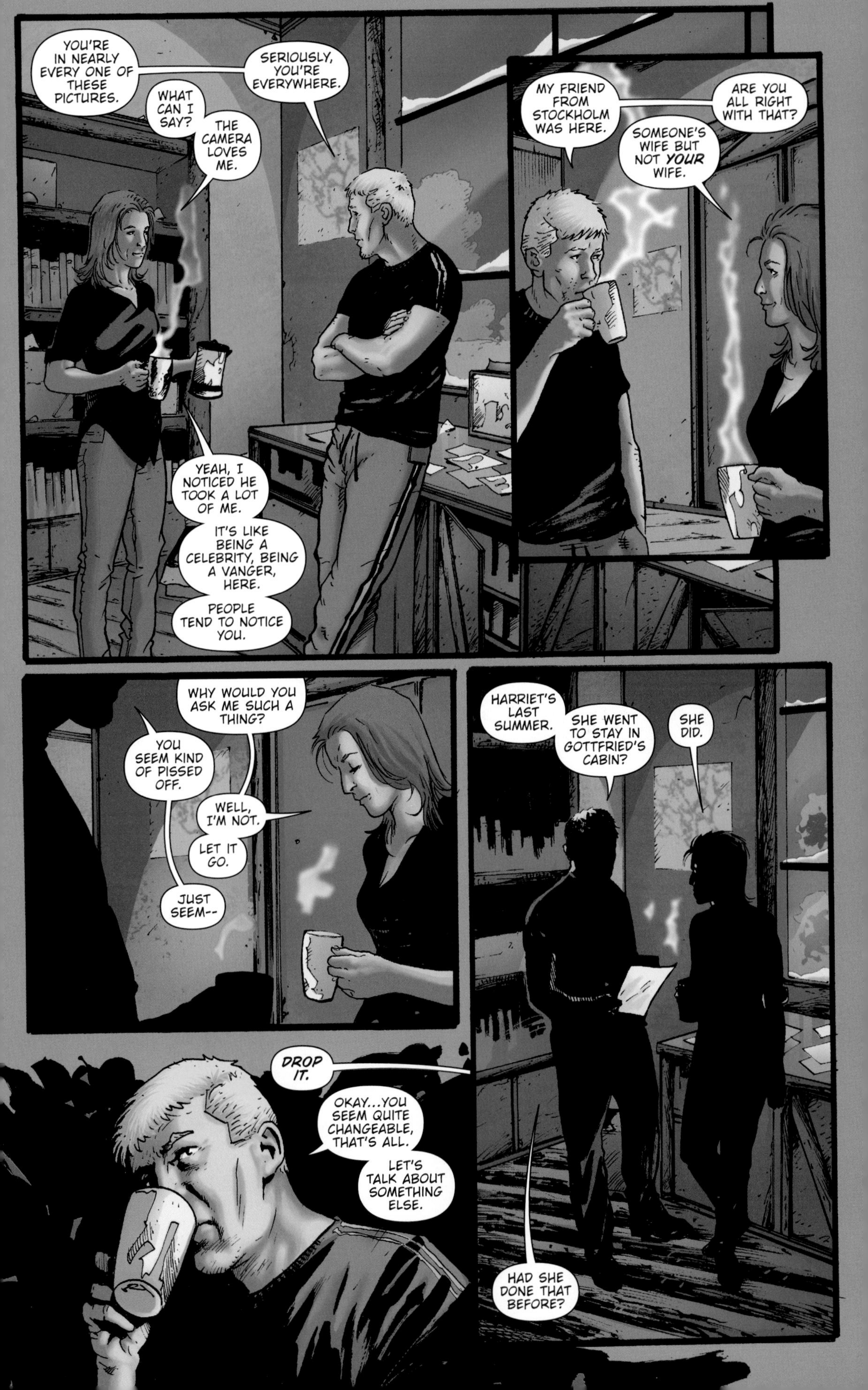
YOU'RE IN NEARLY EVERY ONE OF THESE PICTURES.
SERIOUSLY, YOU'RE EVERYWHERE.
WHAT CAN I SAY?
THE CAMERA LOVES ME.
YEAH, I NOTICED HE TOOK A LOT OF ME.
IT'S LIKE BEING A CELEBRITY, BEING A VANGER, HERE.
PEOPLE TEND TO NOTICE YOU.
MY FRIEND FROM STOCKHOLM WAS HERE.
ARE YOU ALL RIGHT WITH THAT?
SOMEONE'S WIFE BUT NOT YOUR WIFE.
WHY WOULD YOU ASK ME SUCH A THING?
YOU SEEM KIND OF PISSED OFF.
WELL, I'M NOT.
LET IT GO.
JUST SEEM--
DROP IT.
OKAY...YOU SEEM QUITE CHANGEABLE, THAT'S ALL.
LET'S TALK ABOUT SOMETHING ELSE.
HARRIET'S LAST SUMMER.
SHE WENT TO STAY IN GOTTFRIED'S CABIN?
SHE DID.
HAD SHE DONE THAT BEFORE?

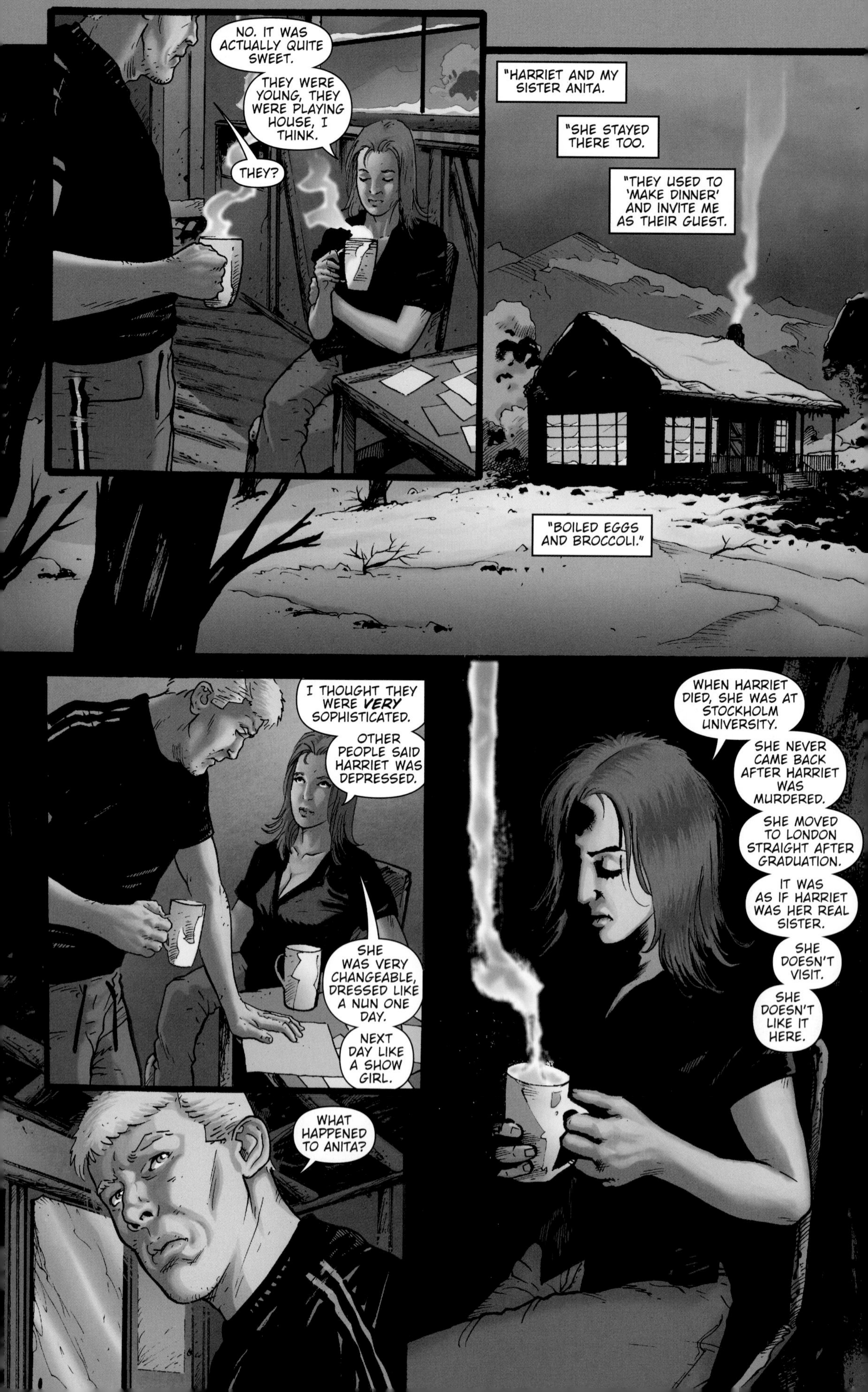
NO. IT WAS ACTUALLY QUITE SWEET.
THEY WERE YOUNG, THEY WERE PLAYING HOUSE, I THINK.
THEY?
"HARRIET AND MY SISTER ANITA.
"SHE STAYED THERE TOO.
"THEY USED TO 'MAKE DINNER' AND INVITE ME AS THEIR GUEST.
"BOILED EGGS AND BROCCOLI."
I THOUGHT THEY WERE VERY SOPHISTICATED.
OTHER PEOPLE SAID HARRIET WAS DEPRESSED.
SHE WAS VERY CHANGEABLE, DRESSED LIKE A NUN ONE DAY.
NEXT DAY LIKE A SHOW GIRL.
WHAT HAPPENED TO ANITA?
WHEN HARRIET DIED, SHE WAS AT STOCKHOLM UNIVERSITY.
SHE NEVER CAME BACK AFTER HARRIET WAS MURDERED.
SHE MOVED TO LONDON STRAIGHT AFTER GRADUATION.
IT WAS AS IF HARRIET WAS HER REAL SISTER.
SHE DOESN'T VISIT.
SHE DOESN'T LIKE IT HERE.

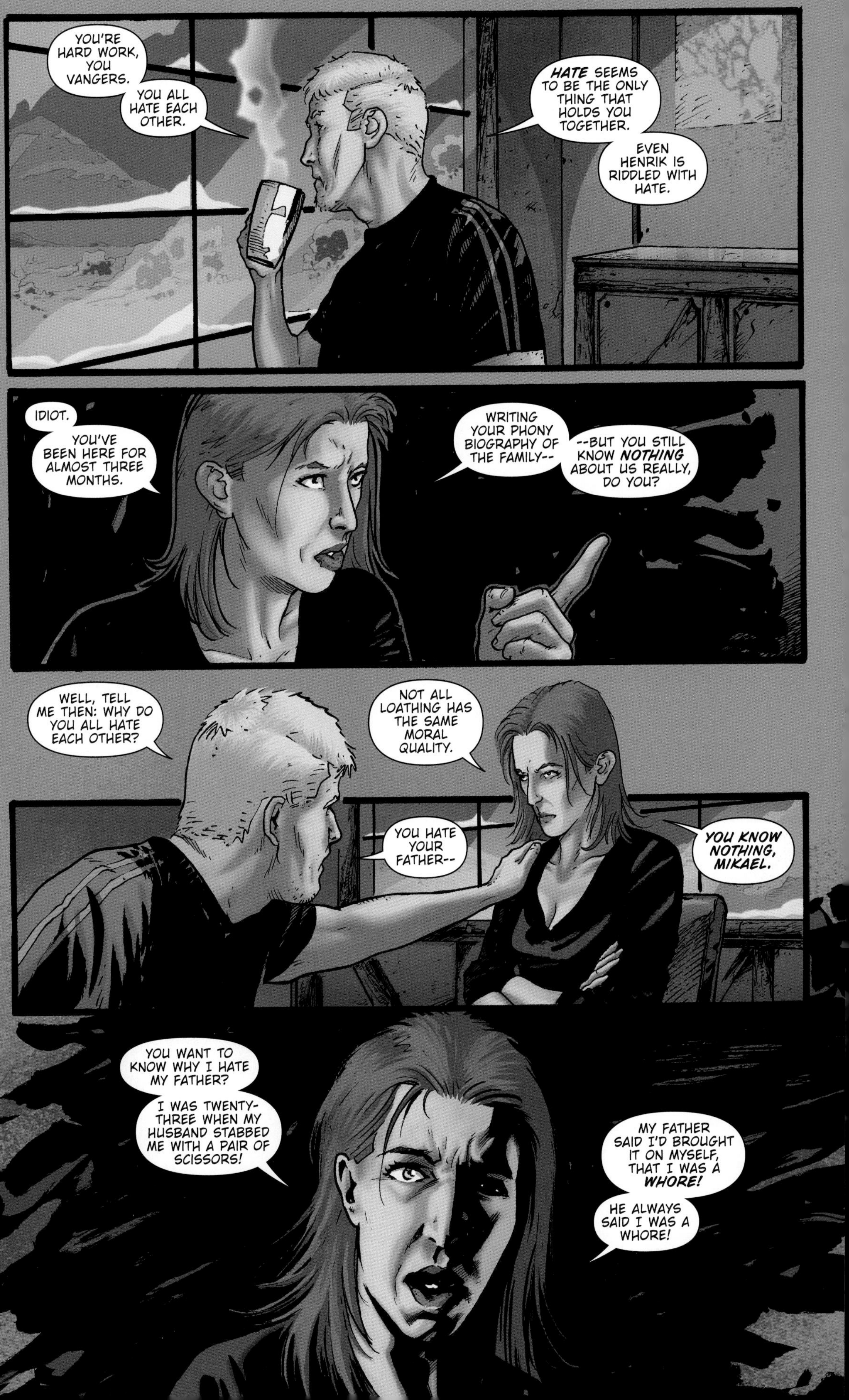
YOU'RE HARD WORK, YOU VANGERS.
YOU ALL HATE EACH OTHER.
HATE SEEMS TO BE THE ONLY THING THAT HOLDS YOU TOGETHER.
EVEN HENRIK IS RIDDLED WITH HATE.
IDIOT.
YOU'VE BEEN HERE FOR ALMOST THREE MONTHS.
WRITING YOUR PHONY BIOGRAPHY OF THE FAMILY--
--BUT YOU STILL KNOW NOTHING ABOUT US REALLY, DO YOU?
WELL, TELL ME THEN: WHY DO YOU ALL HATE EACH OTHER?
NOT ALL LOATHING HAS THE SAME MORAL QUALITY.
YOU HATE YOUR FATHER--
YOU KNOW NOTHING, MIKAEL.
YOU WANT TO KNOW WHY I HATE MY FATHER?
I WAS TWENTY-THREE WHEN MY HUSBAND STABBED ME WITH A PAIR OF SCISSORS!
MY FATHER SAID I'D BROUGHT IT ON MYSELF, THAT I WAS A WHORE!
HE ALWAYS SAID I WAS A WHORE!

SO YOU DON'T GET ON AND HE'S AN ANGRY OLD MAN?

WHEN I WAS NINETEEN I WENT OUT ON A DATE.

I WENT TO GET MY PURSE.

WHEN I CAME BACK...

...HE HAD INTERVIEWED THE GUY

A *QUARTER* JEW.

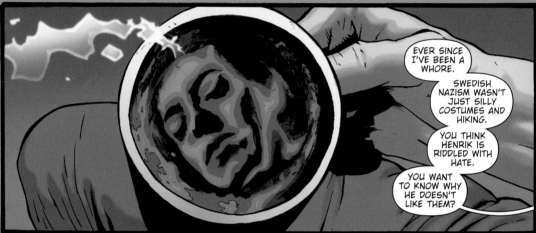

EVER SINCE I'VE BEEN A WHORE.

SWEDISH NAZISM WASN'T JUST SILLY COSTUMES AND HIKING.

YOU THINK HENRIK IS RIDDLED WITH HATE.

YOU WANT TO KNOW WHY HE DOESN'T LIKE THEM?

HENRIK'S WIFE, EDITH, CAME FROM MUNICH WITH HIM IN 1939.

HE KNEW WHAT THEY WOULD SAY.

HE ONLY MEANT TO SAVE HER LIFE.

BUT THEY FELL IN LOVE ON THE VOYAGE OVER.

HE MARRIED HER KNOWING THAT HIS BROTHERS WOULD NEVER SPEAK TO HIM AGAIN.

HE DOESN'T HATE THEM.

HE JUST KNOWS WHAT THEY ARE.

EDITH WAS A JEWISH REFUGEE?

WORSE: EDITH WAS A JEWISH *LADY*.

SHE HAD MORE BREEDING AND GRACE THAN ANY OF THEIR WIVES.

THEY NEVER FORGAVE HENRIK.

THAT'S WHY THEY MURDERED HARRIET.

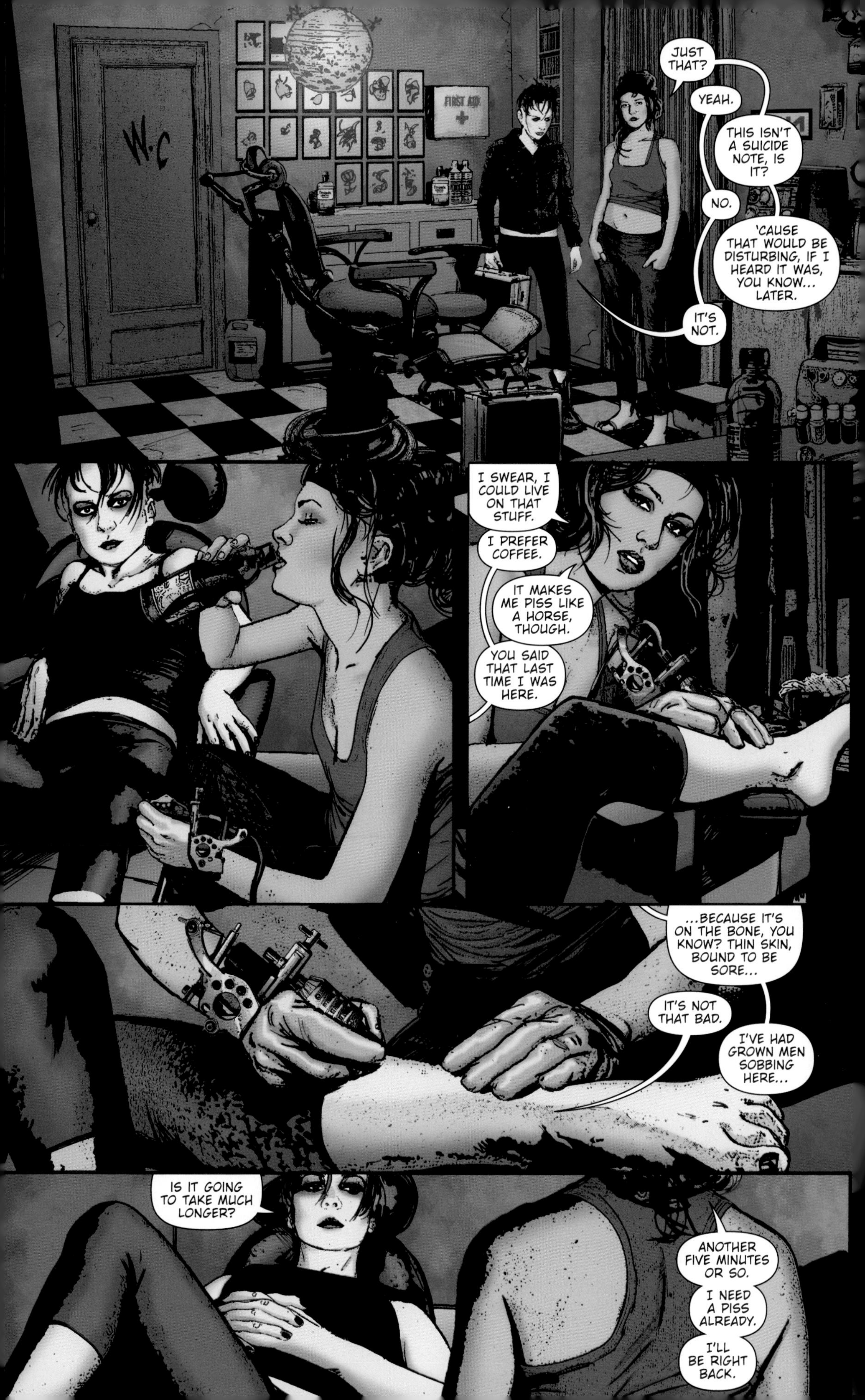
JUST THAT?
YEAH.
THIS ISN'T A SUICIDE NOTE, IS IT?
NO.
'CAUSE THAT WOULD BE DISTURBING, IF I HEARD IT WAS, YOU KNOW... LATER.
IT'S NOT.
I SWEAR, I COULD LIVE ON THAT STUFF.
I PREFER COFFEE.
IT MAKES ME PISS LIKE A HORSE, THOUGH.
YOU SAID THAT LAST TIME I WAS HERE.
...BECAUSE IT'S ON THE BONE, YOU KNOW? THIN SKIN, BOUND TO BE SORE...
IT'S NOT THAT BAD.
I'VE HAD GROWN MEN SOBBING HERE...
IS IT GOING TO TAKE MUCH LONGER?
ANOTHER FIVE MINUTES OR SO.
I NEED A PISS ALREADY.
I'LL BE RIGHT BACK.

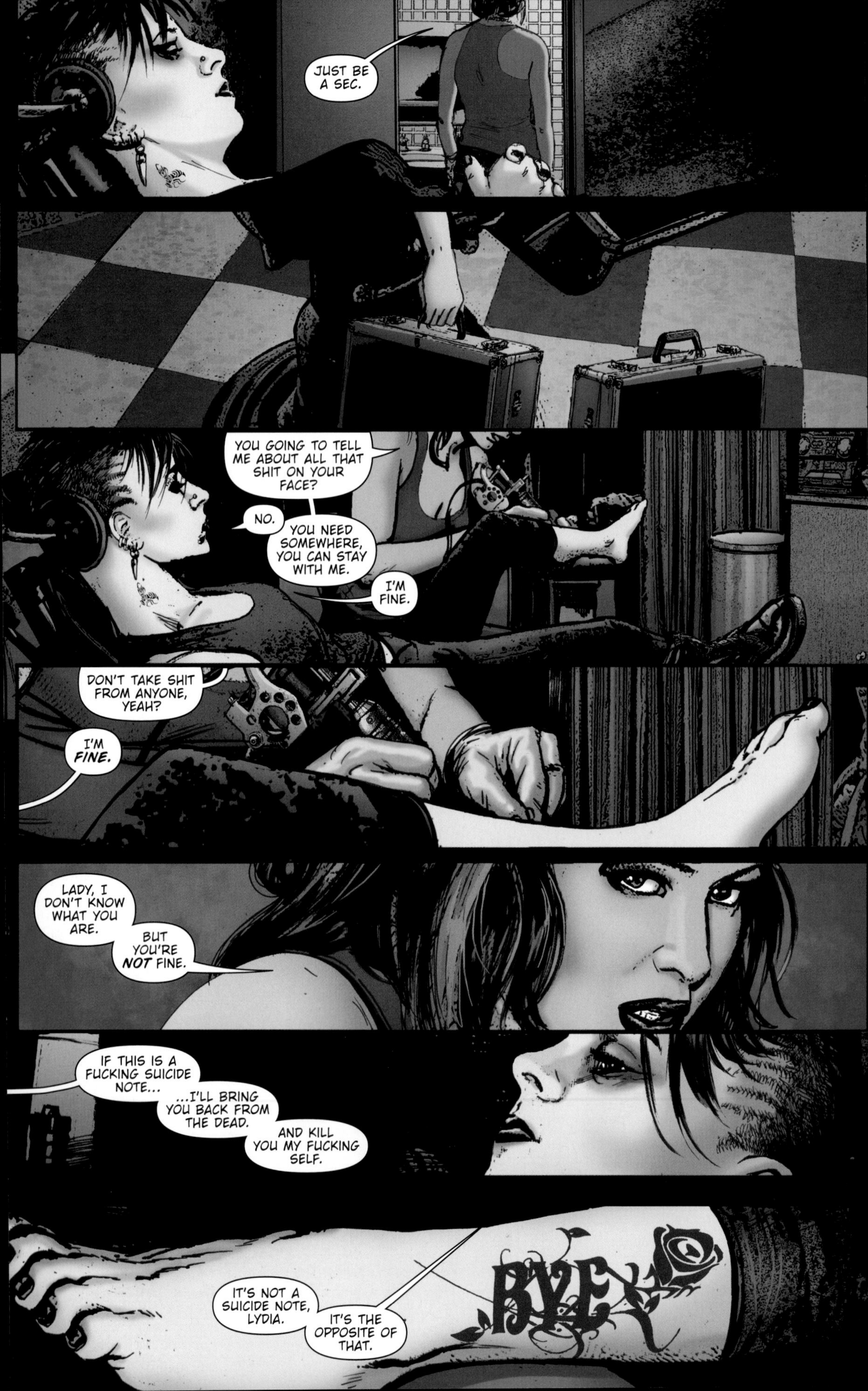
JUST BE A SEC.
YOU GOING TO TELL ME ABOUT ALL THAT SHIT ON YOUR FACE?
NO.
YOU NEED SOMEWHERE, YOU CAN STAY WITH ME.
I'M FINE.
DON'T TAKE SHIT FROM ANYONE, YEAH?
I'M **FINE.**
LADY, I DON'T KNOW WHAT YOU ARE.
BUT YOU'RE **NOT** FINE.
IF THIS IS A FUCKING SUICIDE NOTE...
...I'LL BRING YOU BACK FROM THE DEAD.
AND KILL YOU MY FUCKING SELF.
BYE
IT'S NOT A SUICIDE NOTE, LYDIA.
IT'S THE OPPOSITE OF THAT.

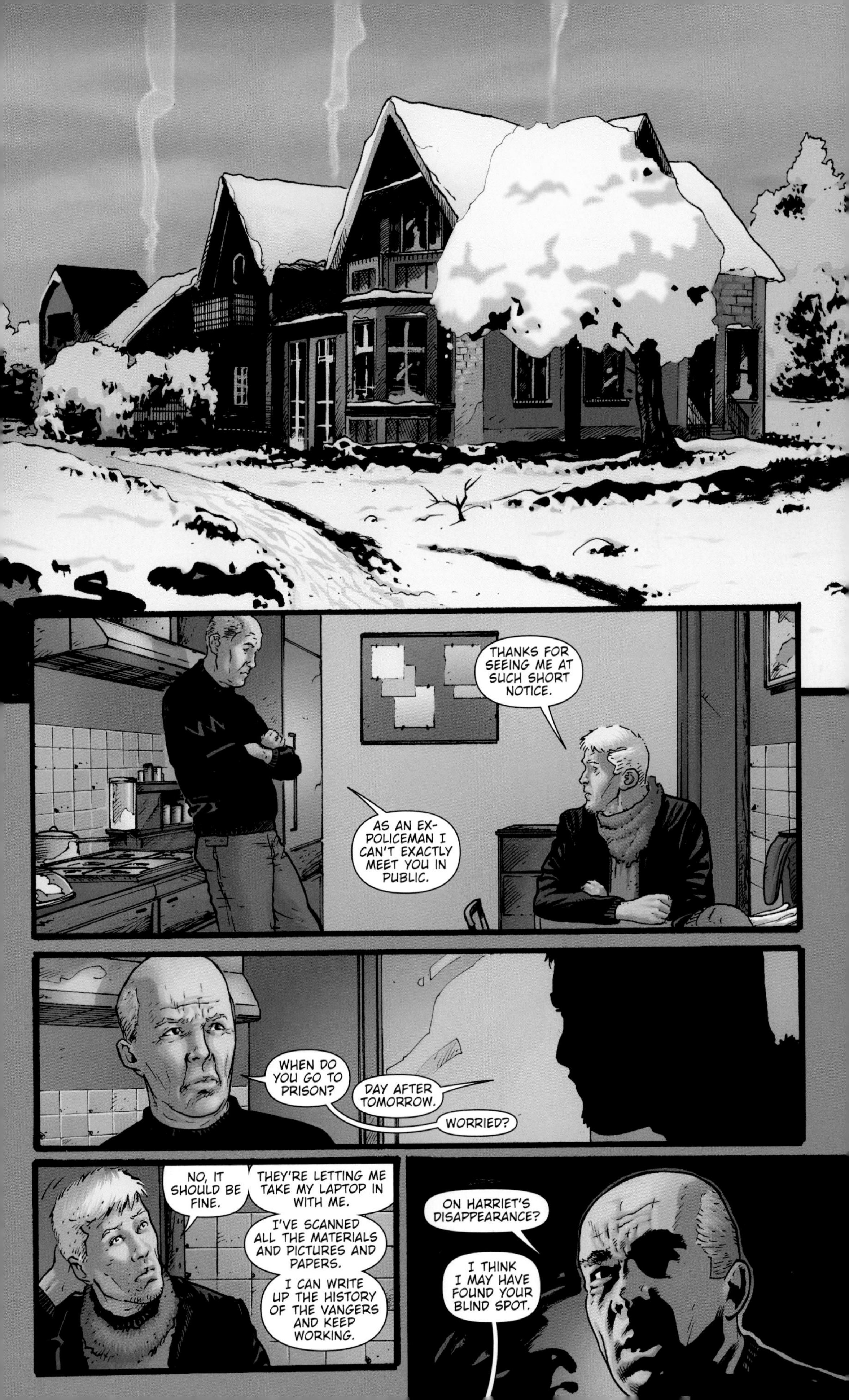
THANKS FOR SEEING ME AT SUCH SHORT NOTICE.
AS AN EX-POLICEMAN I CAN'T EXACTLY MEET YOU IN PUBLIC.
WHEN DO YOU GO TO PRISON?
DAY AFTER TOMORROW.
WORRIED?
NO, IT SHOULD BE FINE.
THEY'RE LETTING ME TAKE MY LAPTOP IN WITH ME.
I'VE SCANNED ALL THE MATERIALS AND PICTURES AND PAPERS.
I CAN WRITE UP THE HISTORY OF THE VANGERS AND KEEP WORKING.
ON HARRIET'S DISAPPEARANCE?
I THINK I MAY HAVE FOUND YOUR BLIND SPOT.

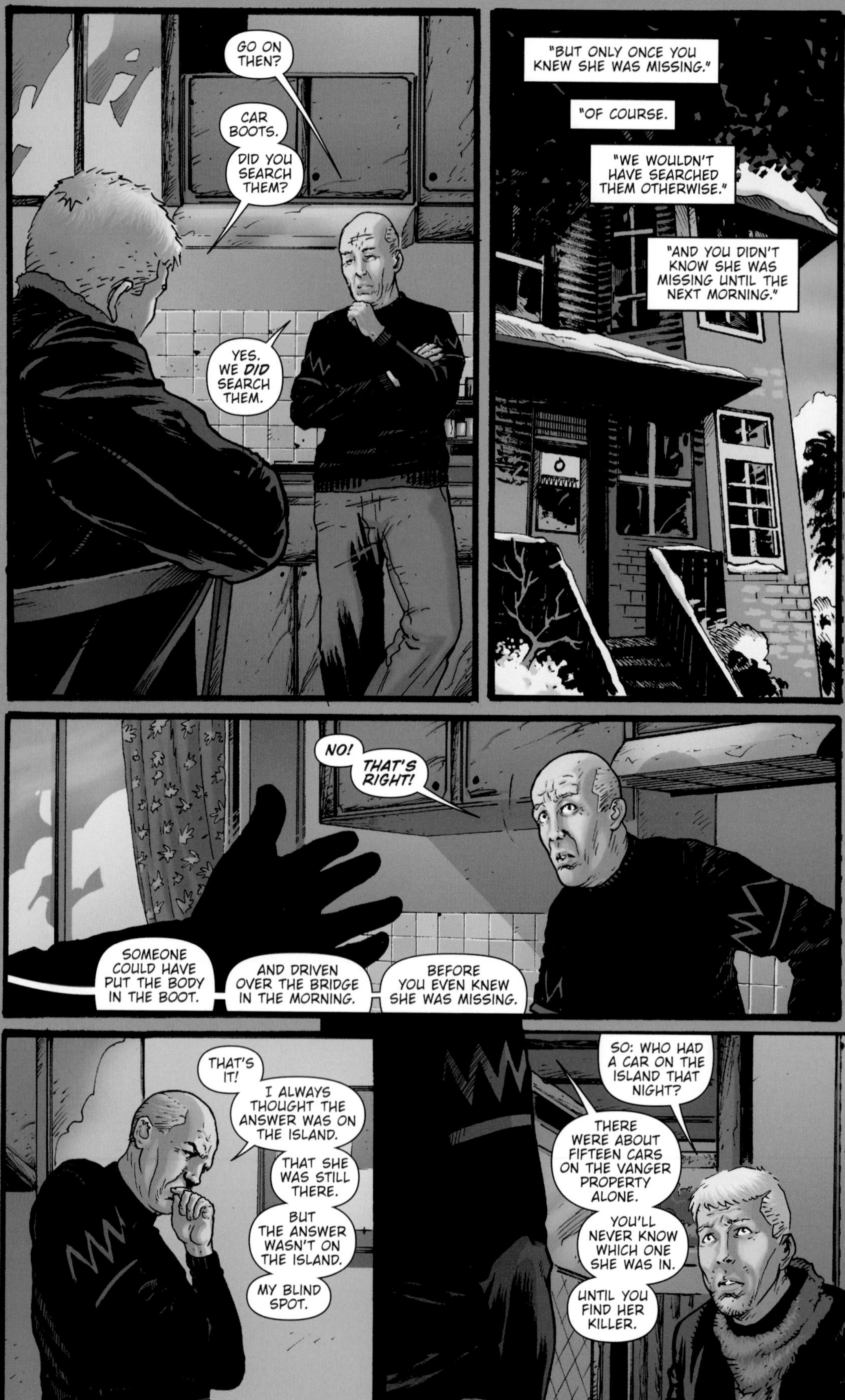
GO ON THEN?
CAR BOOTS.
DID YOU SEARCH THEM?
YES. WE *DID* SEARCH THEM.
"BUT ONLY ONCE YOU KNEW SHE WAS MISSING."
"OF COURSE.
"WE WOULDN'T HAVE SEARCHED THEM OTHERWISE."
"AND YOU DIDN'T KNOW SHE WAS MISSING UNTIL THE NEXT MORNING."
NO!
THAT'S RIGHT!
SOMEONE COULD HAVE PUT THE BODY IN THE BOOT.
AND DRIVEN OVER THE BRIDGE IN THE MORNING.
BEFORE YOU EVEN KNEW SHE WAS MISSING.
THAT'S IT!
I ALWAYS THOUGHT THE ANSWER WAS ON THE ISLAND.
THAT SHE WAS STILL THERE.
BUT THE ANSWER WASN'T ON THE ISLAND.
MY BLIND SPOT.
SO: WHO HAD A CAR ON THE ISLAND THAT NIGHT?
THERE WERE ABOUT FIFTEEN CARS ON THE VANGER PROPERTY ALONE.
YOU'LL NEVER KNOW WHICH ONE SHE WAS IN.
UNTIL YOU FIND HER KILLER.

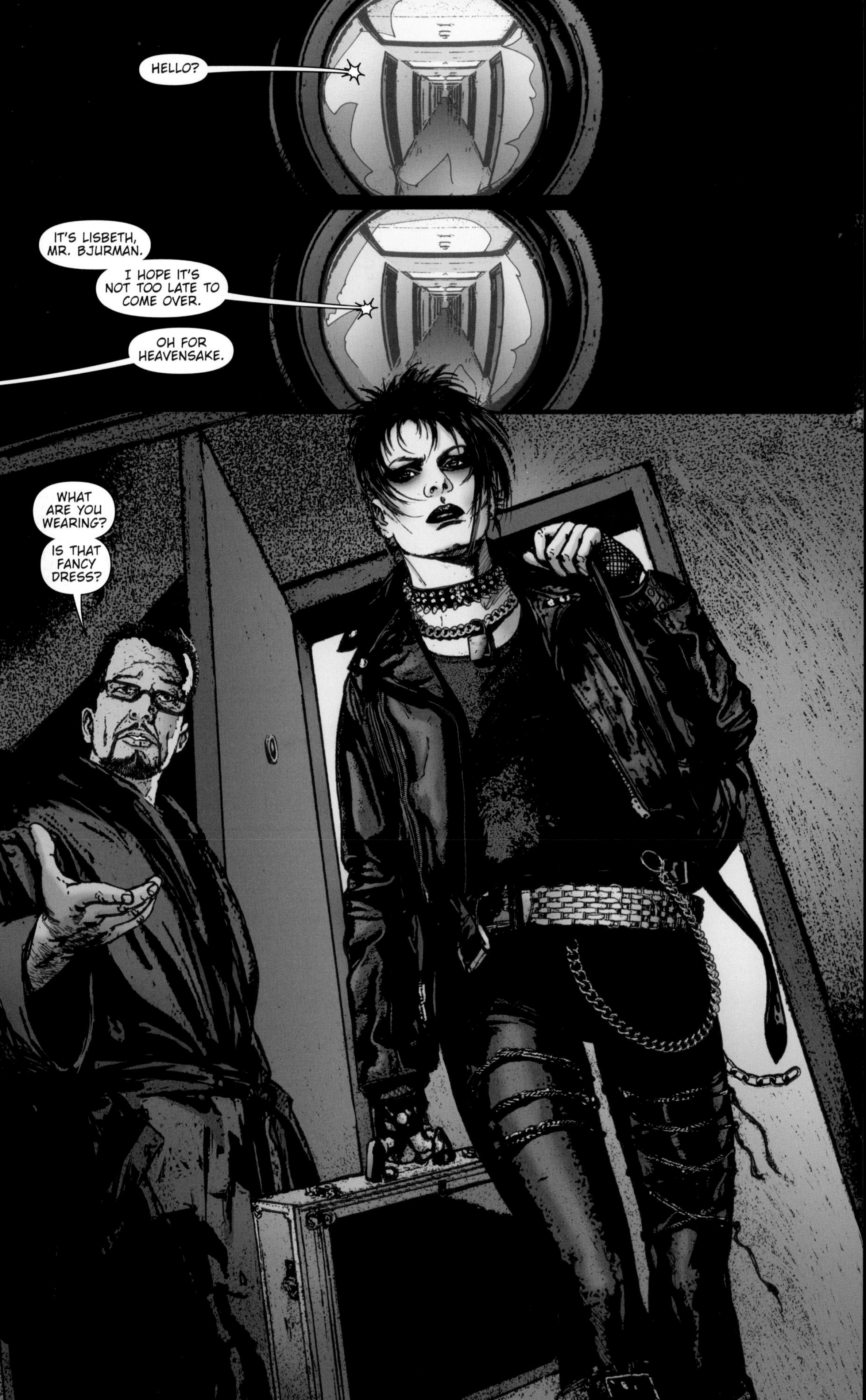
HELLO?
IT'S LISBETH, MR. BJURMAN.
I HOPE IT'S NOT TOO LATE TO COME OVER.
OH FOR HEAVENSAKE.
WHAT ARE YOU WEARING?
IS THAT FANCY DRESS?

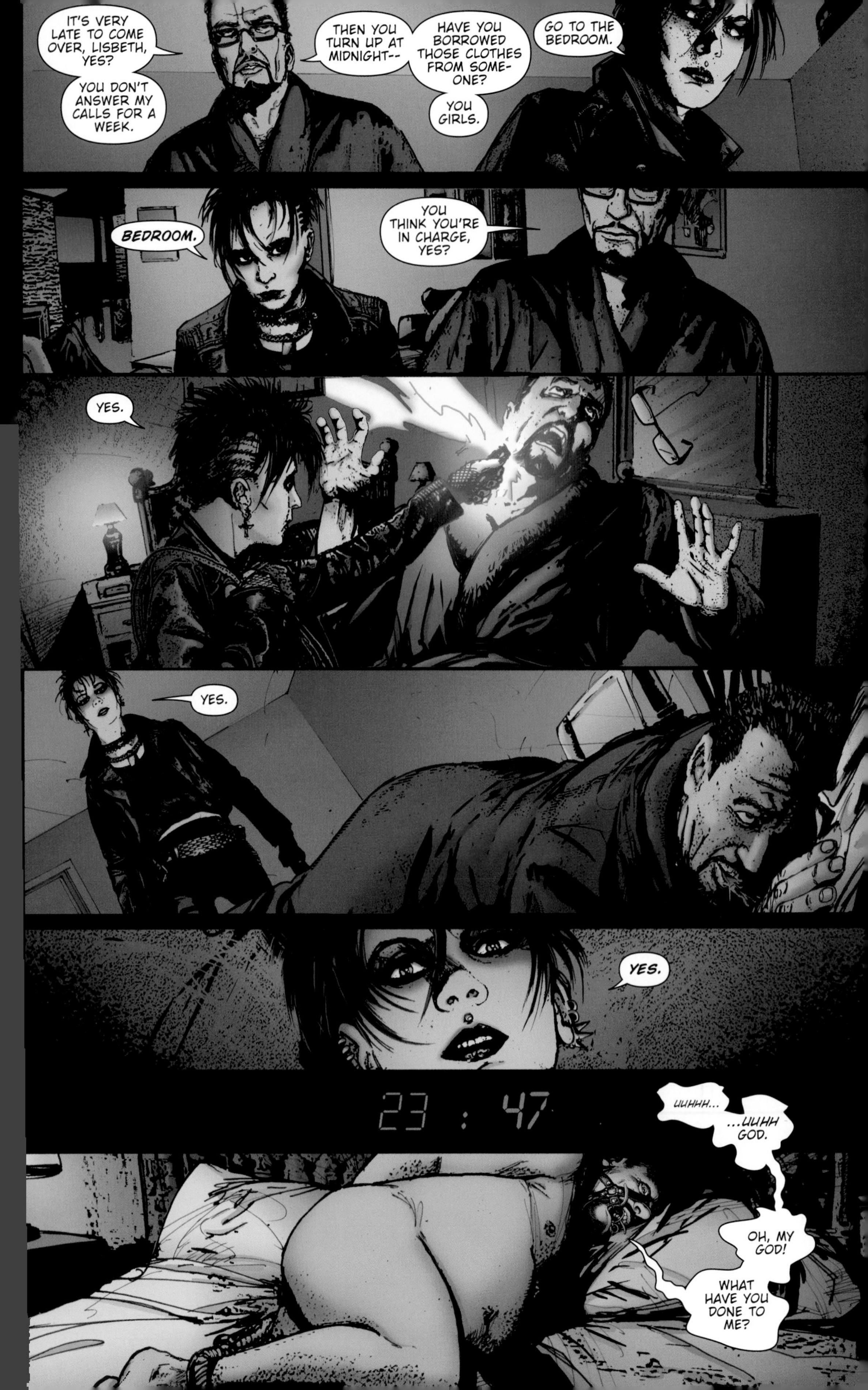
IT'S VERY LATE TO COME OVER, LISBETH, YES?
YOU DON'T ANSWER MY CALLS FOR A WEEK.
THEN YOU TURN UP AT MIDNIGHT--
HAVE YOU BORROWED THOSE CLOTHES FROM SOME-ONE?
YOU GIRLS.
GO TO THE BEDROOM.
BEDROOM.
YOU THINK YOU'RE IN CHARGE, YES?
YES.
YES.
YES.
23 : 47
uuhhh...
...uuhh god.
OH, MY GOD!
WHAT HAVE YOU DONE TO ME?

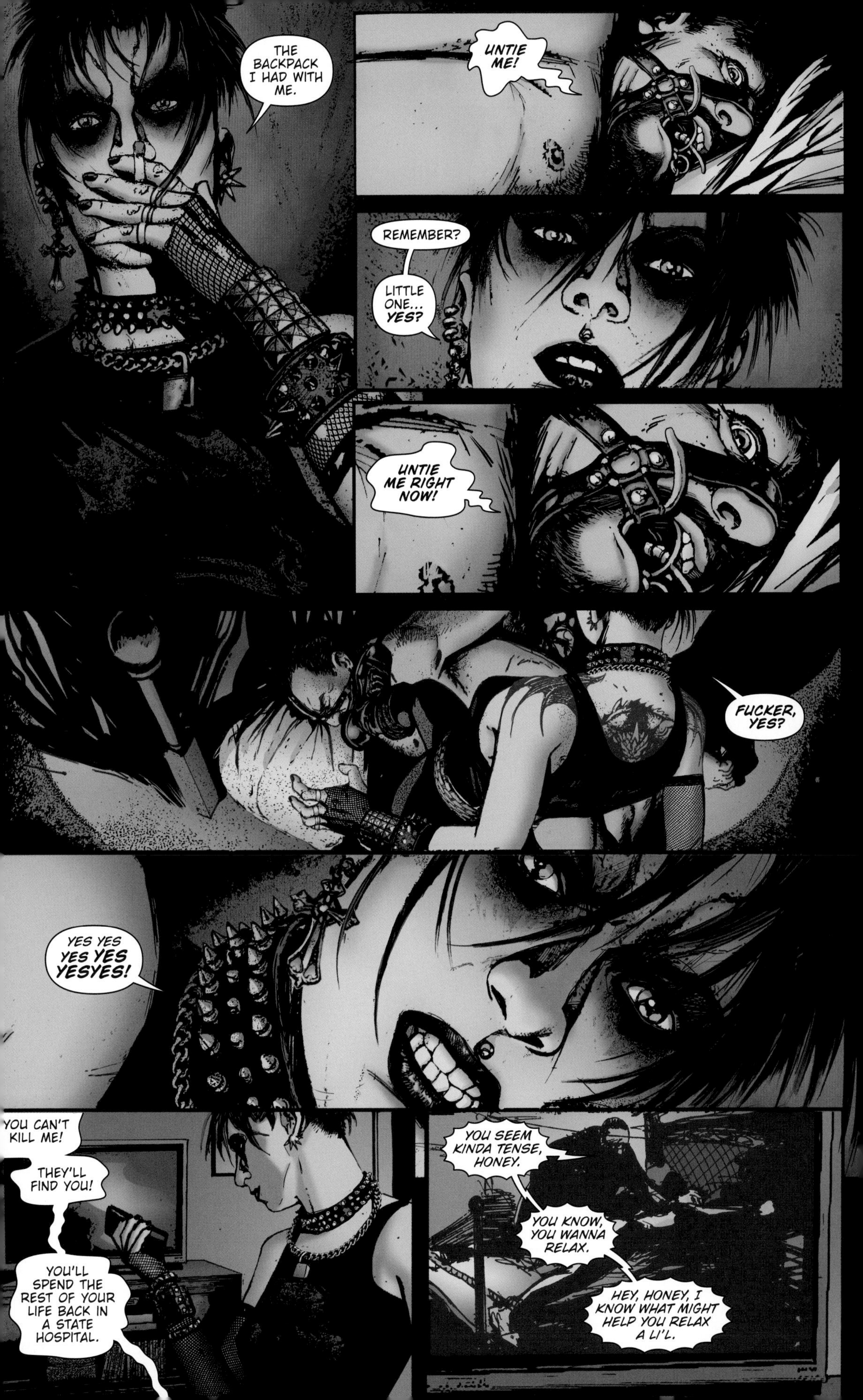
THE BACKPACK I HAD WITH ME.
UNTIE ME!
REMEMBER?
LITTLE ONE... YES?
UNTIE ME RIGHT NOW!
FUCKER, YES?
YES YES YES YES YESYES!
YOU CAN'T KILL ME!
THEY'LL FIND YOU!
YOU'LL SPEND THE REST OF YOUR LIFE BACK IN A STATE HOSPITAL.
YOU SEEM KINDA TENSE, HONEY.
YOU KNOW, YOU WANNA RELAX.
HEY, HONEY, I KNOW WHAT MIGHT HELP YOU RELAX A LI'L.

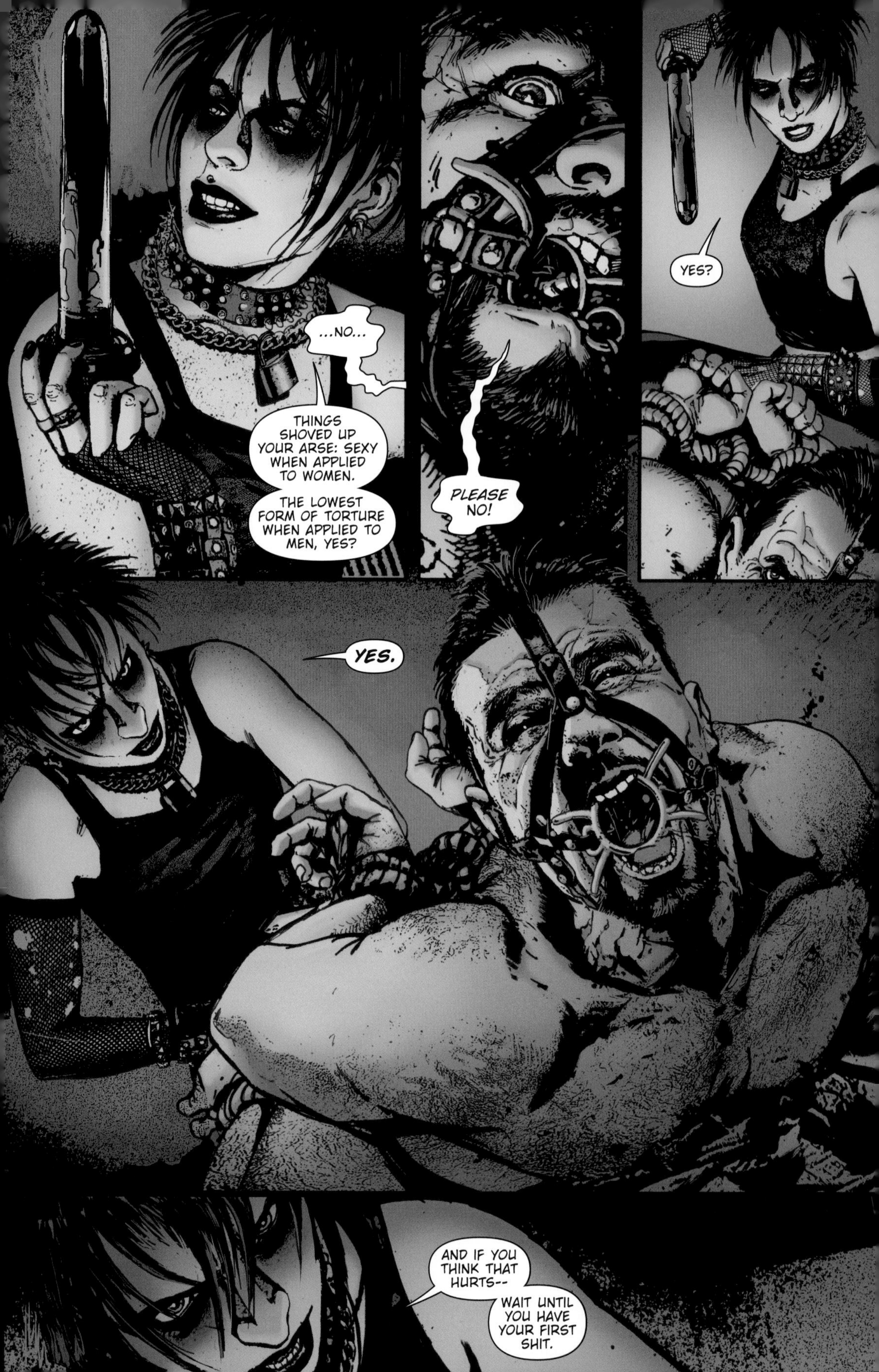
...NO...
THINGS SHOVED UP YOUR ARSE: SEXY WHEN APPLIED TO WOMEN.
THE LOWEST FORM OF TORTURE WHEN APPLIED TO MEN, YES?
PLEASE NO!
YES?
YES.
AND IF YOU THINK THAT HURTS--
WAIT UNTIL YOU HAVE YOUR FIRST SHIT.

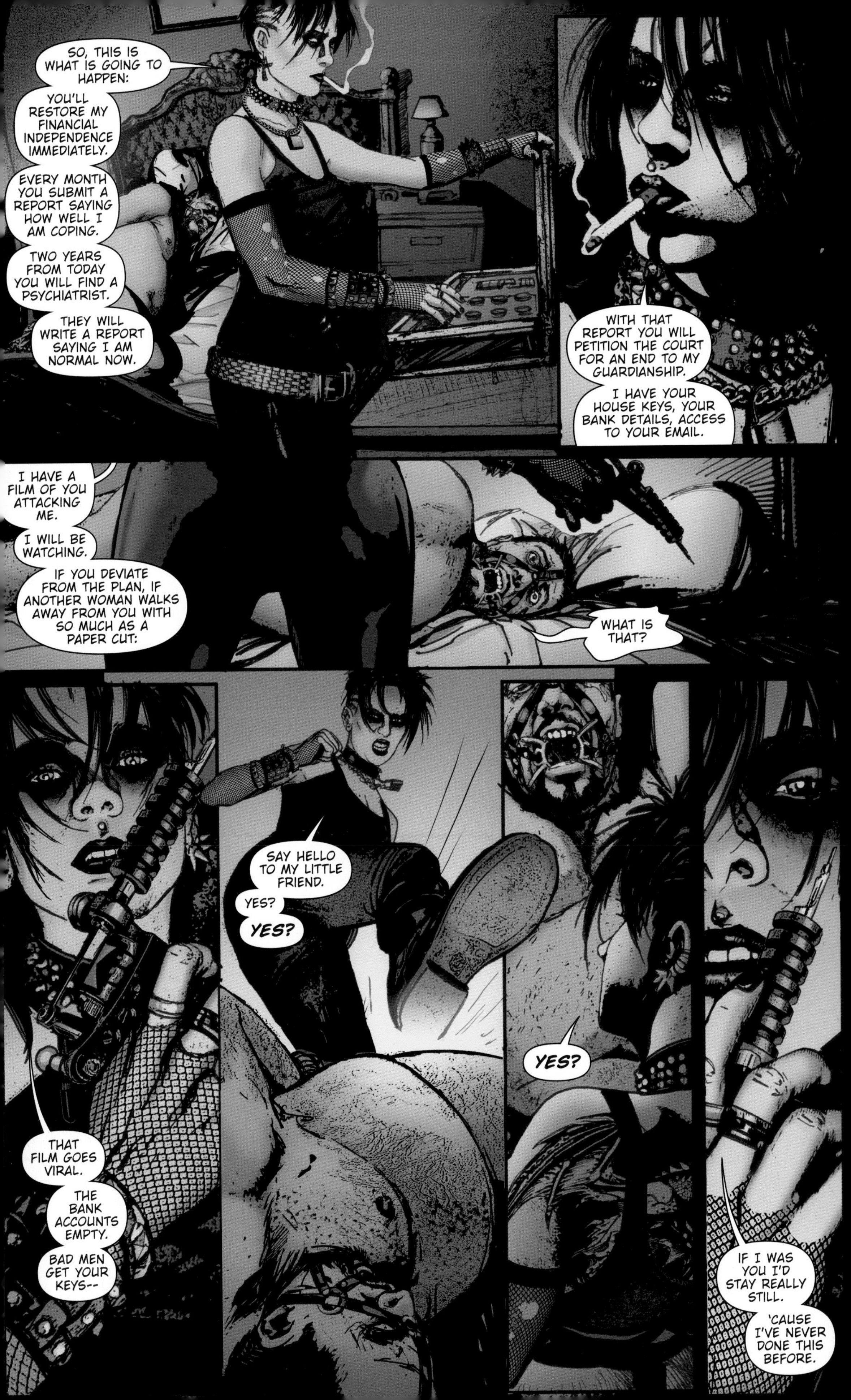
SO, THIS IS WHAT IS GOING TO HAPPEN:
YOU'LL RESTORE MY FINANCIAL INDEPENDENCE IMMEDIATELY.
EVERY MONTH YOU SUBMIT A REPORT SAYING HOW WELL I AM COPING.
TWO YEARS FROM TODAY YOU WILL FIND A PSYCHIATRIST.
THEY WILL WRITE A REPORT SAYING I AM NORMAL NOW.
WITH THAT REPORT YOU WILL PETITION THE COURT FOR AN END TO MY GUARDIANSHIP.
I HAVE YOUR HOUSE KEYS, YOUR BANK DETAILS, ACCESS TO YOUR EMAIL.
I HAVE A FILM OF YOU ATTACKING ME.
I WILL BE WATCHING.
IF YOU DEVIATE FROM THE PLAN, IF ANOTHER WOMAN WALKS AWAY FROM YOU WITH SO MUCH AS A PAPER CUT:
WHAT IS THAT?
THAT FILM GOES VIRAL.
THE BANK ACCOUNTS EMPTY.
BAD MEN GET YOUR KEYS--
SAY HELLO TO MY LITTLE FRIEND.
YES?
YES?
YES?
IF I WAS YOU I'D STAY REALLY STILL.
'CAUSE I'VE NEVER DONE THIS BEFORE.

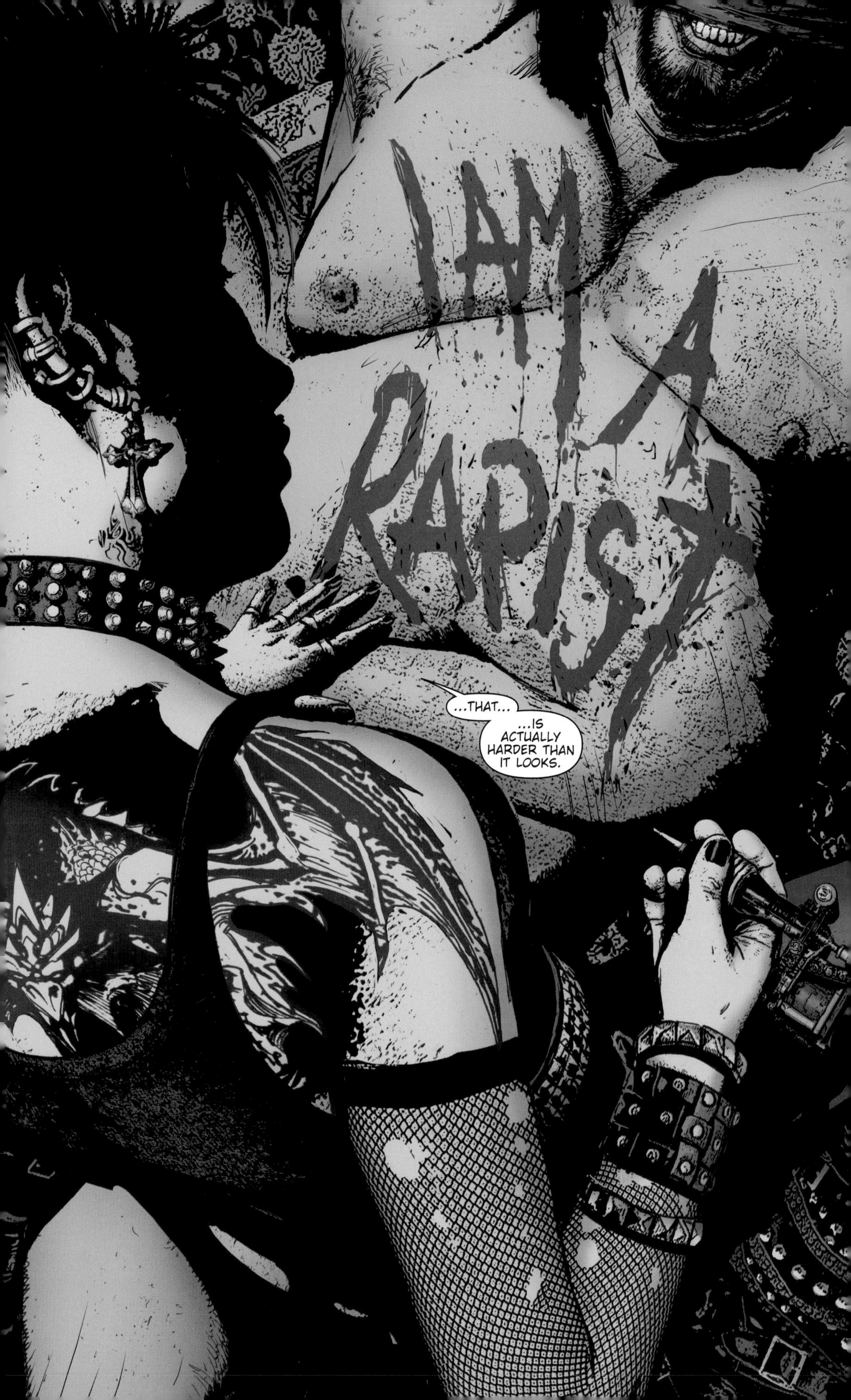
I AM A RAPIST
...THAT...
...IS ACTUALLY HARDER THAN IT LOOKS.

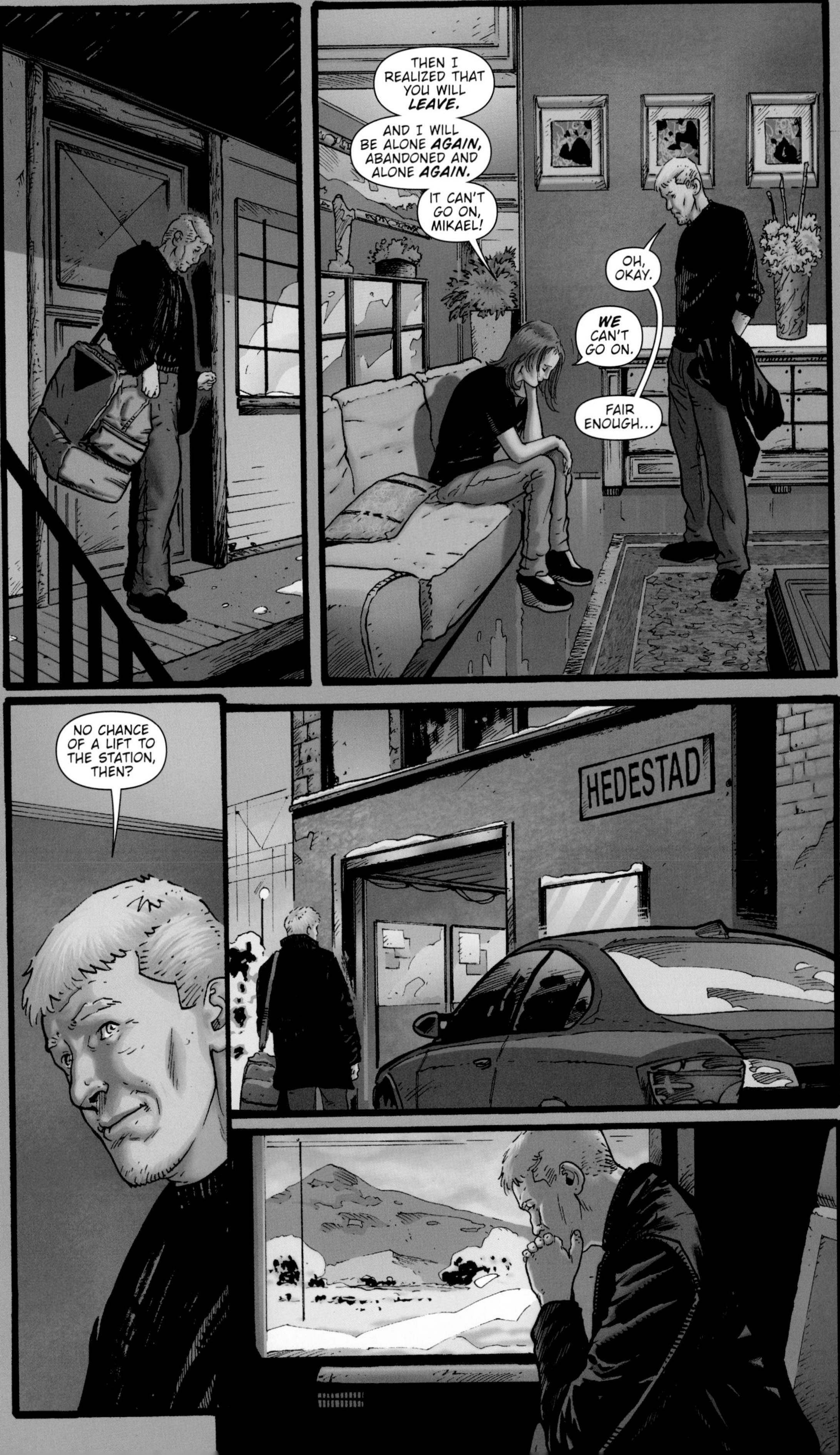
THEN I REALIZED THAT YOU WILL LEAVE.
AND I WILL BE ALONE AGAIN, ABANDONED AND ALONE AGAIN.
IT CAN'T GO ON, MIKAEL!
OH, OKAY.
WE CAN'T GO ON.
FAIR ENOUGH...
NO CHANCE OF A LIFT TO THE STATION, THEN?
HEDESTAD

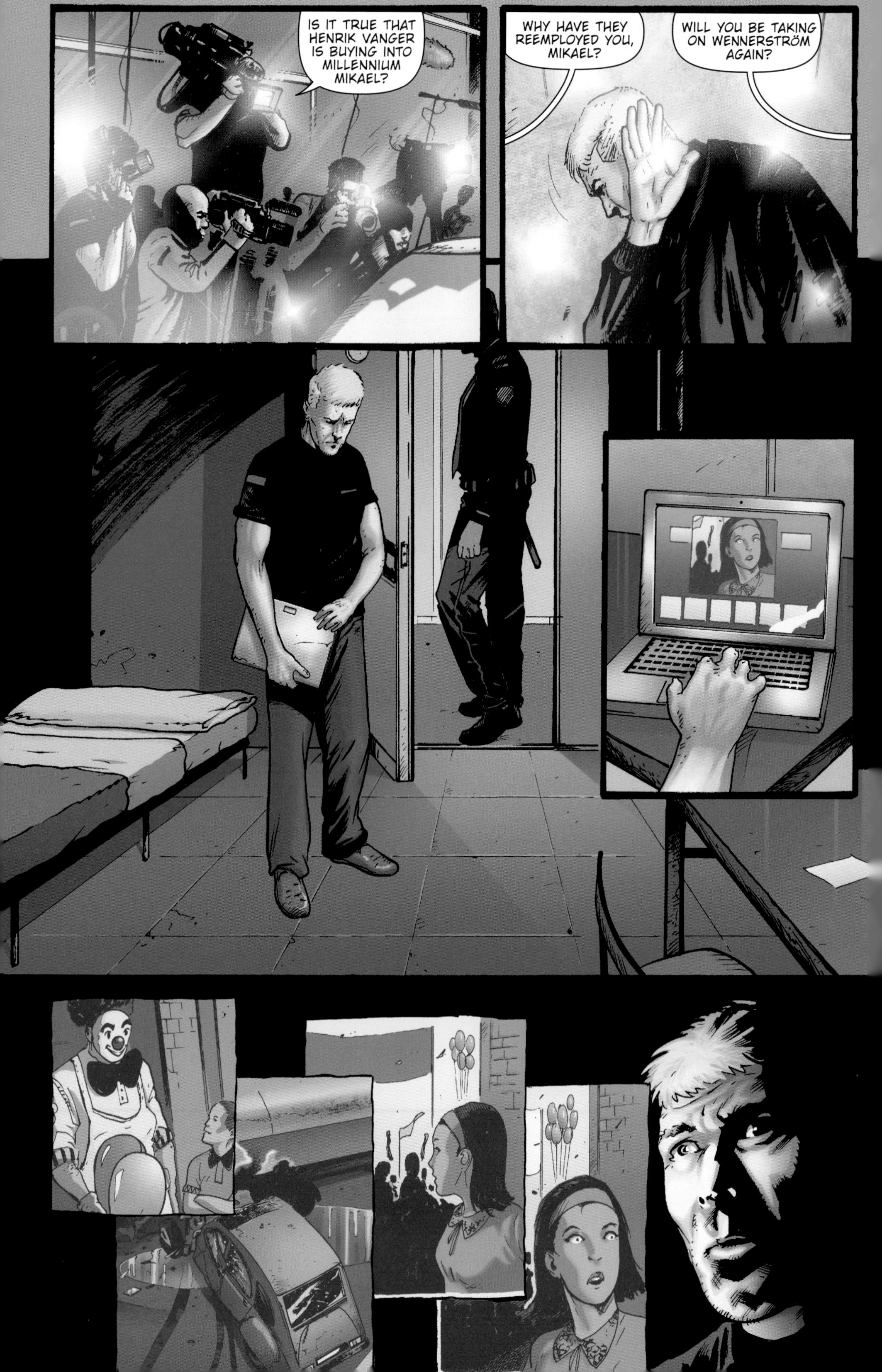
IS IT TRUE THAT HENRIK VANGER IS BUYING INTO MILLENNIUM MIKAEL?
WHY HAVE THEY REEMPLOYED YOU, MIKAEL?
WILL YOU BE TAKING ON WENNERSTRÖM AGAIN?

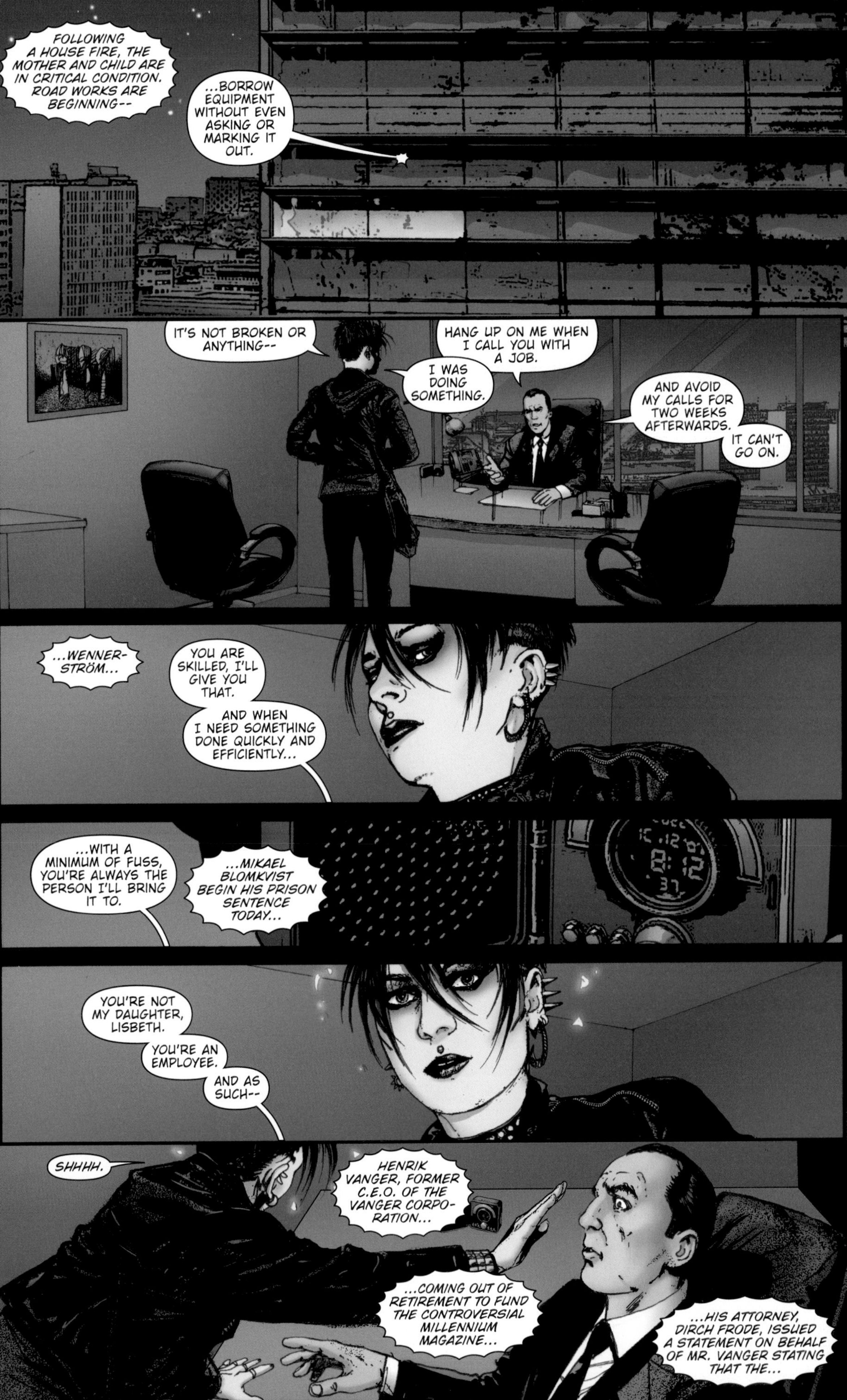
FOLLOWING A HOUSE FIRE, THE MOTHER AND CHILD ARE IN CRITICAL CONDITION. ROAD WORKS ARE BEGINNING--
...BORROW EQUIPMENT WITHOUT EVEN ASKING OR MARKING IT OUT.
IT'S NOT BROKEN OR ANYTHING--
HANG UP ON ME WHEN I CALL YOU WITH A JOB.
I WAS DOING SOMETHING.
AND AVOID MY CALLS FOR TWO WEEKS AFTERWARDS.
IT CAN'T GO ON.
...WENNER-STRÖM...
YOU ARE SKILLED, I'LL GIVE YOU THAT.
AND WHEN I NEED SOMETHING DONE QUICKLY AND EFFICIENTLY...
...WITH A MINIMUM OF FUSS, YOU'RE ALWAYS THE PERSON I'LL BRING IT TO.
...MIKAEL BLOMKVIST BEGIN HIS PRISON SENTENCE TODAY...
YOU'RE NOT MY DAUGHTER, LISBETH.
YOU'RE AN EMPLOYEE.
AND AS SUCH--
SHHHH.
HENRIK VANGER, FORMER C.E.O. OF THE VANGER CORPO-RATION...
...COMING OUT OF RETIREMENT TO FUND THE CONTROVERSIAL MILLENNIUM MAGAZINE...
...HIS ATTORNEY, DIRCH FRODE, ISSUED A STATEMENT ON BEHALF OF MR. VANGER STATING THAT THE...

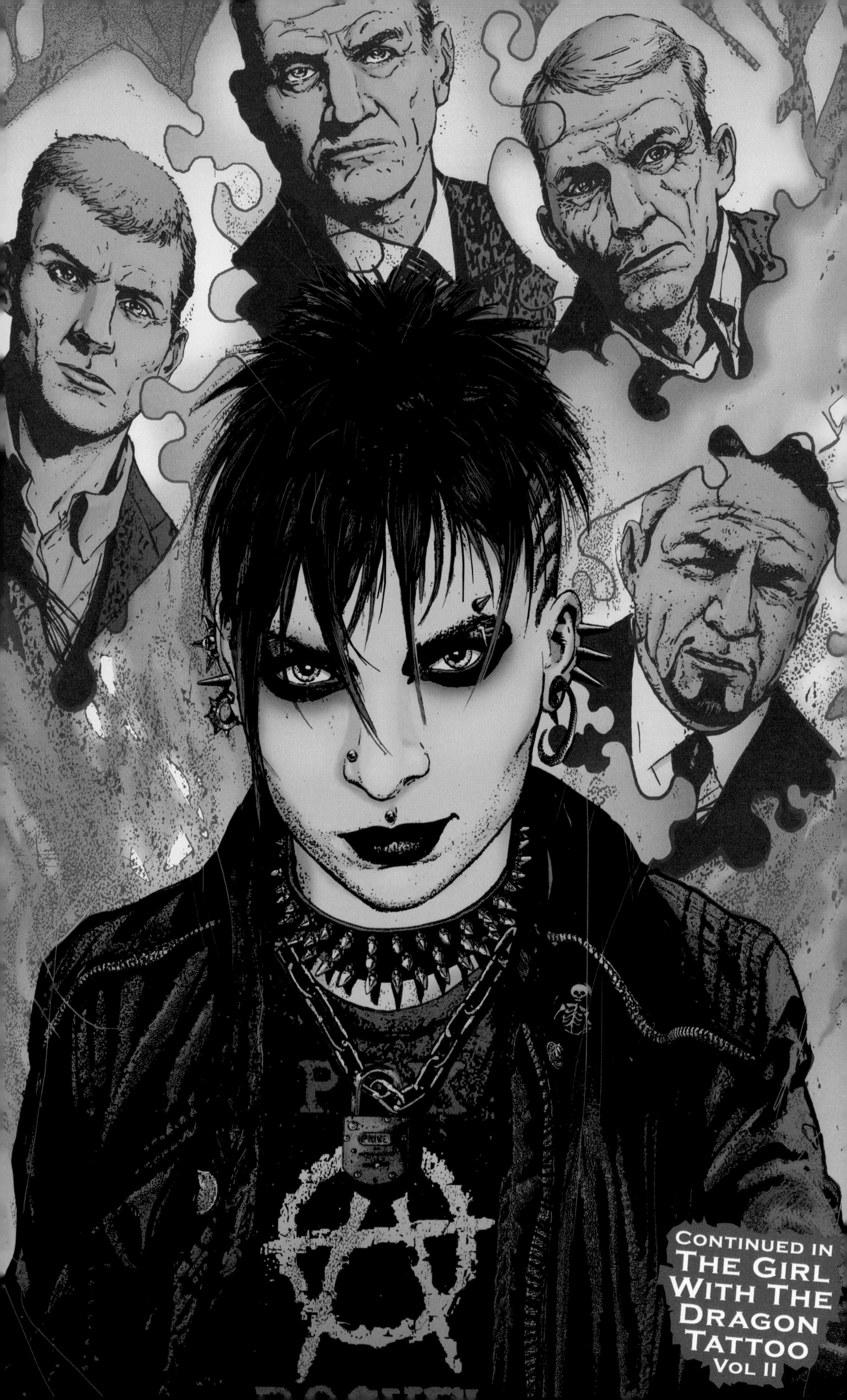
CONTINUED IN
THE GIRL
WITH THE
DRAGON
TATTOO
VOL II

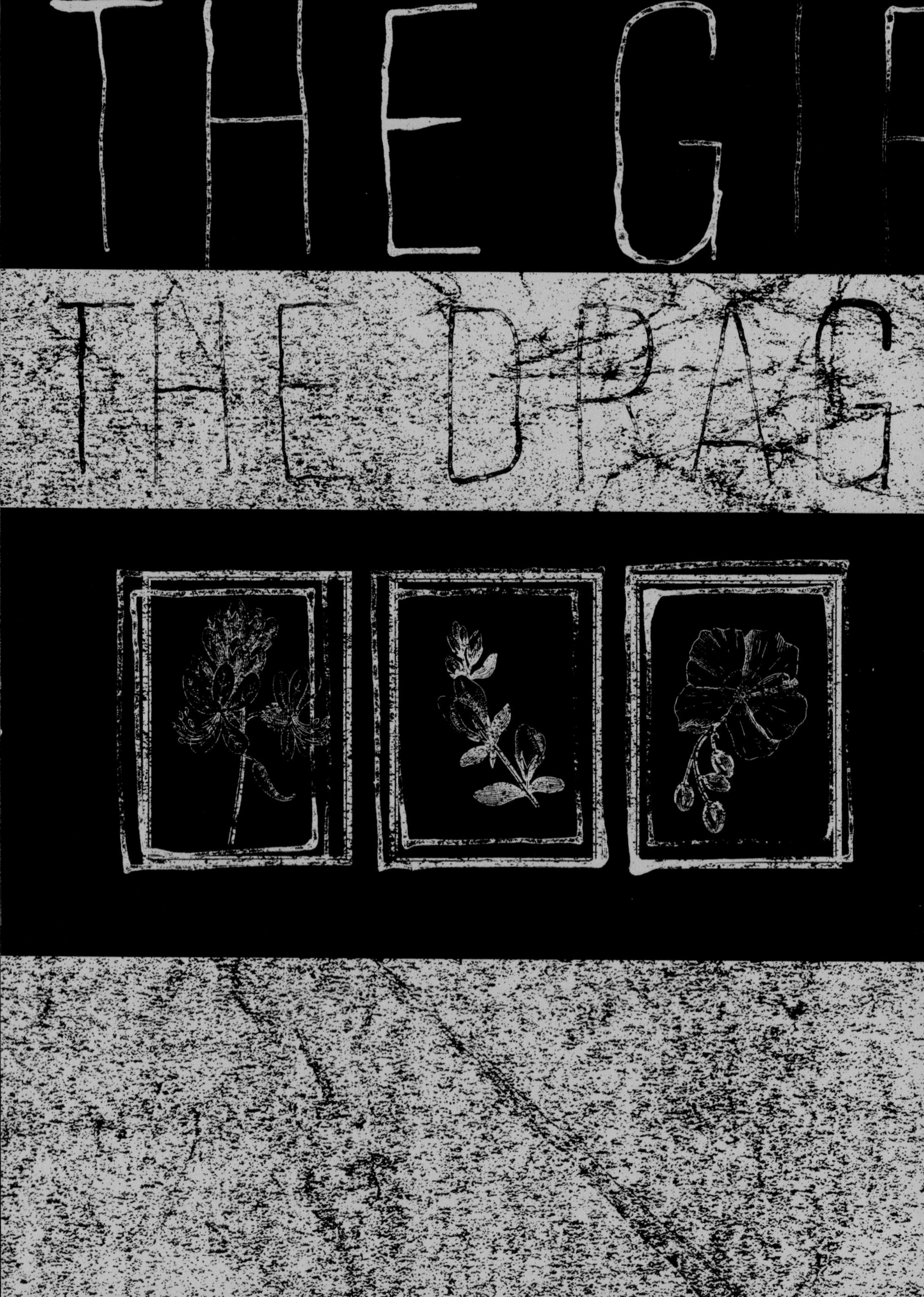
THE G
THE DRAG

Denise Mina is a Scottish crime writer and playwright. Her first novel, Garnethill, won the Crime Writers' Association John Creasy Dagger for the best first crime novel. She is also known for writing the DC Comics series HELLBLAZER and the graphic novel A SICKNESS IN THE FAMILY.

Leonardo Manco is an Argentine comic book artist and penciller best known for his dark and gritty style. Titles include Blaze of Glory, Apache Skies, Deathlok, and HELLBLAZER.

Andrea Mutti attended the International School of Comics in Brescia. He has worked extensively for the French market and is known for his work on the DC/Vertigo series DMZ and THE EXECUTOR.

TO BE CONTINUED IN...

A GRAPHIC NOVEL BOOK TWO DENISE **MINA** LEONARDO **MANCO** ANDREA **MUT**

STIEG LARSSON'S
THE GIRL WITH THE DRAGON TATTO

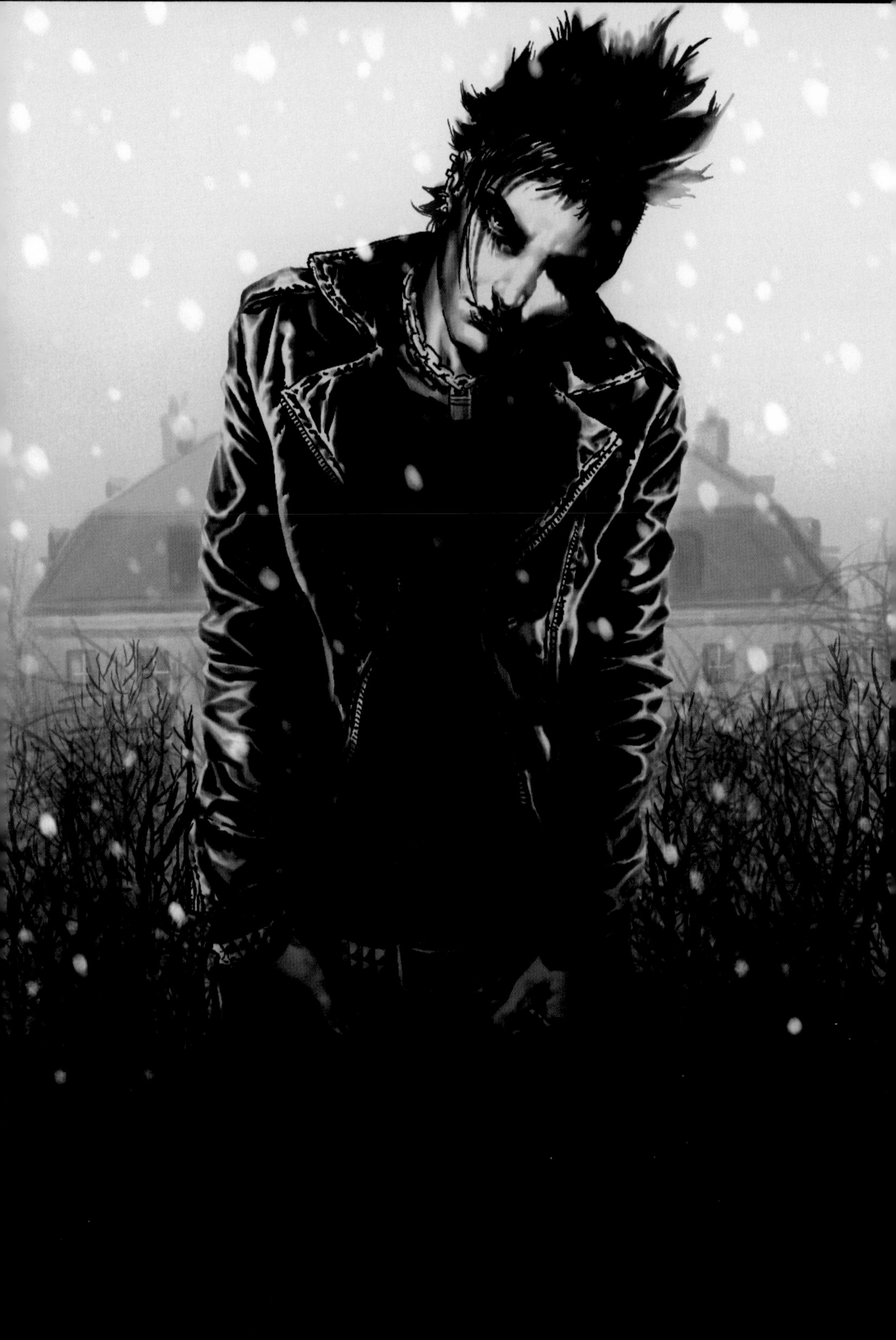

VERTIGO

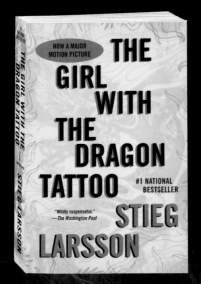
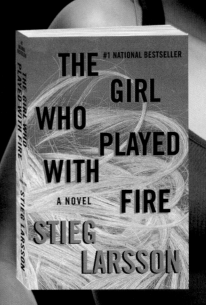
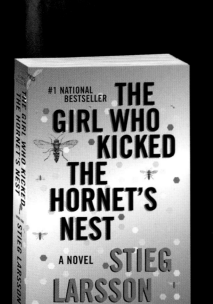

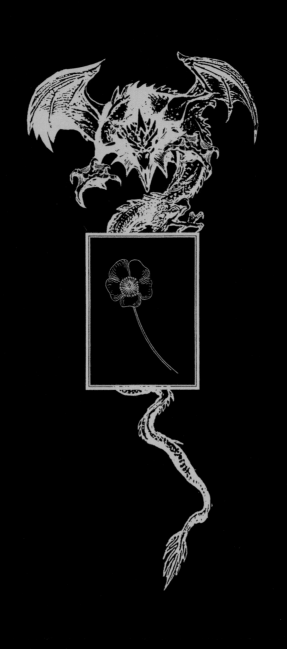